HISTORY OF
United States Naval Operations
IN WORLD WAR II

★

VOLUME FOUR
Coral Sea, Midway and
Submarine Actions
May 1942–August 1942

Admiral Chester W. Nimitz USN
Commander in Chief United States Pacific Fleet

HISTORY OF UNITED STATES NAVAL
OPERATIONS IN WORLD WAR II

VOLUME IV

Coral Sea, Midway and Submarine Actions

May 1942–August 1942

BY SAMUEL ELIOT MORISON

WITH AN INTRODUCTION BY
Jonathan Parshall

NAVAL INSTITUTE PRESS
Annapolis, Maryland

This book was brought to publication with the generous assistance of
Marguerite and Gerry Lenfest.

Naval Institute Press
291 Wood Road
Annapolis, MD 21402

This edition published by arrangement with Little, Brown and Company,
New York, NY. All rights reserved.
First Naval Institute Press paperback edition published 2010.
New Introduction © 2010 by United States Naval Institute.

Library of Congress Cataloging-in-Publication Data
Morison, Samuel Eliot, 1887–1976.
  History of United States naval operations in World War II / Samuel Eliot
Morison.
    v. cm.
  Originally published: Boston : Little, Brown, 1947–62.
  Includes bibliographical references and index.
  Contents: v. 1. The Battle of the Atlantic, 1939–1943 — v. 2. Operations in
North African waters, October 1942–June 1943 — v. 3. The Rising Sun in the
Pacific, 1931–April 1942 — v. 4. Coral Sea, Midway and Submarine Actions, May
1942–August 1942 — v. 5. The Struggle for Guadalcanal, August 1942–February
1943 — v. 6. Breaking the Bismarcks Barrier, 22 July 1942–1 May 1944.
  ISBN 978-1-59114-547-9 (v. 1 : alk. paper) — ISBN 978-1-59114-548-6
(v. 2 : alk. paper) — ISBN 978-1-59114-549-3 (v. 3 : alk. paper) —
ISBN 978-1-59114-550-9 (v. 4 : alk. paper) — ISBN 978-1-59114-551-6 (v. 5
: alk. paper) — ISBN 978-1-59114-552-3 (v. 6 : alk. paper) 1. World War,
1939–1945—Naval operations, American. I. Title.
  D773.M6 2010
  940.54'5973—dc22   2009052288

Printed in the United States of America on acid-free paper

26 25 24 23   15 14 13 12

To

The Memory of

THE AVIATORS
OF THE UNITED STATES ARMY, NAVY
AND MARINE CORPS
WHO FELL IN THE BATTLE OF MIDWAY

It follows then as certain as that night succeeds the day, that without a decisive Naval force we can do nothing definitive. And with it, every thing honourable and glorious. A constant Naval superiority would terminate the War speedily; without it, I do not know that it will ever be terminated honourably.

GEORGE WASHINGTON TO LAFAYETTE

15 November 1781

Preface

VOLUME IV is the second of this History on the war in the Pacific.[1] The United States Navy, which we left at the end of Volume III battered in body though unbeaten in spirit, now wins an important strategic victory in the Coral Sea; and, within a month, at Midway, inflicts a stunning defeat on a far superior Japanese force. That was a turning point in the war. The Aleutians phase of the Midway operation, an integral part of it although geographically separate, comes next. Part II, devoted to the "Silent Service," covers approximately the first year's exploits of the underwater boats in the Pacific. In Part III, which begins the Navy's first Pacific offensive, we follow Operation "Watchtower" through the planning and amphibious phases and leave United States Marines ashore on Tulagi, Gavutu and Guadalcanal, wondering "What next?" What came next, the six months' struggle for Guadalcanal, is described in detail in Volume V.

Several books and articles about the actions covered by this volume, by able and gifted writers, have already appeared. Most of them contain important errors, largely because the authors lacked sufficient information to tell the story correctly. In particular, they lacked information from the Japanese side; and any attempt to describe air battles — such as Coral Sea and Midway essentially were — from one side only is fatally handicapped. Instead of taking time out to refute these errors, I have simply gone ahead and told the story as it happened, to the best of my knowledge and ability. I do not claim omniscience. As fresh data appear, mistakes

[1] See also the Introduction to Volume I of this History for statement of scope and purpose of this work, and the methods followed by the writer; and the Preface to Volume III, for the general sources of information for World War II in the Pacific.

will be found and later writers will make new interpretations. It is the fate of all historians, especially those who take the risk of writing shortly after the event, to be superseded. Far safer to write about an era long past, in which all the actors are long since dead! But my warm contact with the United States Navy in action has given me the opportunity to see events for myself, to obtain oral information while men's memories are still fresh, and to correct mistakes in the written record. I hope that naval officers and others will not hesitate to point out errors and take issue about conclusions, as they have done very generously in the past.

During the preparation of this volume, my staff has consisted of two naval officers, one former Chief Petty Officer and one yeoman, my civilian secretary, and, for part of the time, a cartographer. Lieutenant Commander Henry Salomon Jr. USNR did the initial research for the Battle of the Coral Sea. He was relieved in September 1947 by Commander James C. Shaw USN, who had collected considerable experience and sixteen battle stars in the Pacific War. Commander Shaw did the initial research for Part II. The rest of the book, including the Battle of Midway, was "untouched by human hand" except my own; but I was tremendously helped in describing Midway by the fact that Commodore Richard W. Bates and staff at the same time were making a blow-by-blow analysis of that great battle for the Naval War College. I was able to profit by their intensive research, and from frequent discussions with Commodore Bates. Lieutenant Roger Pineau USNR, the junior member of my staff, sought out fresh source material of Japanese origin, translated everything that was relevant, and helped in the preparation of the volume in other ways. Mr. Donald R. Martin, with some assistance from Mr. Walton L. Robinson, compiled the task organizations. All the charts were prepared under my direction in the cartographic section of the Naval War College, headed by Mr. Charles H. Ward. The typing was done by Miss Antha E. Card and Yeoman Howard C. Dickens.

This volume, like its predecessor, has been completed under the benevolent oversight of Rear Admiral John B. Heffernan, Director of Naval History, with the moral support of three successive Presidents of the Naval War College: Admiral Raymond A. Spruance, Rear Admiral Allan E. Smith and Vice Admiral Donald B. Beary. Many other officers of the Navy, especially Captain Ralph C. Parker, Captain Tracy B. Kittredge USNR and Captain E. T. Layton, have cleared up various points and helped in countless ways.

During the five years since the first edition of this volume appeared, several officers of the United States Navy, as well as other readers, have sent in suggestions and corrections. These have been checked and collated by Captain John W. McElroy USNR of the Naval History Division and all necessary corrections made.

SAMUEL ELIOT MORISON

ON BOARD YAWL *Emily Marshall*
25 August 1953

The volume has profited by the translation by Roger Pineau & C. Kawakami of Mitsuo Fuchida & Masatake Okumiya *Midway, the Battle that Doomed Japan* (1955), and by a careful scrutiny of the text by Captain T. Ohmae. But I do not accept their contention that *Nautilus* attacked *Kaga*, not *Soryu* (pp. *128–9* below).

BOSTON, *March 1959*

Contents

PART II
SUBMARINE ACTIONS

PART III
THE FIRST AMERICAN OFFENSIVE
10 July–8 August 1942

List of Illustrations

(All photographs not otherwise described are Official United States Navy)

List of Charts

Abbreviations

Officers' ranks and bluejackets' ratings are those contemporaneous with the event. Officers and men named will be presumed to be of the United States Navy unless it is otherwise stated; officers of the Naval Reserve are designated USNR.

Other service abbreviations are: –
RAN, Royal Australian Navy
RN, Royal Navy
USA, United States Army
USMC, United States Marine Corps; USMCR, Reserve of same

Other abbreviations used in this volume: —
AA — Anti-aircraft
A.A.F.— United States Army Air Force
AK — Naval cargo vessel
AO — Naval oiler
AP — Transport; APD — Converted destroyer-transport
ASP — Anti-submarine patrol
ATIS — Allied Translator and Interpreter Section, General MacArthur's Headquarters
Batdiv — Battleship division
BB — Battleship
Buships — Bureau of Ships
CA — Heavy cruiser
CAP — Combat Air Patrol
Cardiv — Carrier division; Crudiv — Cruiser division
C. in C. — Commander in Chief
Cincpac — Commander in Chief, United States Pacific Fleet
CL — Light cruiser
C.O. — Commanding Officer
Com — as prefix means Commander. Examples: Comairsopac — Commander Aircraft South Pacific; Comcrudiv — Commander Cruiser Division; Cominch — Commander in Chief, United States Fleet

CNO — Chief of Naval Operations

CTF — Commander Task Force; CTG — Commander Task Group

CV — Aircraft carrier

DD — Destroyer

Desdiv — Destroyer division; Desron — Destroyer squadron

H.M.A.S. — His Majesty's Australian Ship

H.M.N.Z.S. — His Majesty's New Zealand Ship

H.M.S. — His Majesty's Ship

Inter Jap. Off. — USSBS *Interrogations of Japanese Officials*, 2 vols. (1946)

JANAC — Joint Army-Navy Assessment Committee *Japanese Naval and Merchant Shipping Losses World War II* (1947)

Lt. (jg) — Lieutenant, junior grade

N.A.S. — Naval Air Station

O.N.I. — Office of Naval Intelligence

Op — Operation

O.T.C. — Officer in Tactical Command

PC — Patrol craft

PT — Motor torpedo boat

R.A.F. — Royal Air Force

R.N.Z.A.F. — Royal New Zealand Air Force

Subdiv — Submarine division; Subron — Submarine squadron

TF — Task Force; TG — Task Group

U.S.C.G.C. — United States Coast Guard Cutter

USSBS — United States Strategic Bombing Survey

VF — Fighter plane or squadron

VMB, VMF — Marine Corps bomber or fighter squadron

VP — Patrol plane or squadron

VS — Scout plane or squadron

VSO — Scout-Observation plane or squadron

VT — Torpedo-bomber or squadron

WDC — Washington Document Center

YP — Patrol vessel

Aircraft Designations. Numerals 1, 2 or 4 in parentheses indicate
number of engines.

United States

A-20, Army (2) light bomber, land-based
A-24, Army version of the SBD, land-based
B-17, Flying Fortress, Army (4) heavy bomber, land-based
F4F-3, F4F-4, Wildcat, Navy (1) fighters, land- or carrier-based
OS2U, Kingfisher, Navy (1) Scout-Observation seaplane
P-35, P-36, P-39, P-40, Army (1) pursuit fighter planes, land-based
P-38, Lightning, Army (2) pursuit fighter plane, land-based
PBY, Catalina, Navy (2) patrol seaplane (See chap. vi footnote 46)
SBD, Dauntless, Navy (1) scout or dive-bomber, land- or carrier-based
SB2U-3, Vindicator, Navy (1) scout bomber, land- or carrier-based
TBD, TBF, Devastator, Avenger, Navy (1) torpedo-bombers, carrier-
based

Japanese

"Betty" — Mitsubishi Zero-1 (2) medium bomber
"Emily" — Kawanishi Zero-2 (4) bomber (flying boat)
"Kate" — Nakajima 97-2 (1) high-level or torpedo-bomber
"Val" — Aichi 99-1 (1) dive-bomber
"Zeke" (called "Zero" in 1942–43) — Zero-3 (1) fighter plane

Introduction

THE BATTLE OF MIDWAY is clearly the centerpiece of this particular volume of Samuel Eliot Morison's seminal naval historical series, and rightly so. Midway was without question the single most important battle in the Pacific War because of the enormous and immediate impact it had on the overall strategic balance of forces in that conflict. Midway's verdict literally changed the momentum of the war overnight, serving emphatic notice to both sides that the initial phase of easy Japanese victories had ended. Midway by itself did not equate to overall defeat for the Japanese, but it did create the context for America's eventual victory in the Pacific by opening new offensive possibilities for the United States that simply would not have existed had Japan's carrier fleet emerged intact from the battle. The U.S. Navy was not slow in capitalizing on the radical transformation of its fortunes, quickly initiating the first in a series of counteroffensives that began in the waters around Guadalcanal and ended in the waters of Tokyo Bay. Morison certainly appreciated these dynamics, noting that it "thrust the Japanese war lords back on their heels, caused their ambitious plans for the conquest of Fiji, New Caledonia and New Zealand to be canceled, and forced on them the unexpected and unwelcome role of the defensive" (page 159).

Not surprisingly, Midway has attracted its fair share of attention over the years. The two most important English histories published before the turn of the century were Walter Lord's *Incredible Victory* (New York: Harper and Row, 1967) and Gordon Prange's *Miracle at Midway* (New York: McGraw-Hill, 1982). Both are fine works. Lord's prose is beautiful, and he has a true gift for getting at the heart of his subject matter. He also is to be applauded for beginning the incorporation of Japanese sources on the battle (in the form of interviews of Japanese participants).

Prange's work was actually completed by his graduate students Donald Goldstein and Katherine Dillon after Professor Prange was diagnosed with what would turn out to be his final illness. Goldstein and Dillon are to be complimented for having brought the work to completion; it has served as the main Western account of the battle since its publication.

To these two works, however, must be added two outstanding but underappreciated general histories: Robert Cressman, *A Glorious Page in Our History* (Missoula, MT: Pictorial Histories Publishing Co., 1990), and H. P. Willmott's *The Barrier and the Javelin* (Annapolis, MD: Naval Institute Press, 1983). Cressman, joined by well-known historians Steve Ewing, Barrett Tillman, and others, forged a work that looks meticulously at the American air operations in the battle. It is notable for its accuracy in this respect. Willmott's work provides a superb analysis of the strategic aspects of the battle, as well as of the battle's relation to the Battle of the Coral Sea that was fought just a month before Midway. Serious students of the battle will not want to miss either of those books. To these can also be appended such other general works as Hugh Bicheno's *Midway* (London: Cassell & Co., 2001), Peter Smith's *Midway: Dauntless Victory* (Barnsley, South Yorkshire, UK: Pen and Sword Books, 2007), and several others.

In addition to the general histories on the battle, other more-specialized studies have appeared, such as Edwin Layton's *And I Was There* (Old Saybrook, CT: Konecky & Konecky, 1985) that laid out the veritable cryptographic miracles that were the foundation for Nimitz's battle planning. John Prados' *Combined Fleet Decoded: The Secret History of American Intelligence and the Japanese Navy in World War II* (New York: Random House, 1995) deals with the same subject matter, and in a more detailed fashion. Morison, of course, had no knowledge of the cryptographic breakthroughs into JN-25 when he was writing. Thus, when he writes on page 69 of this volume, "[S]hortly before battle was joined in the Coral Sea, word had reached Admiral Nimitz of a forthcoming enemy offensive in the Central Pacific," one must forgive him the vagaries as to exactly *how* the word had reached Nimitz. The same is true of Nimitz's statement on page 158 that without early information of the Japanese movements "the Battle of Midway would have ended differently." These matters would not be declassified and fully understood until the 1980s.

Around this same time, the first generation of what might be called "serious" Western books on Japanese naval topics began to appear, some of them addressing issues related to Midway. This marked a turning point in the study of Midway: Japanese source materials were finally being addressed more comprehensively. Perhaps the most important scholar in this respect is John Lundstrom. His first work, *The First South Pacific Campaign* (Annapolis, MD: Naval Institute Press, 1976), went largely unread in the late 1970s, unfortunately. But his 1984 work focusing on naval air power—*The First Team: Pacific Naval Air Combat from Pearl Harbor to Midway* (Annapolis, MD: Naval Institute Press, 1984), followed ten years later by *First Team and the Guadalcanal Campaign: Naval Fighter Combat from August to November 1942* (Annapolis, MD: Naval Institute Press, 1994) fundamentally changed the way these sorts of histories were written. These works dramatically raised the bar in terms of their quality of research on *both* the American and Japanese sides of the war. Lundstrom's *Black Shoe Carrier Admiral: Frank Jack Fletcher at Coral Sea, Midway & Guadalcanal* (Annapolis, MD: Naval Institute Press, 2006) again broke new ground, adding important insights into the way admirals Nimitz, Fletcher, and Spruance planned for and fought Midway, as well as balancing the record regarding Fletcher's performance there.

The other important foundation works in this sense were Paul Dull's *Battle History of the Imperial Japanese Navy, 1941–1945* (Annapolis, MD: Naval Institute Press, 1978), followed nearly twenty years later by David Evans and Mark Peattie's *Kaigun: Strategy, Tactics, and Technology in the Imperial Japanese Navy, 1887–1941* (Annapolis, MD: Naval Institute Press, 1997), as well as Peattie's follow-on effort, *Sunburst: The Rise of Japanese Naval Air Power, 1909–1941* (Annapolis, MD: Naval Institute Press, 2001). These three volumes were fundamental to the study of the Pacific War by establishing a framework for understanding how the Imperial

Japanese Navy had evolved, and how it operated during the war. For researchers, these three volumes, in combination with Lundstrom's corpus, pointed out the essential primary sources that would have to be used when undertaking scholarly studies of *any* Pacific War encounter.

In 2005, this author and Anthony Tully published *Shattered Sword: The Untold Story of the Battle of Midway* (Dulles, VA: Potomac Books, 2005). Building on the works mentioned above, *Shattered Sword* marked the first serious attempt in more than forty years to broaden the Japanese account of the battle. Heretofore, all Western accounts had based their treatment of the Japanese side on a trio of sources. The first of those sources was Admiral Nagumo's after-battle report (commonly called "The Nagumo Report") that was captured on Saipan and translated in 1947. The second was the series of postwar interviews of Japanese officers conducted in 1946–47 under the auspices of the United States Strategic Bombing Survey (known as "USSBS," or colloquially as the "Us Bus Reports"). The third was Mitsuo Fuchida's *Midway: The Battle That Doomed Japan* (Annapolis, MD: Naval Institute Press, 1955). Following its initial publication in 1952, *Midway* was quickly translated into English by Roger Pineau, a Japanese language officer during the war and an important naval historian afterwards. Pineau rightly guessed that Fuchida's account would provide an important bird's-eye view of the battle as seen from the vantage of *Akagi*'s bridge. What he could not know was that Fuchida would impart major, and willful, distortions into the historical record, regarding not only Midway, but also Pearl Harbor and other important events during the war.

The most important and damaging of these with respect to Midway was Fuchida's description of the Japanese flight decks in the moments before the climactic 1025 American dive-bomber attack that disabled *Akagi*, *Kaga*, and *Sōryū*. Fuchida painted a dramatic scene wherein the Japanese were mere minutes away from launching a devastating counterattack on the Americans. The Japanese flight decks were supposedly packed chockablock with attack aircraft just waiting for the final signal to take off, only to be interrupted at the last second by the scream of attacking Dauntlesses. In reality, though, as the Japanese operational records subsequently made clear, Admiral Nagumo's force was still at least half an hour away from being ready to launch, and the American attacks caught them essentially flat-footed. Fuchida's story was nothing more than a heroic fairytale. Interestingly, Morison himself painted a scene similar to Fuchida's in his 1949 effort. The difference, of course, is that Morison did not have access to the Japanese operational records, nor did he have first-hand knowledge of the Japanese command decisions of that fateful day.[1] Fuchida did. And it was Fuchida's vivid account, practically made for a screenplay, that cemented the conventional myth of the climactic attack, a myth that would persist for the next fifty-some years.

Fuchida's impact on the study of the battle was incredibly widespread. His account was incorporated into Lord's *Incredible Victory*, Prange's *Miracle at Midway*, and every other Western history of the battle. And because Fuchida's story dovetailed so nicely with the American self-image of the battle—of heroic Dauntlesses coming to the rescue in the nick of time, avenging the slaughter of their torpedo-bomber brethren and snatching victory from the jaws of defeat—Western historians were content to leave well enough alone. Herein lies Fuchida's most pernicious effect: It is not that he lied. Lies can be overturned with new information. Rather, Fuchida essentially froze Western historiography in its tracks regarding the Japanese side of the battle. That condition persisted for decades. The sheer difficulty of finding and using the Japanese primary sources materials to begin with, coupled with the fact that Fuchida's account had apparently been vetted by Prange and others, meant that no one on this side of the Pacific was terribly inclined to do any

---

[1] It is striking that the passage in Morison's work describing the Japanese flight decks during the 1025 dive-bomber attack is without any citation from the Japanese participants that Morison had interviewed. It can only be assumed that Morison was simply extrapolating what had happened on the flight decks from his own naval experiences, or was influenced by the artwork of the battle that was starting to appear. I am grateful to my longtime friend and coauthor Anthony Tully for his insights on this matter.

further digging. As a result, the Battle of Midway's conventional interpretation was essentially set in stone.

On the other side of the Pacific, though, time and research marched on, led by the Japan Self-Defense Forces. Unquestionably, the most important source that Morison did not have access to at the time of his writing was the official Japanese war history series, the *Bōeichō Bōeikenshūjō Senshibu* (originally, *Bōeichō Bōeikenshūjō Senshishitsu*), known in the trade as *BKS* or *Senshi Sōsho*. These volumes (there are more than a hundred) contain the combined wisdom of the Self-Defense Forces' war history department, as compiled from official documentation and extensive interviews with surviving Japanese veterans. They are considered authoritative by most experts in the field. Unfortunately for Morison, they did not begin appearing until the 1970s. The Midway *Senshi Sōsho* volume (vol. 43, *Midowei Kaisen*; Tokyo: Asagumo Shimbunsha, 1974) contained important clarifications that would have been incredibly useful to American researchers had they had access to them at the time.

Almost equally important in the study of the Battle of Midway, however, are the surviving air group records of the Japanese carriers. These records, that escaped destruction by the Japanese after the war (unlike the ship's logs and divisional war diaries from Midway), form the basis for any operational account of the Japanese flight decks. Interestingly, these records were in the hands of the Americans almost from the time of the Japanese surrender. They were captured, carted off to Washington, and subsequently microfilmed. However, they were not used by Western historians because they were seen as the province of specialists since they were handwritten and quite difficult to work with. But in their distilled form they are invaluable: they provide the names, takeoff and landing times, ordnance carried and expended, and other particulars of every sortie during the battle. And from an understanding of what the air groups were doing comes an understanding of what the flight decks were likely doing as well, allowing the historian to construct a very accurate picture of Japanese carrier operations during the battle. Similar records exist for Coral Sea, Philippine Sea, and many other battles, and will doubtless play a part in any similarly detailed account of the major Pacific carrier confrontations.

It should be noted that the Japanese sources are hardly a panacea. The *Senshi Sōsho* has given historians insights into the thinking of Japanese commanders, as well as a wealth of operational detail that were unavailable immediately after the war. However, they have not been translated into English, and are written in an archaic, academic form of the language that even many modern Japanese find difficult to decipher. As such, they are still largely the province of Japanese language specialists, and have yet to be used widely in the West. To this author's knowledge, very few of the volumes have been translated into English. For instance, passages from the Midway volume were used for *Shattered Sword*. Similarly, portions of the Pearl Harbor (*Hawaii Sakusen*) volume have been translated and are being used in a forthcoming comprehensive history of that operation. The Coral Sea volume has been translated, but thus far has been used by only a single historian, and not all the fruits of his research are in print. This points to a central problem with using these sources: the current expense of translating them means that historians are rightly concerned with recouping their costs (by publishing works based on these sources) before releasing them more widely to the historical community. It is to be hoped either that the Japanese authorities eventually will see fit to republish these important works in English (as the Germans did with their official war history series), or that the advent of more-efficient computer-aided translation technology will lower the cost of using such sources to the point where they are not considered beyond the reach of nonspecialists.

In the end, despite more than fifty years having passed since their publication, Morison's volumes remain an important, credible source of knowledge on any of the U.S. Navy's campaigns. In many cases, Morison's orders of battle and other operational details have been corrected and clarified by works that are more recent. But his gift for narrative, and his conveyance of the "big picture," have never been superseded. It is safe to say that Morison's work will be read for another fifty years simply because he had a gift for conveying the importance and immediacy of the crucial events he wrote about.

JONATHAN PARSHALL

PART I

Coral Sea, Midway, Aleutians

CHAPTER I

South from Rabaul

March–April 1942

1. *Delusions of Grandeur*

THE PACIFIC SITUATION is now very grave," cabled President Roosevelt to Winston Churchill on 9 March 1942, the day after the surrender of Java.[1] And so it continued for almost three months. Indeed, the situation was very grave everywhere. In Europe, Germany was preparing a spring drive through the Ukraine into the Caucasus; she might thrust on through Turkey and, with Rommel advancing from the west, take the Suez Canal. During the first three months of 1942 the Allies and neutral nations lost over two million tons of merchant shipping; during the second three months, over two million and a quarter tons, mostly in the Atlantic.[2] In the Pacific, the Japanese now controlled all lands and waters between the Solomons and Burma and China, and everything north of Australia excepting doomed Bataan, where they were closing in, and the south coast of New Guinea, which would be their next objective.

By agreement between the President and the Prime Minister, 17 March 1942, the United States assumed responsibility for the defense of the entire Pacific, including New Zealand and Australia (whither General MacArthur had to retire), while the British undertook to defend the Indian Ocean and the Middle East. The

[1] High command data in this chapter are derived from the files and records of Commander in Chief United States Fleet and Chief of Naval Operations.
[2] Vol. I of this History p. 412.

basic strategic plan of the war, to "beat Hitler first," was confirmed. This meant that the United States was committed to a strategic defensive in the Pacific. But it was well understood by the President, the Prime Minister and the Combined Chiefs of Staff that, while forces were being trained and materials accumulated for a big offensive in Europe or Africa, the Pacific theater would have highest immediate priority for ships, planes and troops in order to hold vital positions and protect communications.[3]

In the Roosevelt Administration and in the armed forces, faith in eventual Allied victory never faltered. Yet, under the impact of defeat after defeat in the Pacific, unbalanced by anything hopeful in the Atlantic, many Americans began to regard the Japanese as endowed with fabulous fighting virtues and infinite military potentialities. Although this feeling was not very articulate, it made a dangerous culture-bed for mischiefmakers who demanded that defeat in the Atlantic be accepted, Europe be left to her fate and American effort be concentrated in the Pacific. For the most part, however, the American people had confidence that leaders like Roosevelt, King, Nimitz and MacArthur would take the offensive against Japan when the time was ripe.

In Japan, the early months of 1942 were pure sunshine. Flushed with victories which had brought *Hakko Ichiu* ("the eight corners of the world under one roof")[4] nearer accomplishment than at any time within recorded history, the Japanese war lords forgot, and the trusting people never knew, that Allied weakness was momentary and that the superior strength of the Imperial Army and Navy could not long be maintained.

As Admiral Hara, the carrier commander at Coral Sea, said, unprecedented success "caused many officials in high positions in Japan to succumb to the so-called 'Victory Disease.'" People stricken with this malady predicted that American counterattack would develop slight strength and come too late, after Japan had

---

[3] For the reallocation of naval forces made in view of these decisions and understanding of 17 Mar. 1942, see chap. xii.
[4] See Vol. III of this History pp. 3–18.

organized her new acquisitions and obtained all the strategic materials that she needed. "Plans for further expansion of the Japanese to the south and east naturally followed these false assumptions." [5]

Initial Japanese war plans were based on the assumption that it would take about five months to conquer the Philippines and Malaya, including the Netherlands East Indies. Logistics experts wanted six months more to get the oil fields operating again with production sufficient for war purposes. Now that the schedule of conquest had been halved, and the "scorched earth" policy as to oil fields had failed, strategic planners believed they could step everything up. Moreover, these marvelous conquests had been cheap. Japanese losses up to 1 May 1942 comprised only 23 naval vessels, none larger than a destroyer, amounting to but 26,441 tons; 67 transports and merchant ships totalling 314,805 tons; [6] a few hundred planes and a few thousand soldiers and sailors. These fell so far short of the anticipated 20 to 30 per cent naval losses that the younger and less farsighted war planners could argue with some logic that they had surplus forces which could be used for further expansion while the earlier conquests were being developed and organized.

Easy success, surplus forces and "victory disease" did not alter the basic Japanese strategy, but speeded it up. They encouraged the Japanese to extend their "ribbon defense" or defensive perimeter at once instead of waiting until Greater East Asia was consolidated. Three new and successive conquests were anticipated: —

1. Tulagi and Port Moresby, in order to secure air mastery of the Coral Sea and its shores.

2. Midway Atoll and the Western Aleutians, in order to

[5] "Supplemental Report of Certain Phases of the War Against Japan, Derived from Interrogations of Senior Naval Commanders at Truk" of whom the most important was Admiral Hara. This "Truk Report," as it is generally called, notes from various Intelligence material by Capt. E. T. Layton, and notes taken in Japan by Lt. Cdr. Salomon Jr. from conversations with Japanese naval officers, supplements the discussion of basic Japanese strategy in *The Campaigns of the Pacific War*.

[6] *Japanese Naval and Merchant Shipping Losses*, which includes transports with merchant vessels.

strengthen the defensive perimeter and bring the United States Pacific Fleet to a decisive engagement.

3. New Caledonia, Fiji and Samoa, in order to cut lines of communication between the United States and Australasia.

The Battle of the Coral Sea came about because the Allies resisted point 1; the Battle of Midway was the principal product of 2; and 3 never came off.

All three moves, and more, were in the Japanese Basic War Plan,[7] which dates from 1938; the only new elements were shortening the timetable for 2 and 3 above, and the objective of a big fleet action.[8] Admiral Yamamoto rejected the traditional Japanese naval strategy of keeping the Fleet in home waters awaiting the enemy's arrival; he was bent on sailing out to seek action. For, he argued, if the Combined Fleet could annihilate our Pacific Fleet and set up air patrols between Wake, Midway and the Aleutians, the Imperial Japanese Navy could cruise at will throughout the Pacific and land troops anywhere. This line of reasoning sounded correct to Japanese disciples of Mahan; and, personally, I see nothing wrong with it. Japan had to smash the Pacific Fleet in 1942 or sustain an irresistible counterattack in 1943–44. If that Fleet had only consented to play the rôle assigned to it by the Japanese, they could have stretched their defensive perimeter to Hawaii without any weakening of their strength. Conversely, unless the Pacific Fleet were knocked out, a mere strategic defensive behind the perimeter would avail nothing in the end; provided, of course, the American will to fight did not abate.

The Coral Sea, appropriately named in 1803 by Captain Matthew

[7] As stated in Combined Fleet Operation Order No. 1, promulgated 5 Nov. 1941, the "Areas which are to be rapidly occupied or destroyed, as soon as the war situation permits," were (1) Areas of Eastern New Guinea, New Britain, Fiji and Samoa; (2) Aleutian and Midway Areas; (3) Areas of the Andaman Islands; (4) Important points in the Australian Area. The whole of this "Op Order" is translated in *Nachi* Documents (recovered from cruiser *Nachi* in 1945) Part viii p. 9 (ATIS No. 39); my translation however is by Capt. E. T. Layton from the original.

[8] Capt. Ohmae in *Inter. Jap Off.* I 176. See Vol. III of this History pp. 389–98 for the Tokyo raid. According to Capt. Layton, that raid delayed rather than speeded up Step 1 (Port Moresby) by about 4 days, because the Combined Fleet wasted time searching the waters east of Japan for Halsey.

Flinders RN, is one of the most beautiful bodies of water in the world. Typhoons pass it by; the southeast trades blow fresh across its surface almost the entire year — raising whitecaps from the lee shores of the islands, that build up to a gentle, regular swell that crashes on the Great Barrier Reef in a 1500-mile line of white foam. There is no winter, only a summer that is never too hot. Almost all the islands on its eastern and northern edges — New Caledonia, the New Hebrides, the Louisiades — are lofty, jungle-clad and ringed with bright coral beaches and reefs. Here the interplay of sunlight, pure air and transparent water may be seen at its loveliest; peacock-hued shoals over the coral gardens break off abruptly from an emerald fringe into deeps of brilliant ame-thyst. Even under the rare overcasts that veil the tropical sun, the Coral Sea becomes a warm dove-gray in color instead of assuming the bleak foul-weather dress of the ocean in high latitudes. Here, too, as at Rossel Island, are some of the last unspoiled island Arcadias, where a stranded sailor or airman might believe himself to be back in the Golden Age.

Only in its northern bight — sometimes called the Solomons or the Bismarck Sea — does the Coral Sea wash somber shores of lava and volcanic ash. That bight had been dominated by Japan since January 1942, from her easily won base at Rabaul. It was now time, in the view of her war planners, that she swing around the corner of New Guinea, through the Louisiades, and move into the dancing waters of the broad Coral Sea. If all went well, the next move would take the warriors of Japan to Nouméa and the south-ern edge of the Great Barrier Reef, so that before the end of 1942 every shore of the sea would be in their possession or under their planes and guns. That is why the Coral Sea, where no more serious fights had taken place in days gone by than those between trading schooners and Melanesian war canoes, became the scene of the first great naval action between aircraft carriers.

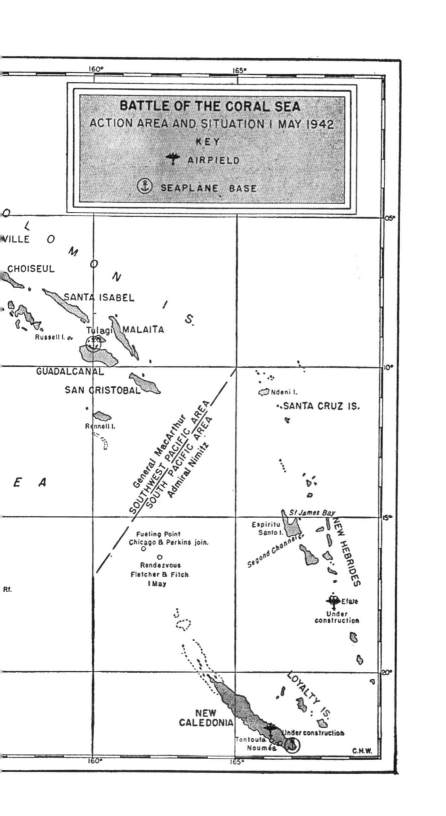

BATTLE OF THE CORAL SEA
ACTION AREA AND SITUATION I MAY 1942
KEY
✈ AIRFIELD
⚓ SEAPLANE BASE

160°   165°   05°

O
L
VILLE   O
M
CHOISEUL
O
SANTA ISABEL   N
I   S.
Russell I.   Tulagi MALAITA
GUADALCANAL   10°
SAN CRISTOBAL   Ndeni I.
Rennell I.   SANTA CRUZ IS.

General MacArthur
SOUTHWEST PACIFIC AREA
SOUTH PACIFIC AREA
Admiral Nimitz

E   A
St James Bay   15°
Espiritu
Santo I.
Fueling Point   Second Channel   NEW HEBRIDES
Chicago & Perkins join.
O
Rendezvous
Fletcher & Fitch
I May
Efate
Under
construction

Rf.
20°
LOYALTY IS.

NEW
CALEDONIA
Under construction
Tontouta
Nouméa   C.H.W.
160°   165°

2. *Plans and Aspirations*

Japan's overall plan for Operation "MO" was so simple that it could be told in three sentences: "With the coöperation of the South Seas Army Detachment and the Navy, we will occupy Port Moresby and important positions on Tulagi and in southeastern New Guinea. We will establish air bases and strengthen our air operations in the Australian area. Successively, an element will carry out a sudden attack against Nauru and Ocean Islands and secure the phosphorus resources located there." [9] The phosphorus was wanted for Japanese agriculture.

Port Moresby was the key to Papua, the tail end of New Guinea; and Papua must be secured in order to bring northern Australia within range of Japanese warships and bombers. The seizure of "important points in the Australian Area" — meaning, presumably, ports and airfields of Northern Queensland down to Townsville — had been recommended but rejected, for as the situation developed, the Japanese decided that smaller and more easily acquired land masses such as Papua, the New Hebrides and New Caledonia, would serve equally well to control the Coral Sea, cut off and force Australia out of the war. Hence the attempt to take Port Moresby by sea. Developed as an air base, it would enable the Japanese air force to bomb Allied supply routes and "Darwinize" the Queensland ports and airfields.

The Japanese expected to run into opposition. They correctly estimated that about 200 Allied land-based planes were spotted on Australian fields and observed that American plane reconnaissance was so active — extending even to Kavieng in New Ireland — that the concealment of Japanese ship movements had "become extremely difficult." They knew that Allied naval forces in the Southwest Pacific were "not large"; but as they assumed only one carrier,[10]

---

[9] "Full Translation of the Port Moresby Operation May 1942 — Volume V" (subtitle "May 1942 MO Operations") ATIS Doc. No. 18665 (WDI 56).

[10] *Saratoga* was still undergoing repairs and modernization in Puget Sound Navy

Saratoga, to be available, these forces were a little stronger than they expected.

No very great force could be spared for Operation "MO" because Yamamoto's Combined Fleet was getting ready for Midway. In mid-April Admiral Nagumo's Carrier Striking Force [11] reached home waters after its Easter raid on Ceylon, with depleted air groups and ships badly in need of upkeep. Rear Admiral Hara's carrier division, *Shokaku* and *Zuikaku*, could, however, be readied in time, and a number of heavy cruisers which had done fine service in the Indies could be spared. The Fourth Fleet (Vice Admiral Shigeyoshi Inouye), based at Truk and Rabaul, could furnish the rest.

As finally constituted, Task Force "MO" comprised (1) the *Port Moresby Invasion Group* of eleven transports carrying both Army troops and a Naval Landing Force, screened by a destroyer squadron; (2) a smaller *Tulagi Invasion Group* for setting up a seaplane base at Tulagi; (3) a *Support Group* built around a seaplane carrier, for establishing a seaplane base in the Louisiades; (4) a *Covering Group* consisting of light carrier *Shoho*,[12] four heavy cruisers and one destroyer, commanded by Rear Admiral Goto; and finally (5) the *Striking Force* of two big carriers, two heavy cruisers and six destroyers, commanded by Vice Admiral Takagi. Admiral Inouye, Commander Fourth Fleet, who exercised the overall command from Rabaul, also controlled four submarines. The naval land-based air force which, though smaller numerically than the United States Army Air Force in northern Australia, was more mobile, but did not come under Inouye's command.

Yard. She had been out of action since 11 Jan. when hit by a submarine torpedo (see Vol. III p. 260). The Japanese then identified her as *Lexington* and thought they had sunk her.

[11] Walton L. Robinson "Akagi" *U. S. Naval Inst. Proc.* LXXIV 579–95 (May 1948) tells the movements of Nagumo's force.

[12] *Shoho* was a converted 12,000-ton carrier of the *Zuiho* class, capable of only 25 knots and so unsuitable to operate with the big carriers. In the early accounts of the battle she is misnamed *Ryukaku*. All Japanese characters are susceptible of two or more transliterations, and we had to catch a Japanese prisoner and get the name from him orally to know what was meant.

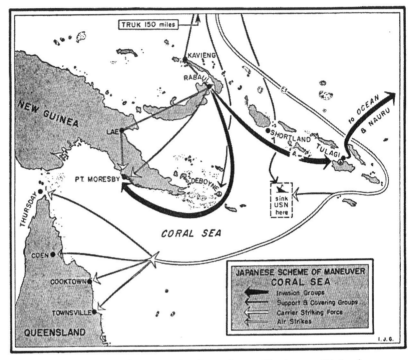

Truk and Rabaul were the jumping-off places. Tulagi was to be occupied first, on 3 May; then the Support and Covering Groups and Striking Forces would cover the Port Moresby Invasion Group, which would leave Rabaul on the 4th and land a sizable army at Port Moresby on the 10th. (A timetable that was never carried out!)

The Japanese expected the United States Navy and the Army Air Force to try to stop them. But the prior occupation of Tulagi and organization there of a seaplane base would make it difficult for the Allies, from their nearest bases at Nouméa and Port Moresby, to follow Japanese ship movements. So, once the Allied Task Force entered the Coral Sea, Admiral Inouye expected to catch and to destroy it by a pincer movement — Goto on the west flank, Takagi on the east — while the Invasion Group nipped through Jomard Pass into Port Moresby. Then, if everything went well, the carriers would proceed to smash up Allied planes and ships at the four Queensland bases, as they had done so successfully at Darwin. Finally, the Tulagi Invasion Group would move up to take Ocean and Nauru Islands.[13]

This complex Japanese plan illustrates a fundamental defect in Japanese naval strategy. Whenever the Japanese planners disposed of sufficient strength, they divided forces and drafted an elaborate plan, the successful execution of which required a tactical competence rare at any time in any Navy, as well as the enemy's passive acceptance of the rôle he was expected to play. That sort of thing worked all right in the Netherlands East Indies, where the Allied forces were heavily outnumbered, and it might have worked here too if the Allies had been surprised. But the Japanese were not sufficiently careful of security. Before 17 April, intelligence reached Cincpac headquarters that a group of transports, protected by light carrier *Shoho* and by a Striking Force that included two large carriers, would enter the Coral Sea, and by the 20th Admiral Nimitz felt certain that Port Moresby was the destination and that trouble would begin on 3 May.[14]

Nimitz and MacArthur properly regarded this Japanese thrust as a major threat. Port Moresby was not simply a place to be denied to the enemy; it was essential for General MacArthur's strategic plans. He intended to develop this advanced outpost as a major air base to block enemy penetration of Australia and as a starting point for his return journey to the Philippines. Although it was clear that whenever battle was joined it would be in the Southwest Pacific Area, on MacArthur's side of the line of demarcation, there was no question of handing the overall command to that distinguished general. According to the strategic arrangements made by the Combined Chiefs of Staff in March, Cincpac must exercise strategic control of any naval operation anywhere in the Pacific; but under no circumstances could he usurp MacArthur's strategic control of ground forces or land-based aircraft within the limits of the latter's command. No ground forces would be involved in this operation (unless the enemy succeeded in landing at Port

[13] Truk Report p. 28–B.
[14] USSBS Summary Report of Pacific War.

Moresby) but about 300 planes of the American Army and Royal Australian Air Forces were under MacArthur's command at Port Moresby, Townsville, Charters Towers and Cloncurry, Australia. Many were nonoperational owing to shortage of spare parts; others had to be used to defend Port Moresby and strike back at Lae and Rabaul. The Navy had only half a dozen Navy Catalinas, based at Nouméa. Thus, Nimitz could not control land-based air searches in this operation. But Inouye, also, had his troubles with the 25th Air Flotilla at Rabaul, as well as all seaplanes, which were under a separate and none too coöperative air command.

In view of the inexperience of Army fliers in over-water work, Nimitz expected to depend mainly on the air groups of *Yorktown* and *Lexington* — fewer than 150 planes — to frustrate the Japanese thrust. These carriers were already familiar with the Coral Sea. *Lexington* was a happy ship. Although commissioned as early as 1927, she still had a number of her original crew (the "plank-owners") on board, and her air group included aviators already famous, such as John S. Thach and "Butch" O'Hare. Their example, as well as combat experience in the air battle of 20 February and the strike on Lae and Salamaua, made all new members of the crew proud to serve in "Lady Lex," as they called her. Captain Frederick C. ("Ted") Sherman, her commanding officer, was a "regular old sea dog" who had taken up air warfare with great zest; officers and men adored him. Rear Admiral Fitch, who relieved Wilson Brown on the flag bridge 3 April, was the most experienced carrier flag officer in the Navy.[15] *Lexington*, moreover, having left Pearl Harbor on 16 April after three weeks' upkeep there, was fresh and taut. Five days later, Cincpac ordered Fitch to rendezvous with Fletcher on 1 May at "Point Buttercup" (lat. 16° S, long. 161°45′ E) west of the New Hebrides.

Rear Admiral Frank Jack Fletcher still commanded the *York-*

[15] See Vol. III of this History pp. 265–68, 381–89. Stanley Johnston *Queen of the Flat-Tops* (1942) is a fine story of *Lexington*, valuable for the description of personalities and life on board a carrier at that period of the war; but it was written too soon after Coral Sea to be reliable as to facts. For Admirals Fitch and Fletcher, see Vol. III p. 236.

town task force (17), then operating out of Nouméa. On 14 April this force was ordered to Tongatabu for replenishment and upkeep in preparation for a fight. *Yorktown*, the Waltzing Matilda of the Pacific Fleet, had been doing turns with her consorts since 14 February except for one week in the not very refreshing advanced naval base at Tongatabu. Her sailors felt that this dance marathon had lasted long enough, and hoped they might continue eastward; but now they must take the old gal over to the Coral Sea and cut in on the Nips.

What else could Cincpac collect? Not Vice Admiral Pye's Task Force 1, consisting entirely of prewar battleships, operating out of San Francisco. Nimitz at one time considered sending them out as a support force; but he could not spare the oilers to fuel them, and anyway they were too slow to keep up with fast-stepping flattops.[16] Vice Admiral Herbert F. Leary, who became Commander of the Southwest Pacific Forces ("MacArthur's Navy"), which absorbed the old Anzac forces,[17] could and did contribute Task Force 44, commanded by that energetic warrior Rear Admiral J. G. Crace RN. At that time the three Australian cruisers of this force were in Sydney; U.S.S. *Chicago* and *Perkins* were at Nouméa. These two were ordered to join Fletcher on 1 May;[18] Admiral Crace to rendezvous with the same task force commander in the Coral Sea on the 4th.[19]

There was a very slim chance of using Admiral Halsey, who blew into Pearl Harbor on 25 April in *Enterprise* with *Hornet*, after carrying Doolittle's Mitchells on the Tokyo raid. His task force (16) comprised half the Pacific Fleet's available carrier

---

[16] TF 1 was ordered to rendezvous with TF 11 near Christmas Island, but on 19 Apr. Cincpac ordered it to remain east of the Line Islands and on the 29th to proceed to San Pedro, California. It is amusing to remember how many people thought the end of the world had come when the Battle Force was sunk at Pearl Harbor, and how little use, until shore bombardment was called for, were the battleships that escaped or were salvaged.

[17] The Anzac organization ceased to exist on 22 April.

[18] *Chicago* War Diary April 1942.

[19] H.M.A.S. *Canberra* was under refit at Sydney. U.S.S. *John D. Edwards* and *Whipple* were to have escorted Admiral Crace's cruisers but *Edwards* developed engine trouble, leaving *Whipple* the sole escort.

strength. Five days was the absolute minimum required for up-keep, the Coral Sea was about 3500 miles away, and the battle was due to break on 3 May. But the enemy might be delayed and Halsey might make it. Admiral Nimitz drew up his operation plan accordingly.

The plan, completed by noon 29 April, simply stated that Admiral Fletcher as officer in tactical command over his own force, Fitch's and Crace's, "will operate in the Coral Sea commencing 1 May." The "how" was up to Fletcher.[20] Coöperating Allied forces not under Fletcher's tactical command were Captain Christie's submarines based at Brisbane, which were to patrol the coastal waters of Papua, the Louisiades and the Bismarcks, and the Allied air forces under MacArthur's command, which were charged with "air reconnaissance of the general area." Although the S-boats' movements were not coördinated with Fletcher's, they added Admiral Shima's flagship and a couple of *Marus* to the Allied bag before the Coral Sea operation was over.

May Day 1942 was anything but cheerful for Admiral Nimitz. Coral Sea was on his hands and something nasty was cooking for the Central Pacific; but he figured that there was time to stop the enemy in the south before deploying to defend the Hawaiian chain. The Australians, apprised of what to expect, saw no point in leaving their meager garrison at Tulagi to be chewed up by the Japanese, and commenced evacuation of that important post in the Solomons on the same day.

[20] Cincpac Op Plan 23-42 of 29 April. If and when TF 16 made rendezvous with TF 17, Halsey as senior to Fletcher would become O.T.C. Crace also was senior to Fletcher, but it had been agreed by the Combined Chiefs of Staff "that the senior United States naval officer commanding a carrier task force will, regardless of relative rank, exercise tactical command of the combined units which operate in the South and Southwest Pacific Areas."

Aubrey Wray Fitch, b. Michigan, Annapolis '06. Served in various ships from 1908, C.O. *Yankton* 1915; gunnery officer *Wyoming* in World War I; C.O. *Luce* and *Mahan* and Comdiv 1 Mine Force. On Naval Mission to Brazil 1922-27; exec. *Nevada;* trained as aviator at N.A.S. Pensacola; C.O. *Wright* 1930; and *Langley* 1931-32. C.O. of N.A.S. Hampton Roads 1932-35; chief of staff to Com Aircraft Battle Force and C.O. *Lexington* 1936. Naval War College senior course 1937-38; Com N.A.S. Pensacola, Comcardiv 1 in *Saratoga* Nov. 1940; CTG 17.5 Mar. 1942; Com Aircraft SoPac Sept. 1942-Apr. 1944; Vice Adm., Dec. 1942. Deputy C.N.O. for Air, Aug. 1944; Supt. Naval Academy 1945-47, when retired as Admiral.

3. *Composition of Forces*

a. Japanese

TASK FORCE "MO"

Vice Admiral Shigeyoshi Inouye (C. in C. Fourth Fleet)
in CL *Kashima*, at Rabaul

LAND–BASED AIR FORCE

Rear Admiral Sadayoshi Yamada (Com 25th Air Flotilla), at Rabaul

Strength and Disposition: 12 VF, 41 VB, 3 seaplanes at Rabaul; 6 VF at Lae; 3 seaplanes at Shortland and 6 at Tulagi, with reinforcement from Tainan and Genzan Air Groups from Truk on 4 May, amounting to some 45 VB and 45 VF.

CARRIER STRIKING FORCE (MOBILE FORCE)

Vice Admiral Takeo Takagi (Comcrudiv 5)

Heavy Cruisers MYOKO, HAGURO

Cardiv 5, Rear Admiral Tadaichi Hara
ZUIKAKU (21 VF, 21 VB, 21 VT)
SHOKAKU (21 VF, 20 VB, 21 VT)
Desdiv 7: USHIO, AKEBONO
Desdiv 27: ARIAKE, YOGURE, SHIRATSUYU, SHIGURE, plus Oiler TOHO MARU

INVASION FORCES

Rear Admiral Aritomo Goto in *Aoba*

TULAGI INVASION GROUP, Rear Admiral Kiyohide Shima

Minelayers * OKINOSHIMA, KOEI MARU
Transport AZUMASAN MARU carrying part of "Kure" Force and a C.B. Unit.
Destroyers * KIKUZUKI, YUZUKI
Converted subchasers TOSHI MARU NO. 3 and TAMA MARU NO. 8 [21]
Converted minesweepers HAGOROMO MARU, NOSHIRO MARU NO. 2,[22] * TAMA MARU
Special minesweepers * NO. 1 and * NO. 2

PORT MORESBY INVASION GROUP

Rear Admiral Sadamichi Kajioka (Comdesron 6) in CL *Yubari*

Destroyers OITE, ASANAGI, UZUKI, MUTSUKI, MOCHIZUKI, YAYOI [23]

* Sunk during this operation; *Okinoshima* by S–42 off Rabaul on 11 May.

[21] Japanese use the same word, *Butai*, for Force, Group or Unit. I have followed U.S. Naval usage in calling subordinate Forces, Groups; and subordinate Groups, Units. On some of the charts, however, Japanese usage has been followed.
[22] Shifted to Port Moresby Group 3 May.
[23] The two DDs in Tulagi Group also belonged to Desron 6.

Transport Unit, Rear Admiral Koso Abe

Minelayer TSUGARU; Fleet minesweeper NO. 20
5 Navy transports carrying major part of "Kure" 3rd Special Naval Landing Force, Base Units, and 6 Army transports carrying South Seas Detachment (Major General Horii)
Converted minesweepers HAGOROMO MARU, NOSHIRO MARU NO. 2, FUMI MARU NO. 2, SEKI MARU NO. 3
Oilers GOYO MARU, HOYO MARU; repair ship OSHIMA [24]

SUPPORT GROUP, Rear Admiral Kuninori Marumo

Crudiv 18 (light): TENRYU, TATSUTA
Seaplane carrier KAMIKAWA MARU [25] and air unit of KIYOKAWA MARU
Gunboats KEIJO MARU, SEIKAI MARU, NIKKAI MARU

COVERING GROUP, Rear Admiral Goto

Heavy Cruisers AOBA, KAKO, KINUGASA, FURUTAKA
Light carrier * SHOHO (12 VF, 9 VT) Capt. Ishinosuke Izawa; destroyer SAZANAMI

SUBMARINE FORCE
Captain Noboru Ishizaki

Patrol Group, I–21, I–22, I–24, I–28, I–29
Raiding Group, RO–33, RO–34 (Capt. Iwagami)

b. Allied Forces [26]

TASK FORCE 17 [27]
Rear Admiral Frank Jack Fletcher in *Yorktown*

TG 17.2 ATTACK GROUP, Rear Admiral Thomas C. Kinkaid (Comcrudiv 6)

MINNEAPOLIS	Capt. Frank J. Lowry
NEW ORLEANS	Capt. Howard H. Good

Rear Admiral William W. Smith (T.F. Cruiser Commander)

ASTORIA	Capt. Francis W. Scanland
CHESTER	Capt. Thomas M. Shock
PORTLAND	Capt. Benjamin Perlman

---

* Sunk during this operation.

[24] In addition, oiler *Iro* was at anchor in Shortland Harbor.
[25] In Vol. III of this History, *Kiyokawa Maru* and *Chitose* are called seaplane tenders; they were, however, seaplane carriers fitted with catapults, a class of which there is no counterpart in the United States Navy.
[26] CTF 17 Operation Order No. 2–42, 1 May 1942, Enclosure B with CTF 17 Action Report 27 May 1942.
[27] As constituted at 0700 May 6. Previously, Kinkaid's and Early's units and *Lexington* belonged to TF 11; Smith's, Hoover's and *Yorktown* were TF 17, and Support Group was designated TF 44.

Destroyer Screen, Captain Alexander R. Early (Comdesron 1)

PHELPS	Lt. Cdr. Edward L. Beck
DEWEY	Lt. Cdr. C. F. Chillingworth Jr.
FARRAGUT	Cdr. George P. Hunter
AYLWIN	Lt. Cdr. Robert H. Rogers
MONAGHAN	Lt. Cdr. William P. Burford

TG 17.3 SUPPORT GROUP, Rear Admiral J. G. Crace RN

H.M.A.S. AUSTRALIA	Capt. H. B. Farncomb RAN
CHICAGO	Capt. Howard D. Bode
H.M.A.S. HOBART	Capt. H. L. Howden RAN

Destroyer Screen, Commander Francis X. McInerney (Comdesdiv 9)

PERKINS	Lt. Cdr. Walter C. Ford
WALKE	Lt. Cdr. Thomas E. Fraser

TG 17.5 CARRIER GROUP, Rear Admiral Aubrey W. Fitch in *Lexington*

YORKTOWN   Capt. Elliott Buckmaster

Air Group, 1 F4F-3 (Wildcat), Lt. Cdr. Oscar Pederson

VF-42:	20 F4F-3	Lt. Cdr. Charles R. Fenton
VB-5:	19 SBD-2, -3 (Dauntless)	Lt. Wallace C. Short
VS-5:	19 SBD-2, -3	Lt. Cdr. William O. Burch Jr.
VT-5:	13 TBD-1 (Devastator)	Lt. Cdr. Joe Taylor

* LEXINGTON   Capt. Frederick C. Sherman

Air Group, 1 F4F-3, * Cdr. William B. Ault

VF-2:	22 F4F-3	Lt. Cdr. Paul H. Ramsey
VB-2:	18 SBD-2, -3	Lt. Cdr. Weldon L. Hamilton
VS-2:	18 SBD-2, -3	Lt. Cdr. Robert E. Dixon
VT-2:	12 TBD-1	Lt. Cdr. James H. Brett Jr.

Destroyer Screen, Captain Gilbert C. Hoover (Comdesron 2) [28]

MORRIS	Cdr. H. B. Jarrett
ANDERSON	Lt. Cdr. J. K. B. Ginder
HAMMANN	Cdr. Arnold E. True
RUSSELL	Lt. Cdr. Glenn R. Hartwig

TG 17.6 FUELING GROUP, Captain John S. Phillips

Oiler	* NEOSHO	Capt. Phillips
Oiler	TIPPECANOE	Cdr. A. Macondray Jr.
Destroyer	* SIMS	Lt. Cdr. Willford M. Hyman
Destroyer	WORDEN	Lt. Cdr. William G. Pogue

* Sunk during this operation.

[28] Desron 2, which also included *Sims* (below), *Walke* (above) and *Moffett, Hughes, O'Brien* and *Mustin*, at this time engaged in other duties, had been one of the pioneer neutrality patrol squadrons and escort-of-convoy squadrons in the Atlantic Fleet. It escorted *Yorktown* to the West Coast after war broke out and participated in the Halsey carrier strike on the Marshalls.

TG 17.9 SEARCH GROUP, Commander George H. DeBaun

Tender TANGIER (at Nouméa)   Cdr. DeBaun
    VP-71 & VP-72: 12 PBY-5 (Catalina) [29]

SOUTHWEST PACIFIC AREA

General Douglas MacArthur USA

ALLIED AIR FORCES, Lieutenant General George H. Brett USA

3rd Light Bombardment Group, 19 B-25, 19 A-24 and 14 A-20, at Charters Towers
22nd Medium Bombardment Group, 12 B-25 and 80 B-26, at Townsville
8th Fighter Group, 100 P-39, half at Port Moresby, half at Townsville
19th Heavy Bombardment Group, 48 B-17, at Cloncurry
49th Fighter Group, 90 P-40, at Darwin
35th Fighter Group, 100 P-39, at Sydney

TF 42 EASTERN AUSTRALIA SUBMARINE GROUP, Rear Admiral Francis
W. Rockwell

TG 42.1, Capt. Ralph W. Christie in tender *Griffin* (Capt. S. D. Jupp)

Subdiv 53, Lt. Cdr. Elmer E. Yeomans	Subdiv 201, Cdr. Ralston B. Van Zant
S-42 Lt. Cdr. O. G. Kirk	S-37 Lt. Cdr. J. R. Z. Reynolds
S-43 Lt. Cdr. E. R. Hannon	S-38 Lt. H. G. Munson
S-44 Lt. Cdr. J. R. Moore	S-39 Lt. F. E. Brown
S-45 Lt. Cdr. I. C. Eddy	S-40 Lt. Cdr. N. Lucker Jr.
S-46 Lt. Cdr. R. C. Lynch	S-41 Lt. Cdr. G. M. Holley
S-47 Lt. Cdr. J. W. Davis	

[29] Half of these arrived 4 May P.M.

CHAPTER II

Into the Coral Sea[1]

1–6 May 1942

East Longitude dates, Zone minus 11 time.

1. *Preliminary Moves*

TO KNOW your enemy's intentions is fine, but such knowledge does not always mean that you can stop him. The solution of the problem in this case lay in applying fleet tactics employed during the first five months of the war — the surprise carrier raid. That was the basis of Nimitz's plan to stop Inouye. Admiral Fletcher was responsible for keeping his command ready for immediate action, and for taking the offensive as soon as he received intelligence of Japanese ship movements, whether from Nimitz, MacArthur or his own pilots. As stated in his own operation order of 1 May, he was there to "destroy enemy ships, shipping and aircraft at favorable opportunities in order to assist in checking further advance by enemy in the New Guinea-Solomons Area."[2]

Fitch's *Lexington* force joined the *Yorktown* force and came under Fletcher's tactical command at 0615 May 1, at a position about 250 miles W by S of Espiritu Santo.[3] Fletcher at once com-

---

[1] *The Battle of the Coral Sea, May 1 to May 11 Inclusive, 1942, Strategical and Tactical Analysis,* a restricted publication by the U. S. Naval War College, 1947, hereafter referred to as *War College Analysis,* is my principal source. This treatise was prepared by Commodore R. W. Bates with the aid of Capt. F. C. Dickey and Capt. S. D. Willingham and Cdr. D. B. Ramage. The information obtained by Lt. Cdr. Salomon at Tokyo was made available to them and they, in turn, made their findings and analyses available for this History.
[2] CTF 17 Op Order 2–42, May 1, 1942.
[3] Lat. 16°16′S, long. 162°20′E.

menced fueling from oiler *Neosho* and directed Fitch to do the same from *Tippecanoe* at a point a few miles to the west and south, where *Chicago* and *Perkins*, which Admiral Crace had sent on ahead, were also to join and fuel. As usual in forces commanded by Admiral Fletcher, fueling was a very leisurely affair, and Fitch did not even start pumping until next day, at the end of which *Chicago* and *Perkins*, first to fill up, peeled off and steamed north to join Fletcher. Fitch, who appears to have been given a bad estimate of how long it would take, informed his O.T.C. that the *Lexington* group could not complete fueling until noon of the 4th. Fletcher, who was receiving intelligence from MacArthur about the approach of enemy forces, felt he could not afford to wait that long, and decided to steam out into the middle of the Coral Sea without Fitch or Crace and try to ascertain the enemy's exact whereabouts by plane search. At 1800 May 2 he headed west [4] at slow speed, leaving Fitch orders to rejoin him at daylight May 4 in lat. 15° S, long. 157° E.[5] By that time all Allied ships would be fueled, ready and in a position to intercept the enemy. At least so Fletcher estimated.

The Japanese, however, pulled a surprise while Fletcher was a good 500 miles from Tulagi. At about 0800 May 3, Admiral Shima's Tulagi Invasion Group made an unopposed landing on the beaches which United States Marines were to win back three months later. In support of the landing, Admiral Goto's Covering Group milled around south of New Georgia, with Admiral Marumo's Support Group sixty miles farther to the westward; but Admiral Takagi's big carriers, with which Fletcher eventually grappled, were well north of Bougainville, keeping out of Allied air-search range, and planning to enter the Coral Sea from the eastward on the 4th.

[4] At 1530 May 2, shortly before Admiral Fletcher turned westward, a scout plane from *Yorktown* sighted an enemy submarine in lat. 16°04′ S, long. 162°18′ E, and three SBDs were vectored out to attack it. Fletcher assumed that his presence would be made known to the enemy, but no report from the submarine ever reached Admiral Inouye. Thus the presence of an American carrier force in this area still remained unknown to the enemy.

[5] The same rendezvous had been arranged with Rear Admiral Crace RN for *Australia* and *Hobart*. CTF 17 Action Report 27 May 1942.

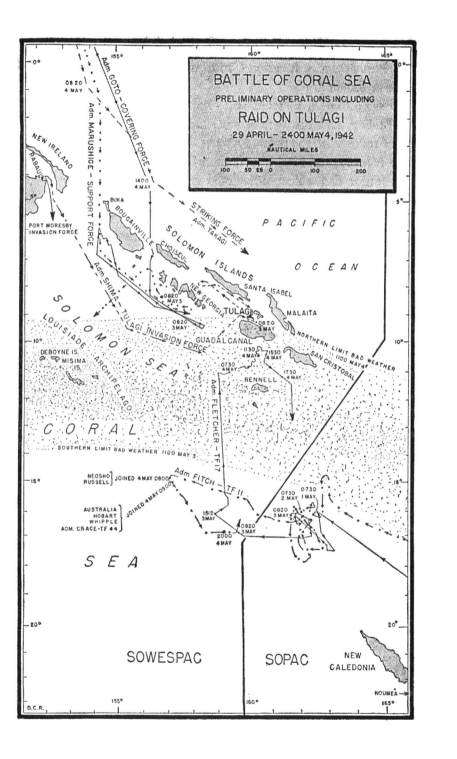

The Port Moresby Invasion Group was still swinging around the hook at Rabaul.[6]

At 0800 May 3, Fletcher and Fitch were about 100 miles apart and fueling, each unaware of what the enemy was doing, and each out of touch with the other. Fletcher was topping off his destroyers from *Neosho*, and Fitch was draining *Tippecanoe* to the last drop. The junior flag officer completed fueling at 1310, twenty-four hours ahead of the predicted time; but he could not break radio silence to inform his senior of this important fact, and for some reason unknown made no attempt to send a message by airplane drop. Instead, he set a course immediately for the planned rendezvous with Fletcher next morning.

Fletcher continued fueling destroyers from *Neosho* during daylight on the 3rd. Then, at 1900, he received an intelligence report from MacArthur that gave him a hot-foot. Australia-based planes had sighted two transports debarking troops off Tulagi, and five or six Japanese warships between that place and Santa Isabel. This startling news brought an immediate change in Fletcher's plans. He directed oiler *Neosho* with destroyer *Russell* as escort to peel off and meet Fitch and Crace at the fueling rendezvous at 0800 May 4, and with them to proceed eastward to join him at a point about 300 miles south of Guadalcanal [7] at daybreak 5 May. One hour and a half after obtaining the word he "had been waiting two months to receive," Admiral Fletcher headed north at 24 knots to which three more were soon added. He had determined to strike Tulagi with the planes of his one available carrier.

The Japanese assumed, on the basis of their easy conquests in the Netherlands East Indies, that once Tulagi was in their hands no one would dare molest it. Consequently Goto's and Marushige's groups that had supported the operation, retired at 1100 May 3, after the island had been secured. Hara's carriers were still north of Bougainville, flying off to Rabaul nine planes they had ferried

[6] *War College Analysis.*
[7] Lat. 15° S, long. 160° E.

down from Truk.[8] The Port Moresby Invasion Group was still anchored at Rabaul, scheduled to leave at 1800 next day. Only the ships of the Tulagi Invasion Force, and not all of them, were in the sound between Tulagi and Guadalcanal.

Fletcher maintained his northerly course throughout the night, and by 0700 May 4 arrived at lat. 11°10′ S, long. 158°49′ E, about 100 miles southwest of Guadalcanal. About the same time, Fitch got the word from *Neosho* and *Russell* concerning his senior's change in plans. At 0900 Crace's force, *Australia*, *Hobart* and *Whipple*, joined him after an uneventful sail from Sydney. So, at this critical juncture, Fitch and Crace were about 250 miles south of Fletcher, unable to support him in case of need; and throughout 4 May, when *Yorktown* was launching and recovering planes, Fitch directed *Lexington* on a southeasterly course, increasing the distance between the two carriers.

2. *Tulagi Strike, 4 May*

As Admiral Fletcher approached a launching position for his Tulagi strike, he ran into foul weather, which for carrier sailors can mean good fortune. The northern edge of a 100-mile-wide cold front which had moved up from Australia had now reached the north coast of Guadalcanal. The sky was overcast, rainsqualls became frequent, and the southeast tradewind blew 25 to 35 knots. It was not good flying weather, but the cold front afforded Fletcher a curtain for his ships and even for his planes until they came within twenty miles of Tulagi. There, fortunately for him, fair weather prevailed.

At 0630 May 4, ten minutes before sunrise, *Yorktown* commenced launching an attack group of 12 TBD (Devastator) torpedo planes and 28 SBD (Dauntless) dive-bombers. Next, a

[8] Report No. 7, Crudiv 6, Battle of the Coral Sea, WDC No. 160,997, July 17 1942.

combat air patrol of 6 F4F–3 (Wildcat) fighters was put in the air. Cruiser float planes flew anti-submarine patrol. *Yorktown* had only 18 fighters operational, and they had to be used for combat air patrol over the carrier, working in three shifts. Thus the attacking bombers had only their own .30-caliber machine guns for protection if they ran into aërial opposition; but the risk had to be accepted.

Each air squadron flew to the target and attacked independently, according to the naval air practice of those primeval beginnings of carrier warfare.[9]

Lieutenant Commander Burch's scouting squadron of SBDs arrived first over Tulagi and began its attack at 0815. As usual throughout the war, the pilots overestimated what they saw; all their swans were geese, and all their geese, ducks or goslings. Admiral Shima's flagship, a fleet minelayer, they took for a light cruiser, the transport for a seaplane tender, the larger minesweepers for transports, and landing barges for gunboats; only the two destroyers present were correctly identified. The scout planes dropped thirteen 1000-pound bombs, damaging destroyer *Kikuzuki* so that she had to be beached,[10] and in addition sending two small minesweepers to Davy Jones's locker. Lieutenant Commander Joe Taylor's torpedo planes came in five minutes later and launched eleven torpedoes but only knocked off sweeper *Tama Maru*. Next, at 0830, Lieutenant Short's bombers dropped another fifteen 1000-pound bombs with possible minor damage to a couple of ships. All planes landed safely on board *Yorktown* at 0931 and rearmed immediately for a second attack. As Burch said, not even time for the pilots to get a cup of coffee![11]

This second strike, consisting of 27 SBDs, each carrying a half-ton bomb, and 11 TBDs, commenced launching an hour after their return. They damaged a patrol craft and destroyed two seaplanes.

---

[9] The air group commander, Lt. Cdr. Oscar Pederson, did not accompany the attack group as his services were needed on board *Yorktown* as fighter-director officer. No other strike group commander was appointed.

[10] Eventually the tide washed her off the beach and she sank.

[11] Washington *Post* 19 Sept. 1942.

The torpedo-bombers came in through heavy anti-aircraft fire and every one launched; but their score was zero and one of them was lost on the return.

As the pilots reported three more Japanese seaplanes anchored off Makambo Island in Tulagi Harbor, Admiral Fletcher sent up four fighter planes that afternoon to get them, which they did. The Wildcats then spotted destroyer *Yuzuki* steaming away, made four strafing runs on her, killed the captain and many others; but the ship got away with only minor damage. As the planes were returning to *Yorktown*, two became separated from the rest and crash-landed on the south coast of Guadalcanal, but both pilots were rescued that night by destroyer *Hammann*.

A third attack group of 21 SBDs launched at 1400 dropped 21 more half-tonners, but sank only four landing barges. By 1632 all had returned to the carrier, and the "Battle of Tulagi" was over.

"The Tulagi operation was certainly disappointing in terms of ammunition expended to results obtained," said Admiral Nimitz, who took this opportunity to emphasize "the necessity for target practice at every opportunity." [12] At any later period of the war their performance would have been laughable, but all hands in Task Force 17 were jubilant. They believed they had sunk two destroyers, one freighter and four gunboats, forced a light cruiser ashore, and severely damaged a third destroyer, a second freighter and a seaplane tender ("may have been a heavy cruiser")! [13] In fact they believed that most of the Japanese fleet headed their way had been destroyed, an illusion that might have been very costly if it had lasted longer. As Fletcher headed south for his next-morning rendezvous with Fitch, he signaled Admiral W. W. Smith, ordering him to designate two heavy cruisers to "go into Savo Island and clean up the cripples the following dawn." *Astoria* and *Chester* were selected; but Admiral Fletcher canceled this order, fortu-

---

[12] Cincpac endorsement on CTF 17 Action Report 17 June 1942. They had expended 22 torpedoes, seventy-six 1000-lb bombs, and about 83,000 rounds of machine-gun bullets.
[13] *Yorktown* Air Group Report of 11 May 1942.

nately so; for if the two cruisers had carried out the assignment they would have encountered enemy carriers and it is unlikely that "Poco" Smith or "Tommy" Shock would have lived to tell the tale.[14]

3. *Interlude, 5–6 May*

When Fletcher's planes hit Tulagi, the Japanese supporting and covering forces were too far away to answer the base commander's call for help. Takagi, commanding the Carrier Force, did not get the word until about noon when he was just completing fueling north of Bougainville. He made best speed to the southeastward but by midnight had only reached a position about a hundred miles north of the southern cape of Santa Isabel. Fortunate indeed that Admiral Fletcher had achieved complete surprise, for if any of these Japanese forces had been within striking distance he could have got no help from Admiral Fitch, who was widening the gap between Fletcher and himself through all three daylight watches.

Yorktown, after recovering her planes, started south fast and met *Lexington* at the scheduled rendezvous, lat. 15° S, long. 160° E, at 0816 May 5.[15] Just at the end of the morning watch, one of *Yorktown's* planes on patrol shot down a Japanese four-engine seaplane which belonged to the 25th Air Flotilla based on Rabaul. Since this air flotilla was not under his command, Admiral Inouye was unaware of this plane's loss or whereabouts, hence he used most of his planes on the 5th for a bombing attack on Port Moresby.

Admiral Fletcher spent the rest of 5 May refueling from *Neosho*,

---

[14] Naval War College interrogation of Capt. T. M. Shock, C. O. of *Chester*, 1 Oct. 1946.

[15] *Hammann* and *Perkins*, left behind to search for survivors of the three lost planes, caught up with TF 17 before it reached the rendezvous. Admiral Fletcher deserves great credit for initiating efforts to rescue aviators downed in combat. As gradually perfected, "air-sea rescue" added immeasurably to the morale of American aviators, and saved hundreds of trained pilots for further combat.

steaming within visual signaling distance of Admirals Fitch and Crace on a southeasterly course. The ships were well out of the cold front, and for two days they enjoyed the perfect weather of tropic seas when fresh trades are blowing — wind from the southeast, force 4; fat cumulus clouds rolling along, casting purple shadows on the opalescent Coral Sea. Task Force 17 was feeling fine. So far as most of the bluejackets knew, they had already turned back the Nips, and scuttlebutt was full of a forthcoming liberty at Sydney.

At 1930 Fletcher changed course to the northwest, assuming correctly that the enemy would be coming out of Rabaul. The Port Moresby Invasion Group and Marumo's Support Group were steaming merrily along on a southerly course aiming at the Jomard Passage through the Louisiade Archipelago. Meanwhile, Admiral Takagi's Striking Force was beating down along the outer coast of the Solomons. At 1900 May 5 it rounded San Cristobal, turned west and passed north of Rennell Island, cruising at 25 knots. By dawn 6 May the enemy carriers were well into the Coral Sea. Goto's Covering Group began refueling from oiler *Iro* at Shortland Island south of Bougainville, completed it at 0830 May 6 and again put to sea. Thus the 5th of May passed peacefully, except for the one plane shot down by *Yorktown*.

Next day, the 6th, was a busy one for all hands, whether Australian, American or Japanese. Everyone was getting a little warmer; something big was bound to happen soon. At 0730 Admiral Fletcher decided it was time to place in effect his operation order drawn up on the 1st, integrating Fitch's and Crace's forces with his own into one task force, 17.[16] The order was little more than a repetition of the injunction to "destroy enemy ships, shipping and aircraft at favorable opportunities." Fletcher was feeling his way along; when the time came he would see what chips the enemy would put on the table and react accordingly. He intended to delegate the tactical command during air operations to Admiral Fitch, who was an experienced carrier sailor; but

[16] CTF 17 Op Order No. 2–42.

by some oversight Fitch was never notified of this until immediately before the action on 8 May.[17]

Meanwhile, Commander G. H. DeBaun in tender *Tangier*, who had charge of the PBY search group in Nouméa, was doing his best. But he had only twelve Catalinas and they were too far away to search the Solomons; to the westward and northwestward their scope was limited by military punctilio – the demarcation line between the South Pacific and Southwest Pacific areas. The western three quarters of the Coral Sea were supposed to be searched by United States Army planes based in Australia, but it was physically impossible for them to do it. And as Fletcher was operating on the MacArthur side of the demarcation line he had to supplement land-based air search by reconnaissance flights of his own carrier-based planes.

Throughout these two days, Fletcher was receiving reports from Brisbane and Pearl Harbor of a large number of enemy ships of practically every type, including three carriers, south of the Solomons; but only by the afternoon of the 6th was it possible for Intelligence to make any sense out of them. Fletcher's staff then confirmed the Admiral's "hunch" that the Port Moresby Invasion Group would turn the corner of New Guinea through Jomard Passage after establishing a forward seaplane base in the Louisiades, and that they would come through next day or the 8th, if not stopped. The Admiral, who had spent a good part of the 6th fueling, cut it short, since in so doing he had to head into the southeast wind, away from the enemy. At 1930 May 6, he resumed his former course to the northwestward in order to be within striking distance of the Port Moresby Invasion Group by daylight May 7.[18] But as Allied Intelligence had but fragmentary knowledge of the movements of Takagi's big carriers, owing to inadequate land-based air search, Fletcher had no knowledge of them, no apprehension of the Japanese plan of envelopment.[19] The Japanese

[17] Statement by Admiral Fitch to Commo. R. W. Bates 30 Nov. 1946.
[18] CTF 17 Action Report 27 May 1942. *Neosho* and *Sims* were detached to operate to the southward.
[19] *War College Analysis.*

Striking Force had changed from a northwesterly to a due south course at 0930 May 6 and was dropping right down on Fletcher's line of advance, but that he did not know. His morning plane search that day turned back just short of the Japanese carriers, and the afternoon search, too, missed them because Takagi was still under an overcast. So *Yorktown* and *Lexington* plodded along on their northwesterly course unobserving and unobserved. By midnight 6 May they had reached a point [20] about 310 miles from Deboyne Island, off the tail end of the New Guinea bird, where the Japanese had established a temporary seaplane anchorage to cover their advance.[21]

Admiral Takagi continued on his southerly course until the second dog watch, when he too had to fuel. At that moment he was only 70 miles distant from Admiral Fletcher; but each was unaware of the other's presence. As nearly as can be ascertained, Takagi ordered no long-range searches on either 5 or 6 May, an amazing omission.[22] Had he done so on the afternoon of the 6th, he would have caught Fletcher fueling, a tough spot for any sailor, and in the bright sunlight at that. Moreover, a failure in communications lost him a wonderful opportunity to catch the American flattops flatfooted. At about 1100 May 6, a Japanese search plane from Rabaul reported Fletcher's position correctly, but Takagi never got the word until too late. So, when he turned north against the light evening breeze to fuel, he was opening range on Fletcher, although closing the Port Moresby Invasion Group which it was his job to protect. The main action of the Battle of the Coral Sea should have been fought on 6 May, and would have been if each force had been aware of the other's presence.

Nevertheless, the 6th day of May did not pass without incident. At 1030, four Flying Fortresses of the 19th Bombardment Group

[20] Lat. 14°03′ S, long. 156°25′ E.

[21] Lt. Cdr. Salomon's notes taken in Tokyo. The Japanese intended to set up two other bases at Samarai Island and Cape Rodney, but never did.

[22] It was the custom of Japanese carrier forces at this time to rely for searches wholly on the float planes of escorting battleships and cruisers. Whether that was done on this occasion I do not know.

from Cloncurry, staging through Port Moresby, dropped twelve bombs at *Shoho* of Goto's Covering Group, then about 60 miles south of Bougainville. Although the carrier had no planes in the air the bombs fell so wide that she was able to launch "Zekes," which drove off the B-17s.[23] Around noon more Allied planes sighted Goto, then heading south looking for trouble; and at 1300 they located the Port Moresby invaders not far south of Rabaul.[24]

Takagi had radio intelligence of what was going on. Inouye now knew that two of his forces had been sighted, estimated that Fletcher was about 500 miles to the southeast of the Japanese forces then moving into the Louisiades, and expected him to attack next day, the 7th. So, at 1520 May 6, Inouye directed all operations to continue according to plan. By midnight the Port Moresby-bound transports were closing Misima Island, almost ready to slip through Jomard Pass. Marumo, who had reached that position well ahead of them, dropped the seaplane carrier *Kamikawa Maru* and retired to the northwestward, up near the D'Entrecasteaux Islands. Goto in the meantime was protecting the left flank of the Port Moresby invaders, *Shoho* furnishing the combat air patrol until sundown at 1815. Four hours later, this light carrier changed course to the WSW for next morning's agreed launching position. By midnight she was about 90 miles northeast of Deboyne Island where *Kamikawa Maru* was ready to fly next day's air search.

This was the day, the 6th of May, that marked the low point of the war for American arms; General Wainwright was forced to surrender his forces in the Philippines. But on the very next day there opened a new and brighter chapter in the Pacific war. The time had come for the Allies to take their first step forward. The transition from Corregidor to Coral Sea is startling, dramatic and of vast importance.

[23] The B-17s claimed only "one near-miss off light cruisers." "AAF Bombardment Group Participating in the Battle of Coral Sea," prepared by the Reference Section, AAF Historical Office, 29 Oct. 1946; *Shoho* War Diary.

[24] At about 0900 May 7, Admiral Inouye postponed the advance of the Port Moresby Invasion Group, owing to the suspected presence of the Allied Task Force.

CHAPTER III

Coral Sea: Actions of 7 May

East Longitude date, Zone minus 11 time.

1. *Loss of* Neosho *and* Sims [1]

WHEN oiler *Neosho* and destroyer *Sims* were detached from Fletcher's task force at 1755 May 6, they headed south for Point "Rye," lat. 16° S, long. 158° E, their next fueling rendezvous,[2] and arrived there about 0810 next morning. Two planes were observed some ten miles away — carrier planes evidently and ours hopefully. Unfortunately, they were Hara's, of Takagi's Striking Force.

That force, as we have seen, reversed course to the northward on the evening of 6 May and maintained it until two hours after midnight, when it turned again and headed south. Since as yet Admiral Takagi had no knowledge of the position of any Allied naval force, he decided on Hara's recommendation to make a thorough search southward in order to make sure no carriers were behind him when he moved westward to provide cover for the Port Moresby Invasion Group. At 0600 May 7 the search went out.[3] Hara, as he ruefully admitted after the war, "was quite pleased

---

[1] "Engagement of U.S.S. *Neosho* with Japanese Aircraft on May 7, 1942; Subsequent Loss of *Neosho*; Search for Survivors," 25 May 1942. *Neosho* and *Sims* survivors' reports disagree but we have for the most part used the *Neosho* reports, as she had many more survivors with more complete information. Compare San Francisco *Chronicle* 10 July 1942.

[2] The Fueling Group, unless otherwise directed, was to pass through Point "Rye" one hour after sunrise on odd days and Point "Corn" (lat. 15° S, long. 160° E) at the same time on even days. At other times it was to operate south of a line joining these two points. CTF 17 Op Order No. 2-42 dated 1 May 1942.

[3] From lat. 13°12′ S, long. 158°05′ E.

with himself at the time for making this change, as by so doing his planes located what they reported as the United States carrier force at the eastern edge of the search sector. . . . In the end it did not prove to be a fortunate decision." [4] Nor was it fortunate for the poor tanker and her single-stack escort, destroyer *Sims*. One of the Japanese search planes reported them at 0736 as a carrier and a cruiser, a compliment to *Neosho* and *Sims* which, if known, would not have been appreciated. Hara accepted this evaluation 100 per cent, promptly ordered an all-out bombing and torpedo attack, and closed distance.

Sims was patrolling about a mile ahead of *Neosho* shortly after 0900 when a single plane appeared and dropped a bomb near by. Both ships went to General Quarters. Half an hour later, 15 high-level bombers dropped, missed and disappeared. At 1038 another group of ten made a horizontal bombing attack on *Sims*, which swung hard right and avoided nine bombs dropped simultaneously. About noon her number came up when 36 dive-bombers arrived. *Sims* went to flank speed and turned left to take position on *Neosho's* port quarter. The planes, aiming for "carrier" *Neosho*, came in from astern in three waves. *Sims* fired away as best she could but one of her four 20-mm guns jammed early and her main battery accounted for only one plane. Three 500-pound bombs hit the destroyer, two exploded in her engine room, and within a few minutes she buckled amidships and sank stern first.[5]

All hands began to abandon ship. Just as the sea reached the top of the single stack, a terrific explosion occurred. What remained of the ship was lifted ten to fifteen feet out of the water. A smaller explosion from depth charges followed. Chief Signalman R. J. Dicken began picking up the few survivors with a damaged whaleboat which the sailors had managed to cut loose; he found only 15

---

[4] Truk Report p. 28–B.

[5] Buships *Summary of War Damage to U. S. Battleships, Carriers, Cruisers and Destroyers, 17 Oct. 1941–7 Dec. 1942* p. 18; Comdespac to Secnav 8 July 1942. In his endorsement to this letter, Admiral Nimitz described this percentage of hits on a high-speed maneuvering destroyer as "extraordinary." It was, compared with ours on destroyer *Tanikaze* at Midway.

men alive. In the meantime, 20 dive-bombers concentrated on the "Fat Lady," as *Neosho* had been nicknamed by the sailors of the fighting ships that she fed.[6] Within a few minutes they scored 7 direct hits and 8 near-misses, one by a suicider who exploded against No. 4 gun station; gasoline burst from the plane's tanks and flowed blazing along the deck. Captain Phillips ordered all hands to "make preparations to abandon ship and stand by."[7] That order does not mean "all hands jump over the side," but that is what a number of sailors did; they had just seen *Sims* blow up and sink. Two whaleboats and some rafts were lowered or thrown overboard and a considerable number of the premature evacuees were brought back on board, but many were drowned and others who had climbed onto rafts drifted away as night fell over the Coral Sea; and it was a rough night for rafts.

These men paid dearly for their lack of discipline; yet many would have been saved but for a bad mistake by the ship's navigator, a lieutenant who shall remain nameless here, although what he did must be inserted as a cautionary tale for young naval officers. During a lull in the engagement this officer took a fix from the sun and Venus but plotted it wrong, getting the position lat. 16°25′S, long. 157°31′E. The correct position, as subsequently plotted by Captain Phillips, was lat. 16°09′S, long. 158°03′E. As a result of this error, search for survivors did not commence at the proper point.

For four days, 7 to 11 May, *Neosho* drifted westerly before the trades. All hands were frantically trying to keep her afloat. The dead were buried and the wounded cared for as well as conditions allowed. Admiral Leary ordered the PBYs based on tender *Tangier* at Nouméa to search for survivors, and early on the 9th sent out destroyer *Henley* to rescue any floaters reported by the

---

[6] A survivor remembered hearing, during a moment's lull in the fight, this monologue from a gun captain: "Oh, come, come, come in and see the Fat Lady! See her qui-v-ver as she laughs! Count her double chins! Come one! Come all! Come in! Bring the missus!" Charles Rawlings and Isabel Leighton "Fat Girl," *Sat. Eve. Post* 6 Feb. 1943 pp. 10–11.

[7] *Neosho* Report.

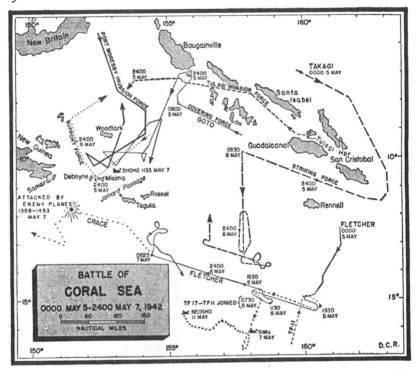

BATTLE OF
CORAL SEA
0000 MAY 5-2400 MAY 7, 1942

Catalinas and take off the rest of *Neosho's* crew. Owing to the navigator's mistake they had the devil's own time accomplishing their mission. The oiler was picked up only about noon 11 May by a PBY. She reported to *Henley,* and that afternoon the destroyer took off the 123 men still on board and scuttled poor "Fat Lady." [8] *Henley* searched for floating survivors the rest of that day and the next, with no luck; and on the 12th headed for Brisbane so that the seriously wounded might have better medical attention than a destroyer could provide.

By this time Captain Phillips had replotted the position of the air attack, and destroyer *Helm* took up the search. On 17 May, three days out of Nouméa, she found a raft with four men alive, last survivors of 68 men in four life rafts that had kept together.[9]

[8] Lat. 15°35′ S, long. 155°36′ E. *Henley* War Diary 9–31 May 1942.
[9] One of the four died later (Medical Officer's Report, Enclosure with *Helm* War Diary May 1942). The position where the raft was found was lat. 15°25′ S, long. 154°56′ E.

This high mortality, excessive for a raft voyage of ten days in tropic seas, was largely due to carelessness and poor discipline. After several such experiences in 1942, the Navy improved the design and equipment of life rafts and provided all hands with rough directions for raft navigation.

Sims and "Fat Lady" did not die in vain. If they had not drawn off this strike, Hara's planes might have found and attacked Fletcher on the 7th when the American planes were working over *Shoho*. In the end this operation caused Hara "much chagrin" and cost him half a dozen of his precious carrier planes.[10]

2. *Crace's Chase*

Admiral Fletcher, when not fueling, steered northwesterly for almost 36 hours until, at 0625 May 7, he reached a point about 115 miles due south of Rossel Island,[11] easternmost of the Louisiade Archipelago which trails off from New Guinea like detached tail-feathers. Twenty minutes later, when the sun rose, he turned north. At the same time he ordered Admiral Crace's Support Group to push ahead, on the same northwesterly course parallel to and south of the Louisiades, and attack the Port Moresby Invasion Group which reconnaissance planes reported to be heading for Jomard Passage, with the obvious intention of whipping into Port Moresby. Fletcher later explained that he had detached Crace because he expected an air duel with enemy carriers, and wished to ensure that the Japanese invasion would be thwarted, even if they finished him. But, if Takagi had stopped Fletcher, Crace's ships would probably have been chewed up too; and, by sending Crace chasing westward, Fletcher weakened his already exiguous anti-aircraft screen [12] and lessened his chances of checking Takagi. Conversely, if Fletcher won the carrier battle he would be in a position to break up the Port Moresby Invasion

[10] Truk Report pp. 28–B, C.
[11] Lat. 13°20′ S, long. 154°21′ E.
[12] Fletcher detached *Farragut* from his own screen and lent her to Crace.

Group even if they did turn the corner. Possibly this diversion served the good purpose of puzzling the enemy and causing him to concentrate his land-based air on Crace's cruisers instead of Fletcher's carriers; but it was only by a special dispensation of Providence that the Support Group escaped a fatal bombing.

Rear Admiral Crace RN, characterized by his American screen commander as an "excellent seaman" and "gallant gentleman who accepted the United States ships into his command with warmth, affection and admiration for their efficiency," assumed a diamond-shaped anti-aircraft formation and steamed on at 25 knots. He had not gone far when, at 0810, *Chicago* sighted a twin-float monoplane swooping around maddeningly, just out of gun range. United States Army reconnaissance planes from Australia were sighted by the Support Group at 0940 and again at 1136.

At 1358, when the group had reached a point south and a little west of Jomard Pass, it was attacked by eleven single-engine land-based planes. All ships opened fire and drove them off. Immediately after, radar picked up twelve "Sallys" (type 96, 2-engine land-based Navy bombers) 75 miles away. Crace ordered radical maneuvers and every ship opened fire as the planes came in low. Eight aërial torpedoes were dropped, but all missed and five of the bombers were shot down.[13] Immediately after the surviving torpedo planes had retired, 19 high-flying "Sallys" dropped their steel eggs from an altitude of 15,000 to 20,000 feet.[14] The ships dodged the bombs as they had the torpedoes, and the planes flew away. Within a few minutes, more trouble developed from an unexpected source. Three bombers jumped *Farragut* and narrowly missed her. Observations by the attacked destroyer, confirmed by photographs taken by the planes themselves, proved beyond possibility of doubt that they were B–17s of the U. S. Army Air Force, from Townsville. Admiral Crace, somewhat upset, com-

---

[13] Three torpedoes were aimed at *Australia*, one at *Hobart*, and four at *Chicago*. CTF 44 (Admiral Crace) "Attack by Torpedo Bombers and High Level Bomber Aircraft" 21 May 1942; *Chicago* Action Report 11 May 1942.

[14] *Chicago* Report says there were 26 planes in this attack.

plained to Admiral Leary, who replied that he had plans to improve Army recognition of naval vessels. But the Army Air commander under General MacArthur insisted that there had been no bombing of Crace's force, declined the plans and prohibited further discussion of the matter.[15]

By midnight Admiral Crace had reached a position about 120 miles south of the New Guinea bird's tail.[16] He continued on his westerly course part of the night and then, having heard that the Port Moresby invaders had turned back, headed south and retired to Australia.

Crace's chase may have served no useful purpose but it was far from inglorious. It proved, as the Abda Command never did, that ships of two nations could be made into an excellent tactical unit. And, as the Japanese attack was of the same type and strength as the one that sank H.M.S. *Prince of Wales* and *Repulse*, on 10 December 1941, the escape of the Support Group without a single hit is a tribute to its training, and to the high tactical competence of its commander. The Japanese, strangely enough, thought they had bettered the score of 10 December. They claimed having sunk an *Augusta* class cruiser (*Chicago*) and a *California* class battleship (*Australia*) and having torpedoed another battleship like H.M.S. *Warspite*. Apparently *Chicago* doubled for her, too; since in the later "Battle of Sydney" she was again reported to be *Warspite*. Ship recognition comes hard to the "fly-fly boys" of every nation; let those who have tried it from 10,000 feet, without previous training, cast the first stone!

3. *"Scratch One Flattop"*

While the planes of Takagi's powerful Striking Force were slaughtering *Neosho* and *Sims* and Marumo's Support Group was

---

[15] Letters from Crace to Leary 12 May; Leary to Crace 16 May; General Brett to Leary 19 May 1942; in "Administrative History Seventh Fleet."
[16] Lat. 12°44′ S, long. 149°59′ E.

herding the Port Moresby invaders toward Jomard Pass, Goto's Covering Group (four heavy cruisers and light carrier *Shoho*) continued on its WSW course until 0700 May 7, when it headed southeast into the wind to launch four reconnaissance planes. Half an hour later *Shoho* launched an additional five planes to cover the Port Moresby Invasion Group, then about 30 miles to the southwestward.

Admiral Fletcher, after detaching Admiral Crace at 0645 May 7, changed course to the northward and launched a search mission. The first important contact, made by a *Yorktown* plane at 0815, reported "two carriers and four heavy cruisers" in lat. 10°03′ S, long. 152°27′ E, a position about 175 miles to the northwestward, t'other side of the Louisiades. Fletcher naturally took this to be the Striking Force and pressed forward, eager to attack. *Lexington* began launching at 0926, when she had reached a point about 160 miles southeast of the "two carriers and four cruisers" reported at 0815; *Yorktown* followed suit half an hour later. Ninety-three planes were airborne by 1030; [17] 47 were left for reserve and combat air patrol. The force had now reëntered the cold front, a gusty wind blew from the southeast and cloud cover increased, although it never became so thick as to hamper launching and recovery. But Goto was out in the broad sunlight, and his position was near enough to the reported one of the "two carriers" to serve very well.

No sooner had *Yorktown's* attack group been launched than her scout planes returned. It was then discovered that, owing to an improper arrangement of the pilots' code contact pad, their reported "two carriers and four heavy cruisers" at 0815 should have read "two heavy cruisers and two destroyers." They had not seen Takagi's force or even Goto's, but Marumo's — then composed of two antique light cruisers screened by two or three converted gunboats! Admiral Fletcher's all-out strike had been

---

[17] *Lexington* group comprised 15 VB, 10 VS, 12 VT, 10 VF and the air group commander with 3 VSB. *Yorktown* group consisted of 17 VS, 8 VB, 10 VT and 8 VF. Her air group commander remained on board as fighter-director officer. The Tulagi strike had cost 3 planes, leaving 140 available on the 7th, and some were not operational.

launched against these feeble ships, in a direction at right angles to that from which the two big Japanese carriers were approaching him. He was in a serious predicament, particularly since his location was well known to the enemy.

Japanese planes had been trailing the United States carriers and reporting to Rabaul. At 0830 Goto knew exactly where Fletcher was, and reported his position to *Shoho*, which promptly prepared for an attack.[18] Other enemy aircraft in the meantime sighted Crace's cruisers pressing westward.[19] The first effect of these contacts, fortunately for Fletcher (and he needed a bit of luck at this point), was to make Admiral Inouye anxious for the safety of his transports. At 0900 Inouye ordered the Port Moresby Invasion Group to turn away instead of entering Jomard Pass. He wished to keep it out of harm's way until Fletcher and Crace were properly handled; but, as it turned out, 0900 May 7 marked the nearest that this or any other Japanese naval force got to Port Moresby.

Commander W. B. Ault's attack group from *Lexington*, well ahead of the *Yorktown* planes, passed Tagula Island, biggest of the Louisiades, about 1100. Shortly thereafter, Lieutenant Commander W. L. Hamilton in one of the scout planes of the attack group, flying at 15,000 feet, had the great good luck to sight one carrier, two or three heavy cruisers and one or two destroyers, 25 to 30 miles on his starboard hand.[20] These were *Shoho* and the rest of Goto's Covering Group. Goto, about the same time, sighted him and began evasive action as Commander Ault with his two wing planes went in for the first attack.[21] A couple of "Zekes" tried

[18] *Shoho* War Diary (WDC No. 160,465) 7 May.
[19] Apparently Hara's contact on *Neosho* and *Sims* was not received by Goto or Inouye until later.
[20] *Lexington* Action Report, Report of Scouting Squadron 2.
[21] American newspapers of 19 June 1942 carried a story from MacArthur's headquarters of U. S. Army bombers, led by Capt. John Roberts USA, attacking the Covering Group a few minutes before the carrier planes did, and hitting a cruiser. But the official history, *Army Air Forces in World War II* i 44, states only that the enemy was sighted first by an Army reconnaissance plane which passed on its position to the carriers' attack groups. It is true that at 1022 Fletcher received a report from MacArthur's headquarters that a B-17 at 0748 had sighted 1 carrier, 16 other warships and 10 transports at lat. 10°35' S, long. 152°36' E,

unsuccessfully to intercept. The three Americans made no direct hits but scored at least one near-miss which blew five planes from *Shoho's* flight deck over the side. Hamilton's ten SBDs attacked at 1110, *Lexington's* torpedo squadron followed seven minutes later, and *Yorktown's* air group piled in at 1125. Ninety-three planes against one light carrier! [22] No ship could have survived such a concentration. After receiving two 1000-pound bomb hits, she burst into flames and went dead in the water. More hits followed, and "by 1130 the entire vessel was damaged by bombs, torpedoes and self-exploded enemy planes," records the *Shoho* war diary; Abandon Ship was ordered at 1131 and the carrier sank within five minutes. [23]

About 160 miles to the southeastward the radio rooms of *Yorktown* and *Lexington* were packed with anxious audiences, for this was the very first attack by American carrier planes on an enemy carrier. Static was bad, and the snatches of pilots' conversation that came over did not tell much. Suddenly the squawking ceased, and over the voice radio, sharp and strong, came the voice of *Lexington's* second SBD leader, Lieutenant Commander R. E. Dixon: —

"Scratch one flattop! Dixon to Carrier, Scratch one flattop!" [24] All but three American planes were safely on board by 1338.

Goto retired to the northeastward. Covering Group now comprised one destroyer and four heavy cruisers, whose float planes were ordered to Deboyne Island, where the seaplane carrier *Kamikawa Maru* of Marumo's Support Group was anchored.

---

steaming westerly. That was the Port Moresby Invasion Group, but Goto was not far away.

[22] Later in the war there would have been a tactical air commander with the strike to divert some of the planes to attack other ships present.

[23] Position lat. 10°29' S, long. 152°55' E; destroyer *Sazanami* rescued about 100 survivors. She carried only about 21 planes, 18 of which were lost. Several U. S. pilots reported the bombing and sinking of a heavy cruiser near the carrier, but no other ship was hit.

[24] Stanley Johnston *Queen of the Flat-Tops* p. 181.

4. *Twilight Tangles and Night Thoughts*

By 1450 May 7, *Yorktown* and *Lexington* were ready to launch a second strike, but Admiral Fletcher wisely decided against it. He estimated that *Shoho's* consorts were not worth it; he had not yet located *Shokaku* and *Zuikaku;* and through radar contacts and radio interceptions of Japanese carrier plane reports he knew that his own position was known to the enemy. Nor did it seem wise to search for the big flattops, because flying conditions worsened and visibility decreased during the afternoon; even if Takagi's Striking Force were located there would hardly be enough daylight left for strike and recovery. So Fletcher decided to rely upon shore-based aircraft to locate Takagi, and steamed to the westward during the night of 7–8 May. He estimated that the Port Moresby Invasion Group would thread the Jomard Pass next morning,[25] not knowing that his own approach and Crace's chase had caused timid Inouye to recall them.

Takagi's initiative changed this American plan. Twelve bombers and 15 torpedo planes took off from *Shokaku* and *Zuikaku* at 1630 to look for Fletcher, with orders to attack at sundown if they located him.[26] Owing to the squally weather they found nothing, and were returning when intercepted by *Yorktown* and *Lexington* fighter planes. In the ensuing series of dogfights nine Japanese planes were shot down at the cost of two Wildcats and Lieutenant (jg) Paul G. Baker, one of the most able and beloved pilots in the Navy.[27] Some of these Japanese planes laid a course for

[25] CTF 17 Action Report.
[26] Capt. Watanabe in *Inter. Jap. Off.* II 539.
[27] There was a story that Lt. Baker deliberately led away the Japanese planes in the wrong direction so they would not find his carrier, and so splashed for want of gas. I have made a careful investigation of this incident and am convinced that it did not occur. A plane, not identified as Baker's, got mixed up with the Japanese aircraft that tried to land on *Yorktown*, was ordered off, and subsequently was heard asking for the carrier's position. This may have been Baker's plane, but others on board *Lexington* think they saw him collide with one of the "Zekes" and fall. In any case, he is credited with shooting down three enemy planes in that action.

"home" right over the American carriers, which they mistook for their own. At 1900, forty-five minutes after sunset, three enemy planes were sighted on *Yorktown's* starboard beam, blinking in Morse code on Aldis lamps, and the carrier obligingly blinked back. They were recognized and fired on as they crossed the flagship's bow, yet they managed to escape. Twenty minutes later, three more tried to join *Yorktown's* landing circle and one was shot down. As Japanese carriers at this time had neither radar nor homing devices, and the American radio telephone inadvertently jammed the frequency used by their aircraft, preventing the pilots from getting a bearing on their carriers, Hara had to turn on his searchlights so the planes could find their way "home." In the ensuing night recovery eleven planes splashed and the remaining six or seven were not recovered until 2100.[28]

At 1930 *Lexington's* radar showed enemy planes orbiting in what appeared to be a landing circle only 30 miles to the eastward. Fitch attempted to pass the word to Fletcher in *Yorktown*, but there was a foul-up in communications and the task force commander did not get it until 2200. He received the report very dubiously. *Yorktown's* radar had given no such indication and, assuming evaluation to be correct, Hara's carriers would be somewhere else by midnight.[29] Actually, at 2200 May 7 they were about 95 miles to the eastward of the American carriers. Fletcher considered detaching a cruiser-destroyer force for a night attack on Takagi but decided against it. The last-quarter moon would not afford much light through thick scudding clouds and the destroyers were needed for anti-submarine protection at night, urgently so for anti-aircraft protection at daybreak. "All things considered," he reported, "the best plan seemed to be to keep our force concentrated and prepare for a battle with enemy carriers next morning." [30]

It is a curious fact that Inouye, too, contemplated night action

[28] Truk Report pp. 28–C, D.
[29] CTF 17 Action Report.
[30] Admiral King criticized Admiral Fletcher for failing to make a night destroyer torpedo attack on the enemy, either that night or the following. Admiral Nimitz replied, defending his task force commander, that the destroyers then

and later thought better of it. He ordered Goto's cruisers and Kajioka's destroyer screen to leave the transports, rendezvous east of Rossel Island and make a night attack on Allied forces; whether Crace's or Fletcher's he failed to specify. But before midnight Inouye canceled this plan, ordered the Port Moresby landing delayed two days, directed two of Goto's cruisers to join Takagi's Striking Force and Goto's other ships to close the invasion transports heading back to Rabaul. The Japanese retreat had begun, although nobody yet admitted the fact.

Admiral Takagi, too, was toying with the idea of night action, to retrieve the "disgrace" of his failure so far. The few planes recovered from his 27-plane flight reported two carriers "about 40 or 60 miles away," an estimate almost as poor as the one Fletcher had on him. On board flagship *Myoko*, Takagi discussed with his staff a possible night attack. He had but two heavy cruisers and six destroyers to protect him and knew not what Fletcher had. His pilots were tired out from their protracted searches. Before any decision had been reached, Rear Admiral Koso Abe, who commanded the retreating Port Moresby transport unit, requested Hara to close and provide air cover, now that *Shoho* was sunk. The carrier commander had other ideas for the employment of his air strength, yet complied because, as he said after the war, "I had my basic mission to fulfill, which was to protect the transports." [31]

At about 2200, when all his surviving planes had been recovered, Hara headed north, and by midnight was in lat. 12°40′ S, long. 156°45′ E, opening range on Fletcher, who about the same time changed course to the southeastward. Neither commander knew what the other was doing that night, but each was thirsty for the other's blood. Before long both would be gratified.

---

with Fletcher were few enough for screening duty, that the possibility of their finding high-speed enemy carriers (they had no radar at this time) was small, that the probability of their not returning to their own force before daybreak was great, and that the fuel situation precluded high-speed destroyer operations at night. Cominch to Cincpac, 11 May and 15 June; Cincpac to Cominch 16 June.

[31] Truk Report p. 36. This incident reveals a curious command relationship. One would suppose that the request should have come in the form of an order from Inouye, and that Takagi, the striking force commander, not Hara the carrier commander, would have made the decision.

CHAPTER IV

Carrier Battle of 8 May

East Longitude date, Zone minus 11 time.

1. *Attack on* SHOKAKU *and* ZUIKAKU

STRIKING FORCE maintained a northerly course throughout the night of 7–8 May. An hour before sunrise, at 0600 May 8, when about 100 miles ESE of Rossel Island,[1] Hara launched a search mission covering the arc 145°–235° to a distance of 200 miles. An hour later an attack group of 90 planes took off to hunt the enemy along the median line of the search arc, which was the S by W rhumb from his flagship. As soon as these planes had been dispatched, around 0825, the Striking Force bent on 30 knots, and headed toward the estimated position of Task Force 17, passing Rossel Island on the starboard hand. The attack group had the good fortune to meet in the air the returning search planes, who guided them to *Yorktown* and *Lexington*.[2]

Admiral Fletcher, who had maintained a southeasterly course during the night, awoke that morning in somewhat more than his usual fighting mood. Unfortunately, owing to the detachment of Crace's force, he had less to fight with than the day before — five heavy cruisers and seven destroyers to support and screen two carriers; but that was one more of each type than Takagi had. More serious, his course had taken him out of the protective cover of a foul-weather front into an area of high visibility. The weather

---

[1] Position lat. 10°25′ S, long. 154°5′ E, according to Hara's memory in Truk Report pp. 28-D, 35-6. War College Analyst, however, believes that his position was farther to the east and south, and I have followed this on our chart.

[2] Same, p. 35. At 0800, TF 17 was in lat. 14°24′ S, long. 154°32′ E, on course 125°.

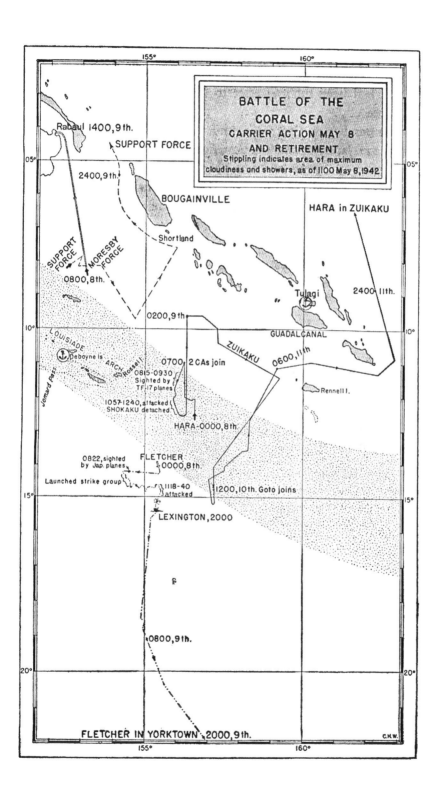

BATTLE OF THE
CORAL SEA
CARRIER ACTION MAY 8
AND RETIREMENT
Stippling indicates area of maximum
cloudiness and showers, as of 1100 May 8, 1942

Rabaul 1400, 9th.

SUPPORT FORCE

2400, 9th.

BOUGAINVILLE

HARA in ZUIKAKU

Shortland

SUPPORT FORCE

MORESBY FORCE

0800, 8th.

0200, 9th.

Tulagi

2400, 11th.

ZUIKAKU

GUADALCANAL

LOUISIADE ARCH.

Deboyne Is.

Rossell I.

0700, 2 CAs join

0600, 11th.

0815-0930
Sighted by
TF 17 planes

1057-1240, attacked
SHOKAKU detached

Rennell I.

Jomard Pass

HARA-0000, 8th.

0822, sighted
by Jap. planes

FLETCHER
0000, 8th.

Launched strike group

1118-40
attacked

1200, 10th. Goto joins

LEXINGTON, 2000

0800, 9th.

FLETCHER IN YORKTOWN, 2000, 9th.

C.H.W.

which had been such an asset to him on May 7 now became a Japanese ally.

The number of planes operational on both sides was almost the same: 121 Japanese and 122 American. The former had the larger proportion of fighter and torpedo planes, and in those types the Japanese excelled. Fletcher, on the other hand, had radar and homing devices which Hara lacked. The enemy carriers had been operating as a division for over six months, while *Yorktown* and *Lexington* had only recently joined and the task force had had no practice in tactical maneuvering. It had the greater number of anti-aircraft guns, the most numerous type being the unsatisfactory 1.1-inch. The aviators on both sides were first-string men.

Before the 8th of May broke, Fletcher's principal concern was to locate *Shokaku* and *Zuikaku*. Intelligence reports received during the night offered nothing specific; radio direction finders indicated that Takagi was either to the eastward or the westward, but that was not much help. A 360-degree dawn search was a necessity, and *Lexington* was given the job.[3] At 0625 she launched 18 planes. No news came in for almost two hours. At 0815 Lieutenant (jg) J. G. Smith obtained the first glimpse of the Japanese Striking Force vouchsafed to any American pilot. By 0838 he had reported the composition, course and speed of the disposition, locating it at lat. 12° S, long. 156°12′ E, 175 miles to the northeastward of Fletcher's position.[4] Before his report came in, *Lexington* had intercepted a radio message from a Japanese search plane giving her own position, course and speed fairly accurately, so it was certain that the enemy was on her tail.

Lieutenant Commander R. E. Dixon, flying an SBD that was searching a sector adjoining Lieutenant Smith's, picked up and verified the enemy contact. At 0930 he sighted the Striking Force steaming due south at a speed of 25 knots, in a position "approximately 25 miles northeast of the 0815 initial contact" by Lieuten-

[3] The search was to be conducted to a distance of 200 miles in the northern semicircle and 150 miles in the southern semicircle.
[4] *Lexington* Action Report, Report of Scouting Squadron 2.

ant Smith, but "about 45 miles north" of Takagi's 0900 position that had been predicted on the strength of that contact.[5] This discrepancy was to cause trouble. Dixon trailed the enemy until 1045 when he had to return to *Lexington* because his fuel was running low.

Within a minute of receiving Lieutenant Smith's amplifying report, at 0838, Admiral Fletcher ordered both carriers to launch air strikes.[6] Unfortunately, his ships were out in the clear sunlight where it was a yachtsman's dream of a perfect tradewind day, but the enemy lay under a protective cover of squall clouds. Before launching was complete, he made Admiral Fitch officer in tactical command "in order to reduce signaling between carriers and to allow him complete freedom of action for his carriers and air groups." At 1000 he radioed to General MacArthur his own location and that of the enemy, hoping that the General would send planes to track and bomb the Striking Force. But Army Air that day made only another non-hit attack on the retreating Invasion Force.

The *Yorktown* group of 39 planes took departure at 0915 and sighted the enemy an hour and three quarters later. *Zuikaku* and *Shokaku*, each screened by two heavy cruisers and two or three destroyers, were steaming southwesterly, 8 or 10 miles apart. While the dive-bombers who had climbed to 17,000 feet on the approach orbited under cloud cover to await the slower, low-flying torpedo planes, *Shokaku* turned into the wind and began launching more combat air patrol, while *Zuikaku* and her attendants disappeared into a rain squall. At 1057, when all *Yorktown* planes were in position, Lieutenant Commander Joe Taylor of Torpedo Squadron 5 led the attack on *Shokaku*. Wildcats pro-

---

[5] *War College Analysis* p. 85.

[6] The numbers and types of planes in this attack were as follows, counting all SBDs as VB: —

	VB	VT	VF	Total
Yorktown	24	9	8	41
Lexington	22	12	9	43
				84

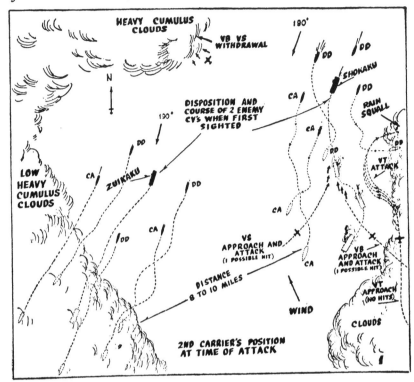

tected the TBDs from "Zekes" as they came in low to launch, and the dive-bombers followed.

This, the first American attack of the war on a large Japanese carrier, fell far short of anticipation. The torpedoes, launched from too great a distance, either missed or failed to explode, and only two bomb hits were scored,[7] one well forward on *Shokaku's* starboard bow, which fired gasoline and damaged the flight deck so that she could only recover planes but not launch; and the other well aft, which destroyed the repair compartment for airplane motors.[8] When Admiral Hara came out of the squall in *Zuikaku*, he saw her sister ship "burning furiously."[9]

[7] *War College Analysis.* The *Yorktown* pilots claimed 6 bomb and 3 torpedo hits.
[8] Capt. Yamaoka, an air staff officer who was on board *Zuikaku*, in *Inter. Jap. Off.* I 54. About a dozen "Zekes" were shot down but 4 of *Yorktown's* SBDs were lost.
[9] Truk Report p. 35.

Nevertheless, the *Yorktown* planes seem to have done better than those of *Lexington*, which took departure ten minutes later and ran into all kinds of trouble. The three Wildcats escorting the SBDs lost them in the clouds and had to return. The torpedo squadron reached the false position predicted from the 0815 contact and naturally found nothing there. By flying a box search, it later picked up the enemy; but the dive-bombing squadron, which ran into a thick overcast, never did locate the enemy and returned when it began to run short of fuel.[10] The rest of *Lexington's* attack group, now reduced to eleven torpedo-bombers, four dive-bombers[11] and six Wildcats, found the enemy at about 1140 after flying eight minutes on the first leg of the box. An approach was made at 6000 feet over a cloud, through a hole in which the torpedo attack was launched in a spiraling glide, followed by the dive-bombers. Three Wildcats fell victim to the "Zekes," which greatly outnumbered them but were usefully drawn off from the bombers, enabling them to attack with relatively little air interference. With the TBDs it was again a case of "slow torpedoes and long range. We could turn and run away from them," a Japanese officer recalled.[12] *Lexington* dive-bombers added one hit on *Shokaku* to *Yorktown's* two,[13] but the report brought back by their pilots that they left one big carrier "settling fast"[14] was greatly exaggerated. *Shokaku* had lost 108 men killed and 40 wounded; but she was not holed below the waterline, all fires were quickly brought under control, many of her planes were transferred to *Zuikaku*, and at

[10] In the urgency of the launching they had not fueled to their capacity load of 250 gals. but were 12 per cent short.

[11] This was the section of the air group commander, Cdr. Ault.

[12] *Inter. Jap. Off.* I 54.

[13] I follow *War College Analysis*, but the evidence is conflicting. Admiral Hara states in Truk Report that his flagship *Zuikaku* became separated from *Shokaku* by about 8 miles while the latter was launching planes, and was not attacked; Capt. Yamaoka states that *Zuikaku* was attacked by bombers and torpedo planes and not hit; Capt. Watanabe in *Inter. Jap. Off.* I 68 says "*Zuikaku* received minor damages and many people killed." Admiral Yamamoto's staff log states that *Shokaku* received 3 bomb hits at 1140 (*Inter. Jap. Off.* II 539), but I believe it means "by 1140," and that Watanabe and Yamaoka confused the two carriers after the war.

[14] Statement by Capt. F. C. Sherman in various newspapers of 13–14 June 1942.

1300 she hightailed it for home. She almost capsized on the way and arrived in bad shape; [15] but she got there, and we shall hear of her again. Admiral Takagi had no qualms about releasing *Shokaku*, for by this time he believed that both United States carriers were well settled on the bottom of the Coral Sea.

2. *Attack on* YORKTOWN *and* LEXINGTON

By the time the American planes began returning to their carriers, both flattops had been hit. Seventy planes from *Shokaku* and *Zuikaku* were beating up the American carriers a few minutes after *Yorktown's* attack on the Japanese carriers ended and before *Lexington's* had commenced. In this strange crisscross air battle, superior success attended the Japanese, whose strike group was larger and better balanced and more accurately directed to its target than that of the Americans.[16]

Retaliation had been anticipated even before the American strike took its departure. Shortly after sunrise, *Yorktown* and *Lexington* began slicing off planes for combat air [17] and anti-submarine patrol. At 1030 Fitch changed course to 28° in order to reduce the distance flown in his returning planes. Topside in *Lexington,* which conducted fighter directions for both carriers, lookouts and airmen scanned the sky and radar sent out its feelers for battle portents. On the strength of Japanese carrier radio activity heard during the forenoon watch, Captain "Ted" Sherman predicted that an enemy strike would come in about 1100. Everyone prepared for action according to doctrine: General Quarters, Flight Quar-

---

[15] Capt. Watanabe, Yamamoto's staff gunnery officer who inspected her for the C. in C., in *Inter. Jap. Off.* I 68; casualties from an ensign's diary secured by Jicpoa.

[16] See comparative table of the two strikes at end of this section. The story current shortly after the battle, that the Japanese and American planes sighted but paid no attention to each other when passing on opposite courses, is not true.

[17] SBDs were used since there were not enough fighters. At 0948 radar picked up an enemy 4-engine flying boat that was promptly shot down by combat air patrol.

ters, ships buttoned up and battened down, additional planes sent aloft to "nip the Nips."

First sign of the attack came as predicted at 1055 when *Lexington's* radar picked up a large group of "bogies" about 70 miles to the northeastward. Despite Sherman's prediction, the fighter-director officer was not prepared. One patrol had just been recovered, and only eight Wildcats were over the carriers at that time; they were too low in fuel both to intercept and fight, so were ordered to stay close by the ships.[18]

The two carriers changed course back to 125°, bent on 25 and then 30 knots, and immediately commenced launching relief combat air patrol of nine Wildcats. Five were sent out on the hopeless mission of trying to stop an enemy many times their strength. Two of them flew low to intercept the Japanese torpedo planes, but escorting "Zekes" kept them too busy to do it. Three others, although flying at 10,000 feet, were not high enough to reach an attack position before the Japanese dive-bombers reached their pushover point. The other four were vectored out 15 miles, but missed the interception and hurried home.[19]

Admiral Fitch had far too few fighter planes, they were not well employed, and his 23 Dauntless dive-bombers which were in the air looking for torpedo planes were inadequately gunned and too slow to double as fighters. Four of them were shot down trying, although they disposed of as many torpedo planes. So the battle quickly resolved itself into a duel between American anti-aircraft gunners and Japanese planes.

At 1118 "the battle busted out," as one of the sailors remarked.[20] The Japanese approached from the northeastward, down wind and down sun. A fresh (16- to 20-knot) tradewind was blowing from half a point north of east; the sea was smooth and visibility high. Torpedo-bombers came in on both bows of *Lexington* to

[18] *War College Analysis* p. 90. But Admiral Sherman disagrees with this.
[19] The War College Analyst severely criticizes this handling of the relief CAP. They were launched too late for successful interception and should have been kept near the carriers, so stacked in altitude as to have an advantage over the attackers.
[20] Henry Milberger in *Houston Press* 19 June 1942.

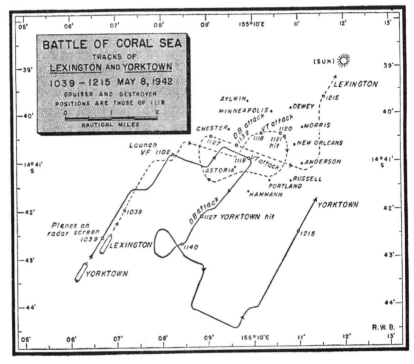

launch their "fish" at half- to three-quarter-mile ranges from an altitude of 50 to 200 feet. One of the first pair was taken apart by 5-inch shells, and the bodies of the crew were seen hurtling through the air.[21] When the first torpedo splashed into the water on *Lexington's* port bow, Captain Sherman ordered full right rudder — a maneuver nullified almost immediately by the appearance of torpedoes on the starboard bow. The Captain made strenuous efforts to swing the huge bulk of the valiant Lady into a safe alignment parallel to the wakes, eleven of which were reported as passing under, alongside and forward. But she was not easily maneuvered. Her tactical diameter was 1500 to 2000 yards, compared with 1000 yards for her consort, and it was impossible to evade so many fast torpedoes. One hit on her port side forward at 1120 was quickly followed by a second on the same side opposite the bridge. To add

[21] Cpl. J. L. Skillings USMC in *San Antonio Express* 17 June 1942.

to her embarrassment, a big dive-bombing attack developed while the torpedo evasion measures were at their height. The "Vals," unmolested except by intermittent anti-aircraft fire, commenced their runs at 17,000 feet and discharged their lethal loads at 2500 feet. One small bomb exploded in a 5-inch ready ammunition box on the port side of *Lexington's* main deck forward, another scored on the smokestack structure. Near-misses ruptured plates and raised huge plumes of ominously black water. The screaming of the ship's siren, jammed in operation by an explosion, added weird shrieks to the cacophony of battle. It was all over in nineteen minutes.

Meanwhile, *Yorktown* was getting her share. The first three of eight torpedoes were dropped on her port quarter at about 1118. She increased speed to 30 knots and maneuvered to avoid. Fortunately, she had a much smaller turning circle than *Lexington*, and on her the Japanese did not use the "anvil" technique on both bows. After a five-minute respite, *Yorktown* was attacked by dive-bombers at 1124. For the next three minutes she dodged steel eggs, then received her one and only hit. An 800-pound bomb struck the flight deck 15 feet inboard of the island and penetrated to the fourth deck. Sixty-six men were killed or seriously injured, mostly by burns.[22] Fires were started but quickly brought under control. A couple of other bombs near-missed but, owing to skillful handling by Captain Buckmaster, *Yorktown* escaped with damage that did not impair flight operations. A single torpedo plane launched a "fish" at her at 1140, and that too was dodged.

During this radical maneuvering it was impossible for the five cruisers and seven destroyers that were screening the carriers to keep formation, especially as the flattops were constantly drawing apart. One group stayed with *Lexington* and one with *Yorktown*, each ship blazing away at the attacking planes and dodging the

[22] Although it had already been proved in the Java Sea that short sleeves and pants exposed men to frightful burns, while even the thinnest covering protected the skin, the lesson had to be learned again at Coral Sea. *Yorktown's* senior surgeon adverted severely against allowing men to wear short-sleeved shirts, rolled-up trousers, etc.

few bombs and torpedoes that came her way. The Japanese were after carriers only and believed they had got them. Exuberant pilots reported to happy Hara that they had sunk one "large" enemy carrier which they identified as *Saratoga,* and one "medium," either *Enterprise* or *Yorktown;* and that they had left burning one battleship or cruiser.[23] Analysis of Japanese reports shows a loss of only 30 planes on 8 May as a result of combat, and 13 more operationally,[24] or a total of 43 against 33 lost that day from all causes by Task Force 17.[25]

The big carrier battle was over by 1145 May 8. If the Coral Sea score had been frozen then and there, the United States could justly have claimed the victory. One Japanese light carrier, one destroyer and several minecraft had been sunk, and a large carrier sent home for repairs, as against the loss of one destroyer, one oiler and two large carriers damaged — apparently not very seriously. But the final score of naval battle is not made up until ships return to port, and the one that never did reversed profit-and-loss in the enemy's favor.

COMPARATIVE TABLE OF CARRIER AIR ATTACKS 8 MAY 1942 [26]

		U. S. Attack			Japanese Attack
		YORKTOWN	LEXINGTON	TOTAL	
Start launching		0840	0840		0822
Take departure		0915	0925		0915
No. planes in strike	VF	8	9	17	18
	VB	24	22	46	33
	VT	9	12	21	18
	Total	41	43	84	69
No. planes that reached target	VF	4	6	10	
	VB	24	4	28	See footnote 27
	VT	9	11	20	
	Total	37	21	58	

[23] *Inter. Jap. Off.* II 539; *War College Analysis.*
[24] These figures do not include the Japanese planes that returned in such bad shape that they could not be flown before extensive repairs had been made.
[25] Not including the 36 planes that went down with *Lexington.*
[26] Compiled largely from *War College Analysis,* Truk Report, and Cincpac-Cincpoa Intelligence Item No. 9718. This table, down to the last line, includes striking planes only, not CAP, ASP or reserve.
[27] It is not known how many, if any, of the Japanese strike group got lost en route.

Time attack began	1057	1136		1113
Time attack over	1101	1140		1140
No. planes recovered ⎰VF	6	6	12	12
⎱VB	20	23	43	18
VT	9	10	19	10
Total	35	39	74	40
Time of recovery	1320–1414	1300–1345		Before 1300
Total planes available to CVs next day	at least 49			39 [28]

3. Loss of "Lady Lex"

The end of the battle found *Lexington* listing seven degrees, with three boiler rooms partially flooded, plane elevators inoperative and three fires burning; but before gun barrels grew cold, the flight deck was readied to launch and recover aircraft. While planes settled on deck, damage control and black gang [29] brought her back to an even keel by shifting oil ballast.[30] An hour passed, and the ship's company had reason to rejoice. The proud Lady was blooded, yet showing a clean pair of heels and conducting nearly normal flight operations. Commander H. R. Healy, the damage control officer, in a telephone report to Captain Sherman, grew facetious: "We've got the torpedo damage temporarily shored up, the fires out and soon will have the ship back on an even keel. But I would suggest, sir, that if you have to take any more torpedoes, you take 'em on the starboard side."[31]

No sooner were those words out of "Pop" Healy's mouth than, at 1247, a devastating internal explosion shook the carrier from stem to stern. Gasoline vapors, released by one of the torpedo hits, had been ignited below by a motor generator left running. More eruptions followed, each more violent than the last. Internal

[28] Capt. E. T. Layton's estimate; "Battle Lessons" p. 2; about 50 others, very largely damaged, were on board *Zuikaku* and *Shokaku* which had pulled out.

[29] This is the term for firemen, watertenders and all engine and fireroom personnel — a holdover from coal-burning days.

[30] Bureau of Ships "Preliminary Report Loss of *Lexington*, May 8, 1942, Coral Sea," War Damage Report No. 16, 15 June 1942 pp. 5–6.

[31] Stanley Johnston in *Chicago Tribune* 17 June 1942.

communications deteriorated rapidly. Central station, the nerve center of damage control, suffered major damage and casualties, Commander Healy among them. Smoke burst from the lower decks.

Even then the situation seemed hopeful to sailors on the bridge. Flight operations continued, planes of the morning attack group were recovered, the last plane being received on board at 1414. The ship still made 25 knots. Only as link after link in the communication system was severed did the officers come to the reluctant conclusion that the Lady was too hot to handle.

A second major internal explosion at 1445, which wrecked the ventilation system of the fire and engine rooms, caused Captain Sherman to ask assistance from other vessels in fighting fires. Half an hour later flight operations were abandoned. *Yorktown* was requested to recover all airborne planes and Admiral Fletcher, who had resumed the tactical command at 1510, was asked to furnish stand-by rescue vessels. Destroyer *Morris* eased alongside and passed fire hoses to the Lady in distress. Engulfing flames made this gesture ineffective. As Captain Sherman reported: —

"By this time the fire was beyond control. Additional explosions were occurring; it was reported the warheads on the hangar deck had been at a temperature of 140 degrees; ready bomb storage was in the vicinity of the fire and I considered there was danger of the ship blowing up at any minute. I had previously directed sick and wounded to be disembarked in our whaleboats and excess squadron personnel had gone on lines to the destroyer alongside." [32]

With engine rooms untenable and communications reduced to one slim telephone line, the black gang was ordered to make its way topside after securing engines and boilers. Steam safety valves were lifted and the ship, drained of her life blood, wallowed to a stop at 1630. All hands prepared to abandon ship; rafts were cast loose, lines trailed in the water, and a search made below for the helpless

[32] *Lexington* Action Report.

wounded. Although the sick bay had to be evacuated and all pa-
tients transferred to the Captain's cabin, there was ample time for
the surgeons and pharmacists' mates to give injections, administer
blood plasma, dress wounds, cover horrible skin burns with tannic
acid, and lower some 150 wounded in basket stretchers into whaleboats.[33]

The curtain for the last act began to descend at 1707 when
Admiral Fitch called down from his bridge to the Captain, "Well,
Ted, let's get the men off." Captain Sherman gave the order that
stabs the heart of every sailor who loves his ship — and this happy
ship was loved as few ships have been before or since. Abandonment was deliberate, methodical and exceedingly reluctant.
"Doughnut" rafts were tossed overboard and the Marines and bluejackets, after setting their shoes in an orderly line on the flight
deck,[34] descended hand over hand on lifelines. Rear Admiral Kinkaid in *Minneapolis* took charge of rescue operations; destroyers
Morris, Anderson and *Hammann* recovered men from the water.
Fortunately the sea was calm and the water warm; it was as luxu-
rious an abandonment as one could expect.[35] One group of men,
awaiting their turn to go over the side, scooped up what ice cream
remained in the ship's service store. Nobody who went overboard
was drowned; even the Captain's dog was saved.

Evening brought "Lady Lex" to her destined end. Admiral
Fitch transferred his flag to *Minneapolis*. Captain Sherman and his
executive officer, Commander M. T. Seligman, made a final inspection to ensure that no wounded were left behind; and while so
engaged had to dodge flying debris from another explosion. Last
three to go down hand over hand were a corporal of Marines,
the Executive Officer and the Skipper, in that order. Admiral

[33] Interview with the senior medical officer, Cdr. A. J. White, in *Washington Star* 18 June 1942.
[34] Capt. Sherman's statement; David Miller in *Providence Eve. Bulletin* 20 June;
Ens. H. B. Shonk in *Manchester* [N. H.] *Union* 19 June. Naval discipline so prevailed that radiomen dusted off their instruments and yeomen tidied up their files
before securing.
[35] William Turner in *Springfield* [Mo.] *Leader and Press*, 18 June 1942.

Fletcher ordered destroyer *Phelps* to administer the *coup de grace* with torpedoes. At about 2000 the battered amazon gave up her ghost with one final and awful detonation as, head up, she slipped into a 2400-fathom deep.[36]

4. *Retirement and Conclusion, 8–11 May*

During the afternoon of 8 May Admiral Nimitz, who had received a radio report of the battle, ordered Task Force 17 to retire from the Coral Sea.[37] That is what Fletcher had intended to do. Next day Nimitz seriously considered canceling this order but let it stand. For, reasoned Cincpac staff, the enemy had retired; his main objective, the invasion of Port Moresby, had been thwarted; any carrier not completely effective is singularly vulnerable, and "inflicting damage on your enemy is no compensation for being sunk yourself." Moreover, Nimitz had to husband his air power for the defense of Midway which was coming up presently.

Admiral Fletcher led his force south during the night, and in the morning began a gradual change of course to the eastward. On the afternoon of 11 May he separated the ships into two groups. One, under the command of Rear Admiral Kinkaid with three cruisers and four destroyers,[38] was sent into Nouméa while Fletcher himself led the rest toward Tongatabu.

Retirement from the scene of battle was not completed without one amusing incident. On the morning of 9 May one of *Yorktown's* planes reported an aircraft carrier 175 miles away from Task Force 17. Dive-bombers were immediately launched from the flag-

---

[36] Jack Smith said, "I couldn't watch her go, and men who had been with her since she was commissioned in '27 stood with tears streaming." *Fort Worth Star-Telegram* 16 June. Seaman Herbert said, "All the fellows were crying and weeping like young girls, so was I." *Wheeling* [W. Va.] *News Register*, 21 June. Her position was lat. 15°12′ S, long. 155°27′ E. The bodies of 216 men and remains of 36 planes went down with her; 19 planes were taken on board *Yorktown* and 2735 men were rescued.

[37] This dispatch is not available, and the exact time is not known. The gist of it was given by Admiral Fletcher to Naval War College analysts in Feb. 1947.

[38] *Minneapolis, New Orleans, Astoria, Anderson, Hammann, Morris* and *Russell.*

ship and, in response to a call for help, 14 Army bombers took off from an Australian base. As luck would have it, on this one occasion when Army and Navy managed to stage a coördinated attack, their target turned out to be a small island or reef. Aside from this false start, during that day and the two following, the Army Air Force concentrated on beating up the enemy seaplane base at Deboyne Island. After these attacks had destroyed most of their planes and shore installations, the Japanese folded up.

Japanese movements after the battle were less consistent. At about 1800 May 8, a few hours after *Shokaku* had departed, Admiral Inouye, assuming Task Force 17 had been liquidated, ordered Takagi to retire to Truk.[39] Before the end of the day, Inouye formally postponed the Port Moresby invasion. The new date, 3 July, turned out to be the equivalent of the classic Greek Kalends. One may well ask what now prevented the Port Moresby Invasion Group from reversing course again and steaming through Jomard Passage to its original destination instead of returning to Simpson Harbor, Rabaul. The Army Air Force may take a bow for that. Inouye did not dare to risk his transports in a second try, because of the intense activity of the A.A.F. along the southern shores of Papua, and the want of air protection now that *Shoho* was sunk and the Striking Force had retired.

Admiral Yamamoto, Commander in Chief Combined Fleet, apparently did not appreciate Inouye's caution, since at midnight May 8 he ordered Takagi to "annihilate" remaining enemy forces.[40] So at 0200 May 9 *Zuikaku* and her consorts turned southeast and later southwest. Takagi could hardly have hoped to intercept Fletcher that late, but orders were orders. At noon May 10 the rest of Goto's Covering Group, which changed missions as often as Inouye changed his mind, joined *Zuikaku;* but, within an hour of picking them up, the carrier countermarched. Next day Takagi received definite orders to leave the area.

On 10 May Admiral Shima's invasion force destined for Ocean

[39] Truk Report pp. 34–5.
[40] Crudiv 6 Action Report (WDC 160,997) p. 14.

and Nauru Islands got underway from Rabaul, only to lose flag-ship *Okinoshima* to United States submarine *S-42* next day and to be recalled to Truk on the 15th when a patrol plane warned Inouye that unfriendly carriers had been sighted some 450 miles east of Tulagi.[41] That was Halsey's task force roaring down from Pearl. But it was too late for *Enterprise* and *Hornet* to change the situation; they never entered the amaranthine waters of the Coral Sea, now unvexed by the keels of fighting ships.[42]

News of the battle, which reached the United States on Saturday 9 May (West Longitude date), caused much speculation. It provoked the conservative *New York Times* to splash streamer headlines across its front page: "Japanese Repulsed in Great Pacific Battle with 17 to 22 of Their Ships Sunk or Crippled; Enemy in Flight, Pursued by Allied Warships." Hanson Baldwin admitted that "the future course of the war in the Pacific — and in the world — may be hanging in the balance . . . and this battle bids fair to be the greatest in American naval history." But he observed that, since we were "fighting a seven-ocean war with a one-ocean Navy," it was "premature to claim a victory or to interpret a defeat."[43] The Japanese claimed, besides sinking mythical battleships in Admiral Crace's force, that they had sent both large carriers to the bottom. Hitler complimented his honorary Aryan allies with what must eventually have seemed a dismal prophecy: "After this new defeat, the United States warships will hardly dare to face the Japanese Fleet again, since any United States warship which accepts action with the Japanese naval forces is as good as lost."

Like Falstaff, when he warned of "villanous news abroad," the Navy Department declared "No credence should be given to claims that have been or may be put out by Tokyo."[44] In order to keep the enemy guessing, it was not until after the Midway victory that

[41] Ocean and Nauru were occupied by the Japanese without opposition on 25–26 Aug. 1942 and held until the end of the war.
[42] Halsey arrived near the New Hebrides 11 May and from 12 to 16 May operated eastward of Efate and Santa Cruz. On 16 May Cincpac ordered him back to Pearl Harbor, and he arrived 26 May.
[43] *New York Times* 9–10 May 1942.
[44] Navy Dept. Communiqué No. 78, 8 May 1942.

the Department released a worthy account of the Coral Sea battle and admitted the loss of *Lexington*. So, for over a month, claims and counterclaims piled up. Prime Minister Curtin of Australia was so alarmed as to warn his people that "invasion is a menace capable of becoming an actuality at any hour." He bluntly reminded the legislature that "men are fighting for Australia today and those who are not fighting have no excuse for not working."

The Battle of the Coral Sea will be ever memorable as the first purely carrier-against-carrier naval battle in which all losses were inflicted by air action and no ship on either side sighted a surface enemy. But the confident prediction of air power enthusiasts that it had set a pattern which would always be followed proved to be premature.

It was a tactical victory for the Japanese but a strategic victory for the United States. The enemy inflicted relatively greater losses than he sustained; *Shoho* and the few small ships sunk at Tulagi were a cheap price to pay for *Neosho*, *Sims* and *Lexington*. On the other hand, the main purpose of the Japanese operation, the capture of Port Moresby, was thwarted. The Louisiades proved to be a barrier beyond which no warship flying the banner of the Rising Sun could ever pass. Tulagi, one of the two secondary objectives of the enemy, had been won and it cost us dear to root him out of it. But in the other scale one must place the temporary elimination of *Shokaku* and *Zuikaku*. The one was so damaged that she could not rejoin the fleet for two months and the other, owing to plane losses, was out of the war until about 12 June, when she went up to the Aleutians. If these two fine carriers with veteran pilots had been able to participate in the Battle of Midway, they might well have supplied the necessary margin for victory.

So many mistakes were made on both sides in this new mode of fighting that it might be called the Battle of Naval Errors; but more were made by the enemy, and he failed to profit by them.[45]

---

[45] "We had personal experience with the tactical ability of the American task forces for the first time in this naval battle, and this had a great effect on our subsequent operations, armament plans and their application. However, the desire

The experience of "Lady Lex," paradoxically, instead of showing that carriers were fragile and easily cracked shells, proved they were tough ships capable of absorbing punishment far beyond pre-war expectation. Her loss merely added another illustration to that old adage beginning, "For want of a nail the shoe was lost." If one electric motor had not been left running, there would probably have been no gasoline explosion and no sinking. Once more the inadequacy of American carrier aircraft was emphasized,[46] but improved models were already coming off the assembly lines. The ratio of fighter planes to bombers and torpedo planes was increased, and in the short month that remained before Midway some improvement was effected in the organization and precision of air attack. There is no teacher of combat that can even remotely approach the value of combat itself; call Coral Sea what you will, it was an indispensable preliminary to the great victory of Midway.

The morale value of the battle to all Allied nations, coming as it did immediately after the surrender of Corregidor, was immeasurable. Captain Sherman's statement, articles by shipboard correspondents and numerous interviews with survivors printed in their home-town papers, told a story of cool efficiency, relentless action, superb heroism and determination. That story of the last fight of "Lady Lex," her calm abandonment, the devotion of her crew to their ship and their captain, transcended mere history; the American people took it to their hearts and stored it up in the treasury of folk memory.

---

to apply this knowledge immediately did not meet with any success; and as in the case of the Battle of Midway, it resulted in nothing but unfortunate results." Report on the Battle of the Coral Sea prepared by Capt. Yamaoka for Lt. Cdr. Salomon.

[46] The "Zeke" was superior to the Wildcat in speed, maneuverability and rate of climb (3000 ft. per minute as against 1100). The TBD was too slow for torpedo-bombing and very vulnerable because its tanks were not leak-proof. The SBD was not quite so fast as the "Val" but had better protection with its twin-mounted .30-cal. machine guns.

CHAPTER V

"Battle of Sydney"[1]

31 May–1 June 1942

TO THE VAST MAJORITY of Americans who had the privilege of spending leave or liberty in that gallant city of the Antipodes, the Battle of Sydney was fought within the confines of the Australia Hotel, Romano's or other well-known "hot spots." Yet there actually was a brief battle in the world's most beautiful harbor, between two American warships and two tiny submarines.

Although the midget submarine attack on Pearl Harbor had been a complete failure[2] and most Japanese naval officers regarded such efforts with contempt, there had been so great a propaganda build-up for the little two-man jobs that the high command decided to make another.

After the Battle of the Coral Sea, Admiral Crace's Support Group was returned to "MacArthur's Navy" of which it then constituted the principal strength. U.S.S. *Chicago* and *Perkins* on 31 May were moored in Sydney Harbor, ready to depart after an unusually pleasant period of upkeep and overhaul. Destroyer tender *Dobbin*, which had arrived a day earlier with a load of torpedoes and warheads, was swinging to a buoy awaiting a chance to land her cargo. H.M.A.S. *Kuttabul*, an old ferry boat converted to a barracks ship, was tied up at a stone dock at the Garden Island

---

[1] *Chicago* Report of 5 June appended to May War Diary; *Perkins* War Diary; a report written for this work by Capt. Francis X. McInerney who was on board *Perkins* as division commander; other details from Capt. George H. Gill RAN, historian of the Australian Navy, and from a personal investigation at Sydney.

[2] See Vol. III pp. 95–98.

Naval Station, close inshore from *Chicago*, with a Royal Nether-lands submarine moored outboard and alongside. Wooloomooloo Pier was filled with the usual laughing throng of Aussies, sailors and girls taking advantage of a Sunday full moon; and although Sydney observed what the city fathers called a "brownout," Garden Island was brilliantly illuminated with high floodlights which beautifully silhouetted the anchored ships for any approaching enemy. The channel from the outer Heads to Port Jackson (of which Sydney Harbor is the lesser part) is a narrow and winding passage some six miles in length, difficult to navigate at the best of times, and the Australian authorities had not yet got around to closing it with anti-submarine nets and boom.

As soon as the Coral Sea operation was over, five I-class Japanese submarines,[3] carrying four midget submarines and one plane, started south. The plane made an unobserved reconnaissance flight over Port Jackson and the midgets were launched off the Heads on 31 May. One or two of them succeeded in making their way up the channel after dark, astern of a fishing vessel. Detected both by the fishermen and by a magnetic underwater loop, their presence was signaled by the naval command at Sydney to ships at anchor by 2230, but nothing was done to douse the lights at Garden Island or stop ferryboats from running. At 2257 lookouts in *Chicago* sighted a conning tower awash 300 yards on her starboard quarter. She illuminated the target and opened fire with her 5-inch battery and machine guns but they could not be depressed for so short a range and some of the shots ricocheted into a residential section of Sydney, where fortunately they did no damage. The story that the only casualty inflicted by *Chicago's* gunfire was a lion in the famous Sydney Zoo, and that Captain Bode was requested to provide a new one out of lend-lease, is the invention of an Australian humorist.

The midget dived, and *Perkins* got under way at 2316 to cover the cruiser and *Dobbin;* but her sound gear was ineffective owing

[3] *I-21, I-22, I-24, I-27, I-29;* Intelligence material based on charts recovered from the midgets.

to the many noises set up by ferryboats and other harbor craft which continued to ply to and fro. Two Australian corvettes also began searching and, when one of them relieved *Perkins*, Captain Bode at 2243 ordered her to pick up her old buoy inshore of *Chicago*. Apparently the skipper of *Chicago* thought he had holed the only midget present.

At half an hour past midnight the wake of a torpedo, evidently aimed at *Chicago*, was observed to pass close aboard the cruiser. It went under the Dutch submarine and the barracks boat and detonated with a great roar and flash against the dock. The concussion blew the bottom out of the ex-ferryboat, killing a number of sailors who were sleeping on board, and left it a total loss.[4] *Perkins* at once resumed patrolling and sent her boats in to fight fires and rescue the wounded.

At 0215 June 1, *Chicago* and *Perkins*, on orders of the naval command at Sydney, stood out to sea. The cruiser, when close to South Head gas buoy, passed the periscope of an entering midget so close that one could almost look down it from the bridge. Whether this midget had already been in and out or was entering for the first time is not known. During the day two damaged and scuttled midgets, complete with the bodies of their four crew members, were discovered on the bottom of Sydney Harbor. They had probably scuttled themselves when their mission was completed.[5] *Chicago* and *Perkins* reëntered the harbor during the afternoon to recover their boats, and promptly left for good.

Japanese Imperial Headquarters issued a communiqué giving a lurid description of H.M. battleship *Warspite* (for which *Chicago* had already been mistaken in the Battle of the Coral Sea) going up in flames and sinking. This bit of misinformation appears to have given the Japanese great satisfaction; the anniversary was cele-

---

[4] A second torpedo which also must have been intended for *Chicago* ran up on the beach at Garden Island and went dead.

[5] One midget's torpedoes had not been fired, as they had fouled her net-cutter. It is not known what became of the other two midgets. The Dutch sub claimed one.

brated with appropriate speeches and newspaper articles in 1943 and 1944.

Apparently the I-boats that brought the midgets south waited around for a week in the hope of recovering them. At about 0020 June 8, seven shells fired from a submarine lying three-and-a-half miles off Cape Banks fell into a Sydney suburb, demolishing one house but killing nobody. The submarine, fired upon by a coastal battery, was last seen heading north on the surface. Air search failed to locate it.

Both this "Battle of Sydney" and a similar midget-submarine attack on Diego Suarez, Madagascar, on the previous day, were doubtless intended as diversions in connection with Midway. Since a midget-submarine attack had heralded the attack on Pearl Harbor, the Japanese wished to create the impression that their next move would be to the south and west, instead of to the north and east. Be that as it may, Admiral Nimitz refused to bite, for he knew that the enemy was about to attack in his direction, not "down under."

CHAPTER VI

Midway Preliminaries

May 1942 [1]

1. *The Hawaiian Sentry*

SHORTLY before battle was joined in the Coral Sea, word had reached Admiral Nimitz of a forthcoming enemy offensive in the Central Pacific that threatened to be far more powerful and dangerous than the one about to be stopped at the Louisiades. There had been some inkling of this two months earlier. On the night of 3–4 March 1942, Oahu was raided by two enemy four-engined flying boats. Owing to a fortunate overcast, they missed Pearl Harbor and dropped four bombs harmlessly into the Punch Bowl crater behind Honolulu. Although these planes were not sighted, experts figured out what they were from the sound and from bomb fragments. And on 10 March one of this type – which

---

[1] The basic sources for the Midway operation on the American side are the Action Reports of Admirals Nimitz, Fletcher and Spruance, of the various ships involved, of Commander N.A.S. Midway, and of Marine Corps units on the atoll. For the Japanese side, the Office of Naval Intelligence has translated Nagumo's official report, the damage reports of the carriers sunk and pertinent extracts from ships' journals and staff diaries as "The Japanese Story of the Battle of Midway," which fills the *O.N.I. Review* for May 1947 (II No. 5). There are several interrogations of key officers in *Inter. Jap. Off.* and USSBS 530. Other reports and track charts were procured for this work in Tokyo by Lt. Cdr. Salomon. For the events on Midway the best account, based on American and Japanese sources, is Lt. Col. R. D. Heinl usmc *Marines at Midway* (1948), a Marine Corps monograph. Most valuable of all is an intensive and thorough study of the operation by Commo. R. W. Bates and staff of the Naval War College, *The Battle of Midway including the Aleutian Phase, June 3 to June 14, 1942. Strategical and Tactical Analysis* (mimeographed book, U. S. Naval War College 1948), referred to here as *War College Analysis*. The official *Army Air Forces in World War II* Vol. I (1948) gives an accurate account of the participation of the A.A.F.

we nicknamed "Emily" — was detected off Midway and shot down after a sharp fight by four Marine Corps Buffaloes.

Where could such planes have come from? By a process of elimination they must have staged through Wotje Atoll and re-fueled from a submarine in the lee of French Frigate Shoals, 490 miles WNW of Oahu and just south of the direct air route to Midway.[2] That estimate was correct. The "Pineapple Navy" — the patrol and other small craft of Hawaiian Sea Frontier forces — then undertook to deny French Frigate Shoals to enemy subma-rines, and the approaches were mined. *YP–277* was blown up by a "friendly" mine off the shoals, and others ran out of fuel when far from home; but they did the job.

Moves of this sort are shadows of events to come — unless they are mere shadows of shadows, deceptive warfare. Nimitz believed that they portended an offensive toward Hawaii, and he was right.

"Midway Island acts as a sentry for Hawaii," said Admiral Nagumo in his report on the great battle. Situated 1135 miles WNW of Pearl Harbor, Midway is the farthest outpost of the Hawaiian chain, excepting the small unoccupied Kure Atoll, 60 miles beyond. Smaller even than Wake, Midway is similarly devoid of Polynesians, coconut palms and the usual attributes of South Sea islands. The entire atoll is but six miles in diameter, and only a small proportion of that is dry land. Of the two islets, Sand and Eastern, the first is less than two miles long and the other a little more than one. A barrier reef rises a few feet above sea level and forms a breakwater around both islets, enclosing one fair harbor and a lagoon that is mostly foul ground.

Midway Atoll, first reported (so far as we know) in 1859 by the American master of an Hawaiian bark and promptly claimed

---

[2] This group of islets, with a total expanse of 30 to 40 acres above water, was discovered by La Pérouse and named after his frigates *Boussole* and *Astrolabe* in 1786. Before the war, the lee was used as an emergency anchorage and seaplane landing. East, the largest islet, with an area of about 10 acres, was developed as an emergency fleet air base before the war. In 1943 Tern Island, at the northern end, was enlarged and developed as an emergency landing strip; from the air it looks like the deck of a carrier.

for his native country, was formally taken into American possession by U.S.S. *Lackawanna* on 28 August 1867, on orders from Secretary Gideon Welles. The Pacific Mail Steamship Company was responsible for this early assertion of "American imperialism," because it wished to establish a coaling station.[3] As the deep lagoon in the center could only be reached over a six-foot bar, the Navy obtained an appropriation of $50,000 in 1869 for dredging a ship channel between Sand and Eastern Islands. Next year, U.S.S. *Saginaw* towed out the first dredges and carried up workers and supplies. At the end of seven months, when the channel was only deep enough for small boats in calm weather, the money had all been spent. *Saginaw* was wrecked on Kure, and during the next thirty years nobody except Japanese feather hunters took an interest in Midway.

A new chapter opened in 1903 when the Pacific Commercial Cable Company decided to establish there a station on its Honolulu–Guam–Manila line. President Theodore Roosevelt issued an order placing Midway "under the jurisdiction and control of the Navy Department," and on 3 June 1903 the redoubtable Hugh Rodman, then a lieutenant commander and skipper of U.S.S. *Iroquois*, using no weapon but his powerful voice and commanding personality, chased off a party of Japanese feather collectors. During that year the cable was laid and a station established. The Navy set out mooring buoys, built a lighthouse on Sand Island, and for four years stationed a twenty-man Marine guard to protect the station. This cable to Honolulu was of immense value to the Navy during the great battle of 1942. It handled most of the heavy traffic incident to a big naval operation, leaving the volume of radio communication normal — so that the enemy did not suspect what was going on.[4]

Superintendents of the cable station brought a few amenities

[3] The Pacific Mail was also responsible for the name Midway; the discoverer, Capt. Brooks, called it Middlebrook Islands. L. S. Shelmidine "History of Midway Islands" *American Neptune* VIII 179–95 (July 1948) is my principal source for the history.

[4] Com Hawaiian Sea Frontier to Cincpac 26 June 1942.

to this desolate atoll. Sand Island, which had hitherto grown little vegetation but the scaevola bush, became a garden spot with Australian ironwood trees, eucalyptus, shrubs, lawns, spacious quarters for the employes, and even tennis courts for their recreation.

From 1920 on the United States Navy occasionally stationed an oiler in Welles Harbor to fuel destroyers. In 1934, when the Naval Limitation Treaty with its anti-defense clauses was denounced by Japan, the Navy studied the possibilities of Midway as a seaplane base. Pan American Airways picked up the ball in 1935, made Sand Island an airport for its trans-Pacific clippers, constructed a seaplane ramp, new quarters, and a small hotel on the lagoon side. Navy seaplanes flew to Midway from Honolulu and Marines "captured" the island during the Fleet Problem of 1935 — the one which pacifists regarded as a menace to Japan. About that time United States Army engineers started to blast out a ship channel between the two islets; it was first used by the minesweeper *Swan* in 1940.

In consequence of the Hepburn Report on Pacific bases, which declared that the Midway air base was second in importance only to Pearl Harbor, construction of facilities for Catalina patrol planes began under naval direction in March 1940. N.A.S. (Naval Air Station) Midway was commissioned 18 August 1941, with Commander Cyril T. Simard as the first C.O. By that time Sand Island had become a populous town with hundreds of contractors' workmen, a defense battalion of the Fleet Marine Force,[5] a large seaplane hangar and artificial harbor, fuel tanks and numerous other buildings. One 5300-foot strip for land-based aircraft had been completed on Eastern Island, and contracts for further construction had been awarded to the amount of $250,000,000.

Midway received the news of the Pearl Harbor blitz at 0630

---

[5] For Marine defense battalions see Vol. III of this History p. 227*n*. The first important detachment of the 3rd Defense Battalion landed at Midway 29 Sept. 1940. The 3rd was relieved by the 6th D.B., 34 officers and 750 men, 11 Sept. 1941. An advance detail of Marine Corps Scout Bombing Squadron 231 arrived 19 Nov. 1941.

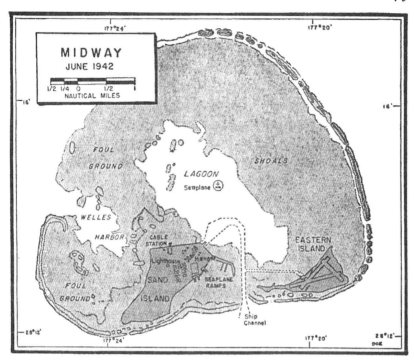

(Zone plus 12 time) 7 December 1941. The Japanese Striking
Force had approached Oahu by a course well outside the cruising
radius of the Catalinas stationed at Midway. But an independent
task group consisting of two new destroyers, accompanied by a
fleet tender, bombarded the atoll that night. A Marine lookout
reported a flashing light to the southwestward at 1842; three hours
later the destroyers opened fire; the Marines' coast defense guns
returned it and claimed three hits. At 2200 the enemy retired after
killing four and wounding ten men, burning the roof of the seaplane hangar and most of the stores therein, knocking out the
Pan American radio direction finder, and destroying one Catalina.[6]

During the week before Christmas, Midway was reinforced by
17 Vought Vindicators (SB2U–3s) and a Marine fighter-plane
squadron (VMF–221). U.S.S. *Tangier*, after landing various sup-

[6] The pilot of the Philippine Clipper which had just evacuated Wake saw one
of the DDs burning about 35 miles from Midway, but both ships got home.

plies and personnel originally intended for the relief of Wake, took away all but a few of the contractors' workmen. This civilian construction gang, described by one observer as "the scum of the West Coast," had been great bullies and fighters up to 7 December, but became demoralized by the brief bombardment. Most of the men scattered into the bush where they made dugouts for themselves and lived on appropriated food; others circulated among the garrison, and the diary of the Naval Air Station shows almost daily commitment of civilians to the local hoosegow for "suspicious or demoralizing attitude, statements, or actions."

As Admiral Nagumo remarked, the importance of Midway was enhanced when we lost Wake; it was now the westernmost American base in the Pacific. By the same token, it was coveted by the enemy. As the atoll lay beyond the range of Wake-based search planes the Japanese could not observe what was going on. Three attempts to bombard the atoll by surfaced submarines were unsuccessful, owing to good shooting by Marine planes and coast defense batteries.[7]

2. *Japanese Strategy and Plans*

The Japanese high command were not much disturbed by their setback in the Coral Sea. Tulagi was in the bag; Port Moresby, they believed, could be captured at leisure; reports of Allied losses in the battle were very satisfactory. No backdoor interference by the British Far Eastern Fleet was anticipated; Nagumo's Easter raid on Ceylon had taken care of that. So, without loss of a day, the Japanese Navy went ahead with its plans to gobble up Midway and the Western Aleutians. The capture of these islands was the most important objective in the second great Japanese offensive that began with the drive on Port Moresby, to end with the conquest of Samoa, Fiji and Nouméa. As the basic strategy of this

[7] 25 Jan., 8 and 10 Feb., 1942; one of the submarines, *I-73*, was sunk two days later by U.S.S. *Gudgeon*. Heinl *Marines at Midway* pp. 17, 18.

offensive has already been discussed, we may now concentrate on the special reasons for taking Midway and the Western Aleutians.

These islands were wanted to repair that rip in the "ribbon defense" through which Halsey had dashed in April to bomb Tokyo.[8] They would serve as key points in a new outer perimeter, Kiska–Midway–Wake–Marshalls–Gilberts–Guadalcanal–Port Moresby. Midway-based patrol planes, in conjunction with others flying out of Kiska and Wake, would be able to detect any task force attempting to raid Japan's inner defense. Midway was an important forward fueling point for the United States submarines, which were beginning to annoy shipping near Japan. But, from Yamamoto's point of view, the principal value of Midway was to draw Nimitz out. Commander in Chief Combined Fleet knew that he must annihilate the United States Pacific Fleet in 1942 or lose the war. For Yamamoto, unlike most of the Nipponese war lords, appreciated American strength and resources. Knowing that these would tell with the passage of time, he argued that Japan must threaten something that America valued, in order to get the Pacific Fleet into a position where it could be wiped out. And what could be better bait than Midway? Nimitz could not let that "sentry to Hawaii" go by default like Wake; and whatever he did about it would involve a movement of the Pacific Fleet westward to a position where the Combined Fleet could strike. Yamamoto converted Admiral Nagano, Chief of the Naval General Staff, to his strategy; and they convinced Imperial Headquarters, which on 5 May 1942 issued the terse order: "Commander in Chief Combined Fleet will, in coöperation with the Army, invade and occupy strategic points in the Western Aleutians and Midway Island." [9]

This was the second phase of the 1942 strategy. Plans for the

---

[8] Certain high-placed Japanese officers still believed that "Jimmy" Doolittle's planes had been based on Midway, which was an additional reason to take the island. Capt. Y. Watanabe, gunnery officer on Yamamoto's staff, in *Inter. Jap. Off.* I 66.

[9] Imperial General Headquarters Orders, obtained in Japan by Lt. Cdr. Salomon; different translation in *War College Analysis*.

third phase — occupation of the Fijis, Samoa and New Caledonia — were activated as early as 18 May.

Pearl Harbor was no objective of the Midway operation. "We wanted to go to Pearl Harbor," said a member of Yamamoto's staff, "but it was not authorized." The Japanese intended to seize French Frigate Shoals and other islets en route to Pearl, and to stage nuisance raids from Midway on the great naval base; but future events would decide whether or not they needed Oahu. It was perfectly clear to these Oriental disciples of Mahan that they must defeat the United States Pacific Fleet before attempting to take and hold Pearl; and that, conversely, if Nimitz succeeded in saving his fleet, Midway could not long be held by Japan.[10]

Although Yamamoto's strategy was logical, not as much can be said of his operation plan. It comprised three separate but mutually supporting actions — (1) occupation of Western Aleutians, (2) occupation of Midway, (3) fleet engagement. These objectives were to be carried by five major forces, some of them subdivided into two or more groups, and all proceeding eastward independently.[11] In brief, these forces were: —

1. *Advance Expeditionary Force*, three groups of submarines.

2. *Carrier Striking Force*, comprising four of the six carriers that had struck Pearl Harbor. Admiral Nagumo still flew his flag in *Akagi*, pride of the Japanese carrier fleet, and the second carrier division was commanded by Admiral Yamaguchi, who had been naval attaché at Washington before the war.[12] Commander Minoru Genda, the most highly esteemed planner of Japanese air tactics, was on Nagumo's staff; he was the one person for whose safety, in the course of the coming battle, Yamamoto expressed concern.

3. *Midway Occupation Force*, Admiral Kondo, Commander in Chief of the Second Fleet, which had played a leading part in the conquest of the Indies. This comprised (*a*) a Covering Group of battleships and heavy cruisers; (*b*) Admiral Kurita's Close Support

---

[10] *Inter. Jap. Off.* II 525; I 66.
[11] See next section for details; chap. ix for Force 5.
[12] Capt. E. M. Zacharias *Secret Missions* pp. 160–83.

Group of four more heavy cruisers; (*c*) a Transport Group carrying the Occupation Force; (*d*) two seaplane tenders; and (*e*) a Minesweeper Group.

4. *Main Body*, under Admiral Yamamoto's personal command, including (*a*) the three latest battleships and a light carrier and (*b*) the Aleutian Screening Force of four battleships and two light cruisers.

5. *Northern Area Force*, Admiral Hosogaya, comprising (*a*) the Second Mobile Force of two carriers and three heavy cruisers and (*b*) the two Occupation Forces for Adak-Attu and Kiska.

The overall plan was as follows: —

1. The Second Mobile Force was to open the battle by delivering a paralyzing air bombardment on Dutch Harbor on 3 June in order to confuse Nimitz and cover the occupation of the Western Aleutians. (We shall have to postpone this part of the story until we are through with Midway.)

2. The Carrier Striking Force, after softening up Midway, was to deliver the first blow at the Pacific Fleet if it challenged, while the Main Body, commanded by Yamamoto in person, moved up for the finish from a supporting position to the westward.

3. In the meantime, after nightfall 5 June,[13] Midway Island would be assaulted by the 5000 ground troops of the Occupation Force, and would be promptly developed as an air base.

4. The Aleutian Support Force was to be detached from the Main Body to take station halfway between Midway and the Aleutians and to intercept any American force that came either way.

There were many other details which never came into operation, such as minesweeping and the setting up of seaplane and midget submarine bases at Kure Atoll northwest of Midway. Land-based air searches were flown from Marcus, Wake and Paramushiro.

If Yamamoto's overall strategy was correct, the actual deployment of his forces to effect this result seems cockeyed. Why did he plan it so? We may never know. Yamamoto was shot down by

[13] The date is from a diary of an officer of the Landing Force, furnished by Capt. E. T. Layton. Actual H-hour in plan was dawn 6 June.

the Solomons Air Command on 18 April 1943, and after the war his flag officers either did not know what had been in the old maestro's mind or believed in the adage *de mortuis nil nisi bonum.* His objectives are well known: occupation of Midway and Kiska and a big fleet action. Why, then, in the name of the sainted Togo, did he not keep his fleet together instead of dispersing it all over the North Pacific, exposing it to defeat in detail by a much weaker American force?

The Combined Fleet was, however, deployed in accordance with Japanese strategic habits. They overvalued surprise, which had worked so well at the beginning, and always assumed they could get it. They loved diversionary tactics — forces popping up at odd places to confuse the enemy and pull him off base. They believed that the pattern for decisive battle was the same at sea as on land — lure the enemy into an unfavorable tactical situation, cut off his retreat, drive in his flanks and then concentrate for the kill. Their manual for Carrier Force commanders even invoked the examples of Hannibal at Cannae and Ludendorff at Tannenberg, to justify just such naval strategy as Yamamoto tried at Midway.[14] Thus, the preliminary air strike on Dutch Harbor was primarily a gambit, intended to pull the Pacific Fleet up north where it would not interfere with the occupation of Midway. But why did Yamamoto hold back his powerful battleships of the Main Body where they could not (as it turned out) get into the fight? Why, if he wanted a fleet action, did he not keep them near the carriers?

Here is the probable explanation. Yamamoto, counting on surprise, expected no opposition to his invasion of Midway. He knew that the Pacific Fleet had no fast battleships, underestimated the number of carriers at its disposal (believing that two had been sunk at Coral Sea), and, never expecting that Nimitz would be wise to his movements, anticipated no challenge to develop until several days after Midway had been secured. By that time substan-

[14] "Japanese Striking Force Tactics — Know Your Enemy," Addendum to *Cincpac-Cincpoa Weekly Intelligence* Vol I No. 10, 15 Sept. 1944.

tial forces in Pearl Harbor might be tearing up north to protect Dutch Harbor; and even if Nimitz had decided to let the situation develop he would be unable to reach Midway until 7 or 8 June at the earliest. Nagumo's carriers would then be in readiness to strike the challenging Fleet; perhaps get between it and Midway, which by that time would be a Japanese fixed airplane carrier. Then Yamamoto's Main Body, and the various battleship and heavy cruiser divisions that had accompanied outlying forces, would close for the kill. His carrier pilots would have been rested, every ship would have had a big drink of oil, and the numerically inferior Pacific Fleet should have been annihilated.[15] Alternately, if Nimitz refused to bite in the first week of June, he would certainly try to recapture Midway within a month or two, and the Combined Fleet would be ready in the Marshalls to pounce on him.

The vital defect in this sort of plan is that it depends on the enemy's doing exactly what is expected. If he is smart enough to do something different — in this case to have fast carriers on the spot — the operation is thrown into confusion.

3. *American Strategy and Preparations*

Admiral Nimitz, in his dual capacity as Cincpac and Cincpoa,[16] exercised strategic and broad tactical direction of all American forces, naval or military, deployed in the Pacific Ocean outside General MacArthur's area. Fortunately he could cut his counter-

[15] This theory of Yamamoto's actions is borne out by Nagumo's Estimate of the Situation (*O.N.I. Review* May 1947 p. 6) which was based on the same intelligence as Yamamoto's. The gist of this was (1) Although the U. S. Navy "lacks the will to fight," it will counterattack if Midway is occupied; (2) "The enemy is not aware of our plans"; (3) he has no carrier force in the vicinity; (4) after attacking Midway by air and destroying American shore-based air strength, the Striking Force would still have enough planes "to destroy any enemy task force which may choose to attack." Additional evidence is in the Japanese submarine operations which will be mentioned shortly.

[16] Nimitz was directed on 3 April to assume command of all Allied armed forces in the Pacific Ocean Area except the land defenses of New Zealand, and assumed it on 7 May; hence the addition of Cincpoa (Commander in Chief Pacific Ocean Areas) to his title. But the MacArthur command always remained separate from his.

strategy to fit the enemy's, since (beginning about 10 May) Intelligence fed him a fairly accurate account of Japanese plans and preparations, deduced from various bits of information from a variety of sources. Nimitz declared a state of "Fleet Opposed Invasion" [17] in the Hawaiian Sea Frontier on 14 May, in agreement with the Commanding General Hawaiian Department; Admiral King on the 15th predicted that an expeditionary force for the capture of Midway would depart Guam about 24 May. Orders were promptly issued from Cincpac headquarters for every ship of the Pacific Fleet that had been engaged at Coral Sea to hasten back to Pearl. But it must not be supposed that these predictions and deductions went unchallenged. Certain important officers, both at Honolulu and in Washington, believed that all these indications were an elaborate hoax of the Japanese to cover another raid on Pearl Harbor or even on the West Coast. Admiral Nimitz made the first vital decision of the campaign in accepting the estimate of his fleet Intelligence officer that Midway and the Aleutians were the enemy's real objectives.

As early as 20 May Admiral Nimitz issued an estimate of the enemy force that was accurate as far as it went — and even alarming.[18] What he did not know was that Admiral Yamamoto himself, in the super-battleship *Yamato*, was to command the Main Body of the Combined Fleet, comprising three new and four old battleships, three light cruisers, a destroyer squadron and a light carrier, to operate between Midway and the Aleutians and cover both. Although the picture was not complete the composition, approximate routes and timetable of the enemy forces that immediately threatened Midway were so accurately deduced that on 23 May Rear Admiral Bellinger, the Naval air commander at Pearl, was able to predict the Japanese plan of attack on the Atoll. But for this early and abundant information and (what was equally im-

[17] This meant that the Navy had principal responsibility for repelling invasion, but left the command of Army ground forces in the hands of Major General Delos C. Emmons USA.
[18] "Reprint of Cincpac Reports of Action and Campaigns Feb. 1942 to Feb. 1943" V (17).

portant) the prompt and intelligent use of it, the Pacific Fleet would have had only a slim chance of winning. As it was, the three weeks preceding Midway were the most tense and anxious experienced by Nimitz's staff during the entire war.

Anxiety was never more justified. The carrier situation was critical. *Saratoga*, her repairs completed, was training her air group at San Diego.[19] *Lexington* had been sunk and *Yorktown* damaged at Coral Sea. After that battle Admiral Fitch estimated it would take about ninety days to repair *Yorktown*, but the Pearl Harbor Navy Yard did it in less than two. She limped into port at 1430 May 27 with her bowels in disorder from a bomb explosion and leaking from near-misses. The big dry dock took her in that afternoon. Over 1400 men — shipfitters, shipwrights, machinists, welders, electricians — poured in, over and under the ship; they and the yard shopmen worked in shifts the rest of that day and the next and during the whole of two nights, making the bulkhead stanchions and deck plates necessary to restore the ship's structural strength, and replacing the wiring, instruments and fixtures damaged in the blast. There was no time to make blueprints or to draft plans; templates of parts that needed replacement were fashioned in wood and hustled ashore to the appropriate shop, where the replacements were made in record time, carried on board "on the double" and installed. At 1100 May 29 the dock was flooded, *Yorktown* moved into the stream with hundreds of men still working on her, fueled that afternoon, took on replacement planes and sailed at 0900 on the following day.[20] Her new air group, a composite from three different carriers, first operated as a unit in the forthcoming battle.

[19] Capt. D. C. Ramsey was eager to get *Saratoga* into the fight, but despite round-the-clock loading of planes, stores, etc., she was unable to leave San Diego until 1 June. *Wasp* was still crossing the Atlantic from Gibraltar. An urgent request to the British Admiralty to lend the Pacific Fleet one of their three carriers then operating in the Indian Ocean, some thousands of miles from the nearest enemy carriers, received the discouraging reply on 19 May that none could be spared, and that their Intelligence reported "no indication" of an attack on Alaska or the Hawaiian Islands.

[20] *Pearl Harbor Banner* 7 Dec. 1943 p. 19; Cincpac War Diary; information from Rear Admiral Furlong.

Enterprise and *Hornet* of Halsey's Task Force 16, which had been rushed down south after the Tokyo raid but arrived too late for the Battle of Coral Sea, came tearing back and reëntered Pearl on 26 May. *Enterprise* was the best of our carriers, with a seasoned air group; *Hornet's* air group had had no battle experience. Vice Admiral Halsey, who had been under great strain for six months, broke out with an irritating skin disease and had to go to the hospital. Admiral Nimitz appointed Rear Admiral Raymond A. Spruance, who had commanded Halsey's heavy cruisers, to relieve him as task force commander.[21] A happy choice indeed, for Spruance was not merely competent; he had the level head and cool judgment that would be required to deal with new contingencies and a fluid situation; a man secure within. Not himself an aviator, Spruance took over Halsey's staff, including his temperamental but highly intelligent chief of staff, Captain Miles Browning.

At that time the Pacific Fleet included not one battleship with the speed to operate with fast-stepping carriers. Vice Admiral William S. Pye's battleship task force, after several weeks' shuttling between West Coast ports, Hawaii and the Line Islands, anchored in San Francisco Bay. Owing, in part, to the insulting attitude of San Franciscans toward battleship sailors on liberty, all hands from the Admiral down were eager to get into the fight. Nimitz, however, refused to include them in the picture because he could afford them no air cover, and because the forthcoming operation promised no suitable occasion for the use of their striking power.[22]

[21] Raymond Ames Spruance of Indiana, born 1886, Naval Academy '07 (graduated 25th) received his first command, of destroyer *Bainbridge*, in 1913. During World War I he was assistant engineer officer at the New York Navy Yard, and, after commanding two destroyers, was attached to the Bureau of Engineering. His specialty was gunfire control. After various duties afloat and ashore, including staff work at the Naval War College (of which he served as President after World War II), he became C.O. *Mississippi* in 1938, Commandant 10th Naval District 1940–41 and, before the outbreak of the war, Rear Admiral in command of the cruiser division in Halsey's Task Force 16. After the Battle of Midway he became chief of staff to Admiral Nimitz and Deputy Cincpac and Cincpoa.

[22] Admiral Pye on his own initiative sent *Maryland, Colorado* and three destroyers 650 miles out on 300° bearing 31 May, under command of Rear Admiral Walter S. Anderson, to search for an enemy converted carrier falsely reported to be

As one of the primary duties of Cincpac was to protect and maintain the lifeline to the antipodes, he did not see fit to halt the regular movement of convoys to and from the West Coast and Panama to Samoa, Nouméa, Australia and New Zealand; and all these had to have destroyer escort.[23]

Thus, Admiral Nimitz had to meet Japanese carriers, battleships and heavy cruisers with a smaller number of every type. The most acute question before his staff was whether to concentrate against the attack on Midway, leaving the Aleutians to their fate, or to do something to protect our far-flung possessions in the north. After much discussion, the Admiral on 17 May decided to form a North Pacific Force consisting of heavy cruisers *Indianapolis* and *Louisville*, light cruisers *Honolulu, St. Louis* and *Nashville*, and ten destroyers, under Rear Admiral Robert A. Theobald.[24]

Besides deducing a large part of his enemy's plans, Nimitz had another strategic advantage over Yamamoto: — shorter distance from base to scene of action. For tactical assets he had first, Midway, which accommodated more planes than a carrier and could not be sunk; and second, radar. Two good search radars were installed on Midway. *Enterprise* had an early type (CXAM); *Hornet, Yorktown* and a few of the cruisers had a slightly later one (SC). The circumstances of this battle were such, however, that radar was of little use afloat.[25]

The operation plan which Admiral Nimitz issued to all task force, squadron and division commanders on 27 May was not one

---

in that area, and which he thought might deliver an air strike on San Francisco. He himself sortied on 5 June with his other four battleships, five destroyers and the escort carrier *Long Island* (carrying only 20 planes), rendezvoused with Anderson about 260 miles west of San Francisco, and returned thither a few days later.

[23] Cincpac War Diary. The San Francisco–Oahu convoys, however, were sailing at this time unescorted.

[24] *Nashville* and five destroyers were already in the Aleutians; the rest had to be pulled out of task forces in the Central Pacific. North Pacific Force or TF 8 was activated 21 May. See chap. ix.

[25] *War College Analysis.* Note later the short distance at which *Hiryu's* air strike on *Yorktown* was detected.

to reassure the fainthearted. He foretold that the enemy would employ 2 to 4 fast battleships, and he had none; 4 or 5 carriers, and he had 3 at most; 8 or 9 heavy cruisers, and he had 7; 4 or 5 light cruisers, and he had one; 16 to 24 destroyers, and he had 14; and at least 25 submarines against his 19. And this estimate of Japanese forces did not include the Main Body, which would have made the balance even less favorable to the United States.[26] Nimitz estimated that the Japanese would make a "full scale attack" for the quick occupation of Midway, that submarines would scout and intercept our forces up to 200 miles west of Oahu, that the carrier planes and battleships would attempt to get at our surface forces, and that the sinking of our carriers would be a prime objective.[27]

Admiral Nimitz's orders to his two commanders of carrier task forces, Fletcher and Spruance, were to "inflict maximum damage on enemy by employing strong attrition tactics," which in the naval language of that day meant air strikes on enemy ships. He cannily ordered Fletcher and Spruance to take initial positions to the northeastward of Midway, beyond search range of the approaching enemy, anticipating that the 700-mile searches by Midway-based planes would locate the Japanese carriers before the presence of his own would be divulged. To this he added a special Letter of Instruction: —

"In carrying out the task assigned . . . you will be governed by the principle of calculated risk, which you shall interpret to mean the avoidance of exposure of your force to attack by superior enemy forces without good prospect of inflicting, as a result of such exposure, greater damage on the enemy."

No commander in chief's instructions were ever more faithfully and intelligently carried out than these, by Admirals Fletcher and Spruance.

Admiral Fletcher, as senior to Admiral Spruance, became O.T.C. (Officer in Tactical Command) as soon as their rendez-

---

[26] Nimitz made a separate estimate of the Northern Area Force, which he sent to Rear Admiral Theobald.

[27] Cincpac Op Plan 29–42.

vous was effected. As he possessed no aviation staff and Spruance had Halsey's, it was probably fortunate that Spruance exercised practically an independent command during the crucial actions of 4–6 June. Neither he nor Fletcher exercised any control over the air and ground forces on Midway Island, over the submarines deployed in their area, or over Admiral Theobald's force in the Aleutians. The overall commander was Admiral Nimitz, who remained perforce at his Pearl Harbor headquarters.

Patrol craft of the Sea Frontier Forces were stationed as aircraft rescue ships at Lisianski, Laysan, Gardner Pinnacles and Necker Island, the islets on the Kauai–Midway line; seaplane tenders *Thornton* and *Ballard* were stationed at French Frigate Shoals.

All available Army bombers at Oahu were alerted to reinforce Midway if needed, and both Army and Navy Air Forces conducted searches 800 miles out from Oahu, in the northwest sector.

Midway itself, the tiny objective of these mastodonic forces, had plenty of attention during the month preceding the battle. Early in May Admiral Nimitz flew up to make a personal inspection of the atoll. He found the defense organization working perfectly under close coöperation between Commander Cyril T. Simard, the atoll commander, and Lieutenant Colonel Harold Shannon usmc, commander ground forces. After asking the Colonel what major items of equipment he needed, the Admiral said, "If I get you all these things, can you hold Midway against a major amphibious assault?" To which Shannon replied with a hearty "Yes, Sir!" [28] And he could have, too. If the Japanese had broken through the Pacific Fleet and tried to land on Midway, they would have met an even hotter reception from the Marines than they gave the Marines at Tarawa.[29]

Sand and Eastern Islands were already ringed with coast de-

[28] Lt. Col. R. C. McGlashan usmc (Shannon's operations officer) two Historical Reports "Defense of Midway" dated 12 Aug. and 19 Sept. 1947, prepared from his personal records and memory.

[29] The composition, organization and equipment of the Japanese defense forces at Tarawa in Nov. 1943 were very similar to those of the Marines at Midway; but the American assault forces at Tarawa were more powerful than those of the Japanese at Midway.

fense, anti-boat and anti-aircraft guns, from 20-mm up to the old Navy 7-inchers, when, about 20 May, Nimitz let the atoll commander know what he had learned of the enemy's plans. All defense activities were then stepped up and a furious reinforcement of the island began. On 25 May U.S.S. *St. Louis* brought two rifle companies of Major Carlson's newly formed 2nd Raider Battalion, which later won fame at Guadalcanal, to augment the small infantry components of the defense battalion, and a 37-mm anti-aircraft battery. Bomb-proof dugouts were constructed to accommodate all hands. On 26 May U.S.S. *Kittyhawk* brought in 16 Marine Corps Douglas dive-bombers, seven Wildcat fighter planes, 22 pilots (mostly fresh out of flight school), more anti-aircraft guns and five light tanks. A few Catalina seaplanes and amphibians were already stationed in the lagoon or on Eastern Island for air patrol; their numbers were now increased to 30-odd. With the cooperation of the Hawaiian Army Command and the VII Army Air Force, 18 B-17s and four B-26s were moved up to augment the six Navy Avengers.[30] Ten motor torpedo boats were dispatched from the Hawaiian Sea Frontier forces. By 4 June there were 121 combat planes, 141 officers and 2,886 enlisted men on the atoll. But the ground crews were not reinforced, and flying personnel had to do a good part of their own fueling and servicing. During the last two weeks before the battle, more coast defense and other guns were mounted for anti-boat and anti-aircraft work, barbed wire was strung, mines and underwater obstacles were emplaced and guns were sited for resisting a landing. "Wreck 'em on the reef!" was Colonel Shannon's slogan, remembering Wake.

A final load of drummed aviation gasoline arrived in the char-

---

[30] The Army was very coöperative, and even proposed a raid on Wake Island with the Flying Fortresses in order to knock it out as a staging point. Cincpac gladly gave his consent (30 May) but the Army withdrew the offer because the distance of over 1,000 miles each way was too much for B-17s. Capt. V. R. Murphy, Cincpac staff war plans officer, doubted the value of sending B-17s and B-26s to Midway; said they would not be worth the room they took up. He was right. If they could have been employed to track the Japanese carrier force when located, they might have been most useful, but their pilots were trained for bombing only. For Gen. Tinker's gallant effort to bomb Wake with Liberators, see chap. viii sec. 2, below.

tered freighter *Nira Luckenbach* on the afternoon of Sunday 31 May. There was a dispute about overtime with the merchant marine crew, but the ship's officers and boatswains manned winches and tended hatches in order that the Marines could unload the cargo that night.[31]

A very careful and comprehensive search plan was drawn up by Captain Simard and placed in effect on 30 May. Weather greatly reduced the effectiveness of air search and exercised a considerable influence on the battle. In May and June the waters to the west and northwest of Midway are often traversed by storms which move northeastward, preceded by weather fronts which produce clouds and rain. Even without a storm, fog can ordinarily be expected about 300 to 400 miles northwest of Midway where the tradewinds strike the Japan Current. The Japanese knew as much about these conditions as we did, and took advantage of the expected fog and weather front to move their carriers as near as possible to Midway undetected. Their Occupation Force, on the other hand, approached through a normally fair weather area to the southwestward.

4. *Composition of Forces*

a. Japanese [32]

COMBINED FLEET

Admiral Isoroku Yamamoto (Commander in Chief) in *Yamato*
Chief of Staff, Rear Admiral Matome Ugaki

ADVANCE EXPEDITIONARY FORCE

Vice Admiral Teruhisa Komatsu (C. in C. Sixth Fleet) in CL *Katori* at Kwajalein

Subron 3: I-168, I-169, I-171, I-174, I-175, deployed between lat. 20° N, long. 166°20′ W, and lat. 23°30′ N, long. 166°20′ W.

[31] Information from the vessel's officers and port abstract. Some wildly inaccurate stories about this ship were current at the time.
[32] Compiled by Lt. Pineau and Mr. W. L. Robinson from Japanese Navy official sources and checked ship by ship from tabular movements of warships, meritorious achievement records, war diaries and logs. CV plane complements from WDC Nos. 161,733 and 161,709.

Subron 5: I-156, I-157, I-158, I-159, I-162, * I-164, I-165, I-166, deployed between lat. 28°20′ N, long. 162°20′ W, and lat. 26° N, long. 165° W.

Subdiv 13: I-121, I-122, I-123, bringing gas and oil to Lisianski Island and French Frigate Shoals.

CARRIER STRIKING FORCE (FIRST MOBILE FORCE)

Vice Admiral Chuichi Nagumo
Chief of Staff, Rear Admiral Ryunosuke Kusaka

Cardiv 1, Vice Admiral Nagumo

* AKAGI (21 VF, 21 VB, 21 VT)   * KAGA (30 VF, 23 VB, 30 VT)

Cardiv 2, * Rear Admiral Tamon Yamaguchi

* HIRYU (21 VF, 21 VB, 21 VT)   * SORYU (21 VF, 21 VB, 21 VT)

Rear Admiral Hiroaki Abe

Crudiv 8: TONE, CHIKUMA
Batdiv 3, 2nd Section: HARUNA, KIRISHIMA

Screen: Rear Admiral Susumu Kimura (Comdesron 10) in CL *Nagara*

Desdiv 10: KAZAGUMO, YUGUMO, MAKIGUMO, AKIGUMO [33]
Desdiv 17: ISOKAZE, URAKAZE, HAMAKAZE, TANIKAZE
Desdiv 4: ARASHI, NOWAKI, HAGIKAZE, MAIKAZE
Supply Unit: Oilers KYOKUTO MARU, SHINKOKU MARU, TOHO MARU, NIPPON MARU, KOKUYO MARU

MIDWAY OCCUPATION FORCE

Vice Admiral Nobutake Kondo (C. in C. Second Fleet)
Chief of Staff, Rear Admiral Kazutaka Shiraishi

COVERING GROUP, Vice Admiral Kondo

Crudiv 4, 1st Section: ATAGO, CHOKAI
Crudiv 5 (Vice Admiral Takeo Takagi): MYOKO, HAGURO
Batdiv 3, 1st Section (Rear Admiral Gunichi Mikawa): KONGO, HIEI

Screen: Rear Admiral Shoji Nishimura (Comdesron 4) in CL *Yura*

Desdiv 2: MURASAME, HARUSAME, YUDACHI, SAMIDARE
Desdiv 9: ASAGUMO, MINEGUMO, NATSUGUMO
Supply Unit: Oilers GENYO MARU, KENYO MARU, SATA, TSURUMI; Repair Ship AKASHI; Light Carrier ZUIHO (12 VF, 11 VB); Destroyer MIKAZUKI

CLOSE SUPPORT GROUP, Rear Admiral Takeo Kurita (Comcrudiv 7)

Crudiv 7: SUZUYA, KUMANO, MOGAMI, * MIKUMA
Destroyers ASASHIO, ARASHIO; [34] Oiler NICHIEI MARU

---

* Lost in this battle. *I-164* sunk en route by U.S.S. *Triton* off Kyushu 17 May.

[33] Before dawn 3 June *Akigumo* was detached to escort of Supply Unit.
[34] *Michishio* and *Oshio* of Desdiv 8, damaged at Lombok Strait, were still under repair.

TRANSPORT GROUP, Rear Admiral Raizo Tanaka (Comdesron 2)
in CL *Jintsu*

12 transports and freighters carrying "Kure" and "Yokosuka" 5th Special Naval Landing Forces and Army Ichiki Detachment; two construction battalions; "survey group," weather group, etc.; about 5,000 officers and men.[35]
Oiler AKEBONO MARU
Patrol Boats Nos. 1, 2, 34,[36] carrying assault detachments, S.N.L.F.

Screen

Desron 2: JINTSU and Destroyers KUROSHIO, OYASHIO; HATSUKAZE, YUKIKAZE, AMATSUKAZE, TOKITSUKAZE; KASUMI, ARARE, KAGERO, SHIRANUHI

SEAPLANE GROUP, Rear Admiral Ruitaro Fujita (Comcardiv 11)

Seaplane Carriers CHITOSE (20 VSO) and KAMIKAWA MARU (8 VSO), carrying seaplane group to be set up at Kure Island; Destroyer HAYASHIO, Patrol Boat No. 35.

MINESWEEPING GROUP

Converted minesweepers TAMA MARU No. 3 and No. 5, SHOWA MARU No. 7 and No. 8; Subchasers Nos. 16, 17, 18; Supply Ship SOYA; Cargo Ships MEIYO MARU, YAMAFUKU MARU [37]

MAIN BODY (FIRST FLEET)
Admiral Yamamoto

Batdiv 1: YAMATO, MUTSU, NAGATO
Light Carrier HOSHO (8 VT); Destroyer YUKAZE; Seaplane Carriers CHIYODA, NISSHIN [38]

Screen: Desron 3, Rear Admiral Shintaro Hashimoto in CL *Sendai*

Desdiv 11: FUBUKI, SHIRAYUKI, HATSUYUKI, MURAKUMO
Desdiv 19: ISONAMI, URANAMI, SHIKINAMI, AYANAMI
Desdiv 20: AMAGIRI, ASAGIRI, YUGIRI, SHIRAKUMO

Detachment from Main Body as Aleutian Screening (Support) Force
Vice Admiral Shiro Takasu [39]

Batdiv 2: ISE, HYUGA, FUSO, YAMASHIRO
Crudiv (light) 9 (Rear Admiral Fukuhara Kishi): KITAGAMI, OI
Supply Units: Oilers TOEI MARU, NARUTO, SAN CLEMENTE MARU, TOA MARU

---

[35] Capt. E. T. Layton has furnished figures; for names of transports see chart of the cruising disposition of Transport Group, below. "Survey group" was usual phrase for midget submarine personnel and base outfit. Two of the freighters were filled with U.S. construction equipment and weapons captured at Wake.
[36] Patrol Boats Nos. 1, 2, 34, and 35 were old destroyers *Shimakaze, Nadakaze, Suzuki,* and *Tsuta,* converted along lines similar to our APDs.
[37] This Group, proceeding from Saipan and Wake, retired upon receiving word that the occupation of Midway had been given up.
[38] Carrying 2 motor torpedo boats and 6 midget submarines.
[39] Part of Desron 3 acted as Screen to this Force.

b. United States

UNITED STATES PACIFIC FLEET AND PACIFIC OCEAN AREAS

Admiral Chester W. Nimitz, Commander in Chief

CARRIER STRIKING FORCE

Rear Admiral Frank Jack Fletcher

TASK FORCE 17, Admiral Fletcher

TG 17.5 Carrier Group, Captain Elliott Buckmaster

* YORKTOWN   Capt. Buckmaster

Air Group,[40] Lt. Cdr. Oscar Pederson

VF–3:	25 F4F–4 (Wildcat)	Lt. Cdr. John S. Thach	*10 lost* [41]
VB–3:	18 SBD–3 (Dauntless)	Lt. Cdr. Maxwell F. Leslie	
VS–5:	19 SBD–3	Lt. Wallace C. Short Jr.	*12 lost*
VT–3:	13 TBD–1 (Devastator)	* Lt. Cdr. Lance E. Massey	*12 lost*

TG 17.2 Cruiser Group, Rear Admiral William W. Smith

ASTORIA	Capt. Francis W. Scanland
PORTLAND	Capt. Laurance T. Du Bose

TG 17.4 Destroyer Screen, Captain Gilbert C. Hoover (Comdesron 2)

* HAMMANN	Cdr. Arnold E. True
HUGHES	Lt. Cdr. Donald J. Ramsey
MORRIS	Cdr. Harry B. Jarrett
ANDERSON	Lt. Cdr. John K. B. Ginder
RUSSELL	Lt. Cdr. Glenn R. Hartwig
GWIN [42]	Cdr. John M. Higgins

TASK FORCE 16, Rear Admiral Raymond A. Spruance

TG 16.5 Carrier Group, Captain George D. Murray [43]

* Lost in this battle.

[40] Including detachments from VB–5 and VF–42 and VS–3 of *Saratoga*. Carrier Air Groups were not numbered until later.

[41] Plane losses in this section are those on 4, 5 and 6 June only, but include both combat and operational losses for those dates. Navy Dept. News Release for 6 June 1948 gives total carrier plane losses for Midway operation as 113, of which 61 were combat, 41 operational and 11 lost when *Yorktown* sank, 7 June.

[42] Joined 5 June; Comdesdiv 22 (Cdr. Harold R. Holcomb) was on board. Capt. Hoover had then been detached from *Hammann*.

[43] Only 35 SBDs on board at time of action, because one wouldn't start at Ewa (but

	ENTERPRISE	Capt. Murray	
	Air Group, Lt. Cdr. Clarence W. McClusky		
VF-6:	27 F4F-4	Lt. James S. Gray	1 lost
VB-6:	19 SBD-2 and -3	Lt. Richard H. Best	11 lost
VS-6:	19 SBD-2 and -3	Lt. Wilmer E. Gallaher	9 lost
VT-6:	14 TBD-1	*Lt. Cdr. Eugene E. Lindsey	11 lost

	HORNET	Capt. Marc A. Mitscher	
	Air Group, Cdr. Stanhope C. Ring		
VF-8:	27 F4F-4	Lt. Cdr. Samuel G. Mitchell	12 lost
VB-8:	19 SBD-2 and -3	Lt. Cdr. Robert R. Johnson ⎱	
VS-8:	18 SBD-1, -2, -3	Lt. Cdr. Walter F. Rodee ⎰	5 lost
VT-8:	15 TBD-1	*Lt. Cdr. John C. Waldron	All lost

TG 16.2 Cruiser Group, Rear Admiral Thomas C. Kinkaid (Comcrudiv 6)

NEW ORLEANS	Capt. Howard H. Good
MINNEAPOLIS	Capt. Frank J. Lowry
VINCENNES	Capt. Frederick L. Riefkohl
NORTHAMPTON	Capt. William W. Chandler
PENSACOLA	Capt. Frank L. Lowe
ATLANTA [44]	Capt. Samuel P. Jenkins

TG 16.4 Destroyer Screen, Captain Alexander R. Early (Comdesron 1)

PHELPS	Lt. Cdr. Edward L. Beck
WORDEN	Lt. Cdr. William G. Pogue
MONAGHAN	Lt. Cdr. William P. Burford
AYLWIN	Lt. Cdr. George R. Phelan

Desron 6, Captain Edward P. Sauer

BALCH	Lt. Cdr. Harold H. Tiemroth
CONYNGHAM	Lt. Cdr. Henry C. Daniel
BENHAM	Lt. Cdr. Joseph M. Worthington
ELLET	Lt. Cdr. Francis H. Gardner
MAURY	Lt. Cdr. Gelzer L. Sims

Oiler Group

Oiler	CIMARRON	Cdr. Russell M. Ihrig
Oiler	PLATTE	Capt. Ralph H. Henkle
Destroyer	DEWEY	Lt. Cdr. C. F. Chillingworth Jr.
Destroyer	MONSSEN	Cdr. Roland N. Smoot

* Lost in this battle.

---

pilot Lt. W. J. Widhelm got on board) and one (Ens. R. D. Milliman) was lost operationally en route.
[44] Light, anti-aircraft cruiser; the others in the group are heavies.

SUBMARINES [45]

Under Operational Control of Rear Admiral Robert H. English,
Commander Submarine Force Pacific Fleet, at Pearl Harbor

TG 7.1 Midway Patrol Group

CACHALOT	Lt. Cdr. G. A. Lewis
FLYING FISH	Lt. Cdr. G. R. Donaho
TAMBOR	Lt. Cdr. J. W. Murphy
TROUT	Lt. Cdr. F. W. Fenno
GRAYLING	Lt. Cdr. E. Olsen
NAUTILUS	Lt. Cdr. W. H. Brockman Jr.
GROUPER	Lt. Cdr. C. E. Duke
DOLPHIN	Lt. Cdr. R. L. Rutter
GATO	Lt. Cdr. W. G. Myers
CUTTLEFISH	Lt. Cdr. M. P. Hottel
GUDGEON	Lt. Cdr. H. B. Lyon
GRENADIER	Lt. Cdr. W. A. Lent

TG 7.2 "Roving Short-Stops"

NARWHAL	Lt. Cdr. C. W. Wilkins
PLUNGER	Lt. Cdr. D. C. White
TRIGGER	Lt. Cdr. J. H. Lewis

TG 7.3 North of Oahu Patrol

TARPON	Lt. Cdr. Lewis Wallace
PIKE	Lt. Cdr. W. A. New
FINBACK	Lt. Cdr. J. L. Hull
GROWLER	Lt. Cdr. H. W. Gilmore

SHORE–BASED AIR, MIDWAY

Captain Cyril T. Simard, as of 4 June

Detachments from Patrol Wings 1 and 2, Cdr. Massie Hughes
and Lt. Cdr. Robert Brixner

32 PBY–5 and PBY–5A Catalinas [46]   *1 lost*
VT–8 Detachment: 6 TBF (Avenger)   Lt. L. K. Fieberling   *5 lost*

MARINE AIRCRAFT GROUP 22, 2nd Marine Air Wing,[47]

Lt. Col. Ira E. Kimes USMC

VMF–221: 20 F2A–3 (Buffalo — *13 lost*); 7 F4F–3 (*2 lost*), *Maj. Floyd B. Parks USMC, Capt. Kirk Armistead USMC

VMSB–241: 11 SB2U–3 (Vindicator — *5 lost*); 16 SBD–2 (*8 lost*), * Maj. Lofton R. Henderson USMC, * Maj. Benjamin W. Norris USMC, Capt. Marshall A. Tyler USMC

* Lost in this battle.

[45] Compiled from the "Submarine Operational History World War II," prepared by Comsubforpacflt, the O.N.I. Combat Narrative and the Pacific Fleet Confidential Notice 10CN–42, 6 May 1942.

[46] The PBY–5 is a seaplane that can alight on or take off from water only. The PBY–5A is an amphibian that can be land-based. Both have the familiar fat Catalina fuselage and carry a crew of 10 to 12.

[47] These numbers, checked at Marine Corps Headquarters, are less than those stated

DETACHMENT OF VII ARMY AIR FORCE
Major General Willis H. Hale USA

4 B-26 (Marauder)	Capt. James F. Collins USA	*2 lost*
13 B-17 (Flying Fortress)	Lt. Col. Walter C. Sweeney Jr. USA	*2 lost*
6 B-17	Maj. G. A. Blakey USA	

MIDWAY LOCAL DEFENSES, Captain Simard [48]

6th Marine Defense Battalion (reinforced), Fleet Marine Force,[49]
Col. Harold D. Shannon USMC
Motor Torpedo Boat Squadron 1, Lt. Clinton McKellar Jr.
8 PT Boats at Midway, 2 at Kure. Also 4 small Patrol Craft

Deployed along lesser reefs and islands of Hawaiian Group

Tender	THORNTON	Lt. Cdr. Wendell F. Kline, French Frigate Shoals
Tender	BALLARD	Cdr. Ward C. Gilbert, French Frigate Shoals
Destroyer	CLARK	Cdr. Myron T. Richardson, French Frigate Shoals
Oiler	KALOLI	Lt. Cdr. G. H. Chapman Jr. USNR, Pearl and Hermes Reef
Cvt. Yacht	CRYSTAL	Lt. Cdr. O. B. Drotning, Pearl and Hermes Reef
Sweeper	VIREO	Lt. James C. Legg, Pearl and Hermes Reef

4 YPs (cvt. tuna boats) at Lisianski, Gardner Pinnacles, Laysan and Necker

MIDWAY RELIEF FUELING UNIT,[50] Commander Harry R. Thurber

Oiler	GUADALUPE	Cdr. Thurber
Destroyer	BLUE	Cdr. Harold N. Williams
Destroyer	RALPH TALBOT	Cdr. Ralph Earle Jr.

5. *Movements of Forces, 10 May–3 June 1942*

East Longitude dates for the Japanese; West Longitude dates for the American forces; Zone plus 12 time at Midway.

During the last week of May, all forces destined for this great battle were on the move. Japanese submarines were the first to get under way. An advance reconnaissance unit comprising *I–121* and *I–123*, 1400-ton minelaying submarines, departed Japan in early

---

elsewhere, the difference being represented by old planes that were inoperative or being "cannibalized." Only 2 fighter planes were operational 5 June.
[48] Under Hawaiian Sea Frontier, Rear Admiral David W. Bagley.
[49] For complete list of units and C.O.s, see R. D. Heinl *Marines at Midway* p. 55.
[50] Departed Pearl Harbor 3 June, arrived Midway 6th.

May, each laden with about 40 tons of aviation gasoline and 12 tons of lubricating oil. After calling at Kwajalein they made for French Frigate Shoals in order to service "Emilys," the big 4-engined bombers. Arriving there on 26 May (East Longitude date) they found already in the anchorage a seaplane tender which Admiral Nimitz had sent up in anticipation. After hanging about for four days and seeing no Japanese planes, *I–121* and *I–123* returned to Kwajalein. Another submarine of the same class reconnoitered Laysan, and possibly Lisianski Island. The main force of submarines was sent first to scout Oahu, then to move northwesterly; on 3 June it deployed along a NNE–SSW line between lats. 26° and 32° N, and longs. 165° and 170° W. This was supposed to be in good time to intercept any Pacific Fleet task force that might move out; for, as we have seen, Yamamoto did not expect Nimitz to react until he heard of the attack on Midway Island. That was a bad guess; these submarines were behind Fletcher and Spruance all the way, and gave the Japanese no information whatsoever.[51]

The first surface group to get under way was Rear Admiral Kakuta's Second Mobile Force, assigned to the Aleutians. Of those destined for Midway, with which we are immediately concerned, Nagumo's Carrier Striking Force sortied from the Inland Sea of Japan on the evening of 26 May. Yamamoto, with the Main Body, followed them two days later. The transports of the Midway Occupation Force departed Saipan the evening of 27 May. Kurita's Close Support Group of four powerful heavy cruisers and two destroyers left Guam at the same time and steamed 75 to 100 miles ahead of the transports; the seaplane carriers tagged along behind.

Yamamoto was suffering from stomach trouble and "seemed in unusually low spirits," but the Main Body as a whole was feeling very snug and secure behind the 18.1-inch guns of *Yamato*

---

[51] Cdr. Fujimori of *I–121* in *Inter. Jap. Off.* II 465, with chart; also in *Campaigns of the Pacific War* p. 62. Capt. Watanabe of Yamamoto's staff adduced the faulty location of this submarine patrol as one of the main reasons for the defeat. *Inter. Jap. Off.* I 67.

and the 16-inchers of the other fast battleships. All hands were "singing war songs at the top of their lungs," [52] confident of annihilating the Pacific Fleet. Sailors whose duties did not involve much exercise were put through daily calisthenics and there was much sun-bathing topside until the Main Body entered the weather front on the afternoon of 1 June. [53]

Commander Striking Force was feeling none too easy despite his tactical superiority. [54] His carriers had returned to home waters on 23 April after their Indian Ocean raid and so had had barely a month for upkeep and repair of ships, refresher training for anti-aircraft crews and flight training for aviators. That, to be sure, was three weeks more than Fletcher and Spruance had. "We participated in the operation," wrote Nagumo after the battle, "with meager training and without knowledge of the enemy." [55]

Of course he knew where to find Midway, his first objective. Striking Force orders were to "execute an aërial attack on Midway . . . destroying all enemy air forces stationed there" on 4 June, in preparation for the landing on the 5th. This looked like an easy assignment, and the high command was so confident of success that it provided the Occupation Force with new Japanese names for the two islets and for Midway itself, the last meaning "Glorious Month of June." So it was, but not for them!

Midway was so crowded with Marines, planes, supply and oil dumps and other installations that there was scarcely room for the "gooney birds," whose hoarse dissent from these goings-on could be heard above the humming of plane motors and the booming of the surf. Captain Simard and staff, Colonel Shannon and his staff had their hands full with defensive preparations such as mining all likely approaches and landing beaches. Radio traffic, most of

---

[52] "Yamamoto's Yeoman's Story." This yeoman was captured during the war and his story was told to Capt. Layton. Many of his "recollections" proved false.
[53] Diary of sailor on board *Fuso*, same source.
[54] Admiral Nagumo's Battle Report (*O.N.I. Review* May 1947) and statement made for this History by his chief of staff, Rear Admiral R. Kusaka (ATIS translation No. 16647 B).
[55] *O.N.I. Review* May 1947 p. 9.

which had to be coded or decoded, air-search operations, unloading ships, and "housekeeping" on an immense scale kept everyone busy. A demolition plan was tested shortly before the battle, and somewhat too realistically; a sailor threw the wrong switch and 400,000 gallons of aviation gasoline went up in flames. The fire was kept under control and over half a million gallons were left; but thereafter all planes, including B–17s, had to be refueled by hand from 55-gallon drums.

The first consideration was air search. It was imperative that the enemy be discovered at the earliest possible moment in order to prevent him from sneaking within plane-launching distance and "pulling a Pearl Harbor" on Midway. Beginning 30 May, 22 Catalinas searched daily the sector SSW to NNE 700 miles out, and another PBY took off during the graveyard watch in order to be at the expected launching position of the enemy carriers at dawn.[56] As Intelligence had reported that two enemy forces would rendezvous 700 miles west of Midway, there was added a daily search-attack mission by Army Flying Fortresses, to arrive at that point around 1500 each day. Nothing was sighted until 3 June. About 300 miles to the northwestward of Midway there was a "weak front," rendered almost stationary by a large high-pressure area centered northeast of the island, and affording perfect cover for Nagumo's carriers. More than once they could hear the motors of American search planes in the clouds above them; but most of the Midway-based aircraft were not yet equipped with radar and could pick up ships only visually. It was so thick around the Japanese Striking Force at noon 2 June that Admiral Nagumo lost visual contact with his own ships; at 1330, when his staff navigator

[56] Statement by Cdr. W. L. Richards, 1947. On the morning of Decoration Day 2 Catalinas about 450 to 480 miles W and SW from Midway were attacked by a twin-engined and a 4-engined bomber patrolling from Wake, and were badly damaged. Cincpac finally admitted what the airmen had long been saying, that PBYs were too slow and vulnerable for such work, but there were no other planes to do it at that time except the B–17s whose pilots were trained for attack not search. One result of this battle was an insistent demand by the Navy for an allocation of B–17s to make searches and maintain contacts; they could defend themselves.

figured that the designated point for a change of course toward Midway had been reached, the Admiral had to break radio silence to give the order.[57]

Rear Admiral Robert H. English, Commander Submarines Pacific Fleet, had charge of deploying the 25 submarines at his disposal. Twelve boats were collected for a Midway Patrol Group by sending some out from Pearl between 21 and 24 May and pulling in others from the Mandates and elsewhere. These were assigned patrol stations west of Midway. Three more, the "roving short-stops" of the disposition, patrolled a scouting line 200 miles north of the Hawaiian chain and halfway between Midway and Oahu, in case the enemy should attempt a diversionary attack on Pearl Harbor. Four submarines were sent to patrol about 300 miles north of Oahu, and six more supported the Aleutians Force.[58]

Admiral Spruance's Task Force, built around *Enterprise* and *Hornet*, departed Pearl 28 May "to hold Midway and inflict maximum damage on the enemy by strong attrition tactics." Admiral Fletcher's *Yorktown* force sortied at 0900 on the 30th, with orders "to conduct target practice and then support Task Force 16."

Spruance on the last day of May and Fletcher on the first of June met oilers *Cimarron* and *Platte* and had their last fueling until after the battle. Spruance then doubled back to meet Fletcher at 1600 June 2 at lat. 32° N, long. 173° W, about 325 miles northeast of Midway. The carriers were now beyond the scope of land-based air searches and had to protect themselves. *Hornet* flew a search mission 150 miles out on 1 June, with no contacts; *Enterprise* searched the sector west to northwest on the morning of the 2nd, but all planes returned early on account of bad weather. The enemy carriers were still behind their protective weather front.

That day, Admiral Spruance made the following visual signal to the ships of his Task Force: —

[57] *O.N.I. Review* May 1947 pp. 14, 15. Nagumo believed that this was what gave him away, but actually we did not pick up that transmission.
[58] "Submarine Operational History World War II" I 174-89.

An attack for the purpose of capturing Midway is expected. The attacking force may be composed of all combatant types including four or five carriers, transports and train vessels. If presence of Task Forces 16 and 17 remains unknown to enemy we should be able to make surprise flank attacks on enemy carriers from position northeast of Midway. Further operations will be based on result of these attacks, damage inflicted by Midway forces, and information of enemy movements. The successful conclusion of the operation now commencing will be of great value to our country. Should carriers become separated during attacks by enemy aircraft, they will endeavor to remain within visual touch.

First air contacts on the enemy were made by Midway-based planes on the Occupation Force. Ensign Jack Reid was flying a Catalina almost 700 miles from Midway shortly before 0900 June 3. His sector covered the point at which Intelligence expected two Japanese forces to rendezvous; the pilots used to draw straws to see who would fly it at dawn. Reid had run down to the end of his arc, on the westerly bearing from Midway. It was time to turn back, but he decided to go on for a few minutes. Suddenly he sighted 30 miles ahead what appeared to be the main enemy fleet, looking like miniature ships in a backyard pond. "Do you see what I do?" he asked his co-pilot. "You're damned right I do!" was the reply. Popping in and out of clouds, they tracked the force for several hours,[59] and by 1100 were able to report eleven ships making 19 knots to the eastward. This was probably the combined transport and seaplane groups of the Midway Occupation Force, which was then indulging in a final battle drill including the arming of flame throwers. United States Marines will learn with envy that their opposite numbers of the "Kure" Special Naval Landing Force, in one transport, were supplied with ten cases of beer after the drill, and got away with it all.[60]

Captain Simard at Midway reacted immediately to the contact

[59] Cincpac broadcast and press release No. 56, 16 June 1942. About 11 minutes earlier another PBY had sighted the Japanese minesweepers.

[60] Diary of a member of the S.N.L.F. furnished by Capt. Layton.

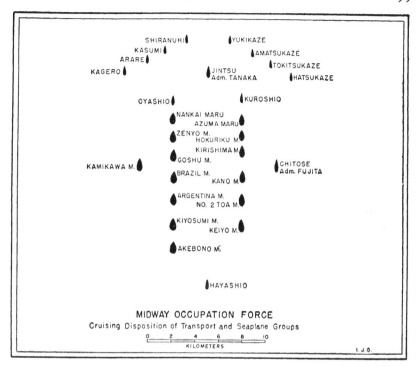

report, sending out nine B–17s. At 1624 the same day, 570 miles out, they found the transports, made three high-level (8,000 to 12,000 feet) bombing attacks and reported having hit "two battleships or heavy cruisers" and two transports; but actually these planes made no hits.[61] Next, four amphibious Catalinas, each armed with one aërial torpedo, were sent to attack this formation. A radar contact at 0115 June 4 led them to where the transports were set forth in bright moonlight. At 0143 three torpedoes were dropped and one hit the oiler *Akebono Maru*. The explosion

[61] Combat Report of *Argentina Maru*, a transport that was attacked (WDC 160,232), and the testimony of Japanese officers interrogated (especially Capt. Toyama and Lt. Cdr. Yunoki, who was in a destroyer of the transport screen, USSBS 195 Navy No. 46) is unanimous on this point, and also admits the later hits on *Akebono Maru*. As a result of this report, Commander Submarines at Pearl ordered U.S.S. *Cuttlefish* to search for and destroy the damaged "battleships."

killed or wounded 23 men and slowed the ship temporarily, but she regained formation.[62]

The battle was on. "The whole course of the war in the Pacific may hinge on the developments of the next two or three days," recorded the Cincpac annalist on receipt of this news. It did. The action about to be joined was one of the most decisive of the war.

---

[62] Capt. Toyama (who was in *Jintsu*) in *Inter. Jap. Off.* I 250; Report of Lt. W. L. Richards who led the flight, and conversation with him in 1947. The pilot whose plane made the hit was Ens. Gaylord D. Probst USNR. The PBYs were back near Midway just when the Japanese raid on the island was beginning, and so came down at or near Lisianski and Laysan, after 13 hours or more in the air.

CHAPTER VII

The Battle of the Fourth of June[1]

Because the Battle of Midway was fought across the International Date Line, much confusion has arisen as to dates and times. The Japanese were using East Longitude date and Tokyo time (Zone minus 9); "The Japanese Story of the Battle of Midway," based on Admiral Nagumo's Battle Report and other sources,[2] is in that date and time. United States forces used West Longitude date and, for the most part, Zone plus 10 time, that of the Aleutians; but ground and air forces based on Midway used the time of Zone plus 12, in which Midway is located. *In the following narrative West Longitude date and Zone plus 12 time are used consistently.*[3]

1. *Fast Carrier Forces Converge*

At 1800 June 3, after the first air attacks had been made by Midway-based planes on the Japanese transports, *Yorktown*, *Enterprise* and *Hornet* were a good 300 miles ENE of Midway, 400 miles east (and a little south) of the point where Nagumo's carriers were steaming at 25 knots toward their planned plane-launching point. Admiral Fletcher had received the first reports of contact

---

[1] See chapter vi footnote 1 for sources.
[2] *O.N.I. Review* May 1947.
[3] For example, the first planes to attack Midway took off from the Japanese carriers at 0130 June 5, according to their log. This is equivalent to 0430 June 4 Midway time, and 0630 Zone plus 10, the time which Fletcher and Spruance were using.

with the enemy in good season; and although they were reported to him as the Main Body of the Japanese Fleet, he correctly estimated that our planes had seen only a transport group with escort. He trusted his original Intelligence report to the effect that an enemy carrier force would be approaching Midway from the northwest, to launch an air attack on the atoll at dawn June 4. And that is exactly what Nagumo was doing. So Fletcher changed course to the southwestward (210°) at 1950 June 3 with the object of arriving by break of day at a position about 200 miles north of Midway, whence he could fly an attack against Nagumo's carriers, provided their position had been ascertained. He correctly assumed that his presence was still unknown to the enemy, and that he might avoid detection next morning until Nagumo's planes were already winging their way to Midway. Thus, during the night of 3–4 June, the opposing carrier forces were approaching one another on courses which, if maintained, would have crossed a few miles northwest of the atoll.

Thursday, the Fourth of June, a day fatal to Japan's hopes of victory, began to break shortly after four o'clock. By sunrise, at 0457, there was a gentle (force 3) tradewind blowing from the southeast, enough for launching planes against an enemy to the westward without much loss of distance. Everyone hoped it would breeze up, but by 0800 the wind had fallen away to mere light airs (4 to 5 knots) which forced the carriers to steam at 21 knots away from the enemy in order to launch or recover.[4] Visibility — 35 to 40 miles — was much too good for the carriers' health; the air temperature throughout the day was pleasantly cool, 68° to 70° Fahrenheit.

As it was *Yorktown's* turn to search, at 0430 she launched ten SBDs to cover the northern semicircle to a radius of 100 miles, a

---

[4] *Hornet* Action Report and Deck Log. During World War II, many quartermasters in the U. S. Navy were exceedingly careless in their meteorological log entries; those of *Enterprise* are particularly bad. *Hornet's* other entries for 4 June follow: 0400, SSE force 3; 0500, SE force 2; 0600, SSE force 2; 0700 through 1000, SE force 2; 1100, E force 2; 1200 through 1600, E force 3; 1700 through 2000, ESE force 3 (times changed to + 12). These check fairly well with the deck logs of the cruisers.

proper precaution against being jumped by the planes of unlocated carriers. At that moment, Nagumo was about 215 miles to the westward, sending off his first strike on Midway. He still had the breaks in the matter of weather; from *Kaga's* log it is evident that the Striking Force was not yet out of the "front." Yet, despite a low (50 per cent) cloud cover and visibility of only 15 miles, American search planes from Midway managed to spot their fast-approaching enemy.

At 0534 June 4, the long awaited word was received on board *Enterprise:* "Enemy carriers." [5] This was an intercepted message from a searching PBY to its base at Midway. Next, at 0545 came a plain English dispatch from the same source: "Many enemy planes heading Midway bearing 320° distant 150." [6] Then, at 0603, "Two carriers and battleships bearing 320° distant 180 [miles from Midway] course 135° speed 25." That position was about 200 miles WSW of Task Force 16. These were the first indications received by any United States command afloat as to where the enemy carriers were. The position given was incorrect by about 40 miles and only two of the four flattops were sighted; but at least Fletcher and Spruance now knew the approximate whereabouts of the Striking Force.

Admiral Fletcher wished to recover *Yorktown's* search mission and await further intelligence before launching a strike, and so passed the ball to Admiral Spruance. At 0607, only four minutes after receiving the last contact report, he ordered Spruance with *Enterprise* and *Hornet* to "proceed southwesterly and attack enemy carriers when definitely located," and promised to "follow as soon as planes recovered."

---

[5] *Enterprise* Action Report. Presumably *Yorktown* got it at the same time, but her message file was lost.
[6] These messages were from Lts. Howard Ady and William Chase, co-pilots of a PBY-5. As Ady described it a few days later, sighting the Striking Force was "like watching a curtain rise on the Biggest Show on Earth." The plane slipped back into the clouds, turned around and sighted the carriers from the rear. *Tone,* it later turned out, sighted the PBY and fighter planes took off from all 4 carriers to get it, but in vain (*O.N.I. Review* May 1947 p. 16). For discussion of time of contact, see Heinl *Marines at Midway* p. 27.

Thus, only ten minutes before the air battle over Midway commenced, Fletcher sparked off the train of events that resulted in the loss of four Japanese carriers.

2. *Battle over Midway*

Leaving the American carriers for the moment, let us follow the planes that took off from all four Japanese carriers at 0430, when 240 miles distant from Midway. Lieutenant Tomonaga, flight officer of *Hiryu*, led this formidable attack group consisting of 36 "Kate" torpedo planes armed with 805-kilo bombs, and 36 "Val" dive-bombers escorted by 36 "Zeke" fighter planes.[7] At 0553, when the Midway search radar picked up the vanguard of this flight, it was 93 miles northwest of the island. The air-raid alarm was promptly sounded, and shortly after 0600 every plane able to leave the ground was in the air. The bombers and Catalinas, which would be useless for interception or defense, were ordered to keep out of the way; Major Parks's Marine Corps fighter squadron was sent out against the approaching enemy. At 0616, when 30 miles out and at 12,000 feet altitude, they encountered the first of the 108 Japanese planes, bombers in a rigid "Vee of Vees" and fighters overhead. The Marine Corps fighters climbed to 17,000 feet and swooped down to intercept, but were hopelessly outnumbered. Within a few minutes there were one to five "Zekes" on the tail of each Marine fighter, who were so busy trying to shake them off that they could give no more attention to the bombers. And they did shake off many, or led their attackers right into the anti-aircraft fire being delivered from Midway.[8]

Within a few minutes the high-altitude bombers had hit Midway, releasing from a height of 14,000 feet; the first bomb fell around 0630. "Val" dive-bombers came in next, through "vicious

[7] Compiled from *O.N.I. Review* May 1947 by *War College Analysis*.
[8] Marine Aircraft Group 22 Action Report (by Maj. V. J. McCaul USMC) and Heinl p. 33.

anti-aircraft fire," as Nagumo described it. They destroyed the Marines' command post and mess hall and badly damaged the powerhouse on Eastern Island, destroyed the oil tanks on Sand Island, destroyed the seaplane hangar, set the hospital and storehouses afire and damaged the gasoline system. But their attempts to render the runways unusable were unsuccessful, and they killed very few men on the ground. This one and only attack on Midway was over by 0650.[9]

At 0715, after enemy planes had departed for their carriers and the All Clear had sounded, Colonel Kimes broadcast "Fighters land, refuel by divisions." Pitifully few responded. It was providential, indeed, that any survived this air battle; for the 20 antique Buffaloes and six period Wildcats were outclassed in almost every respect by the Japanese "Zekes" (the Zero Mark-1 fighter). Seventeen with their pilots, including Major Parks, were missing and seven others severely damaged. The Japanese were vague about plane losses in their official reports (since they lost all by next day); but a careful count on the American side indicates that at least one third of the attack group never returned, shot down by the Marine fighter squadron or by anti-aircraft fire.[10]

The Nips had hit first, and hard. They had won the first round, but they entered the ring weaker in the second.

3. *Midway Counterattacks, Nagumo Vacillates*

Almost at the very moment when the enemy hit Midway, the first of a series of counterattacks on Nagumo's Striking Force got under way. Admiral Nimitz had ordered Captain Simard to "go all out for the carriers," leaving defense of the atoll to its own guns.

[9] Except for two "Zekes" which came in at 0701. Admiral Nagumo's Report *O.N.I. Review* May 1947 p. 43; Lt. Col. Shannon's Report 10 June 1942; Heinl *Marines at Midway*.

[10] Compilation by Lt. Col. Heinl. Capt. Kawaguchi, air officer of *Hiryu*, admitted after the war was over that his ship alone lost 10 planes out of 27 in this attack. Interrogation by Capt. J. S. Russell, ATIS Report No. 1.

The six new Avenger torpedo planes (TBFs) and the four Army Marauders (B–26s), also armed with torpedoes, airborne before the air attack, flew off around 0615 without fighter protection. They encountered the enemy carriers at 0710, but the Japanese saw them first and had time to augment combat air patrol. Four or five of the Midway-based planes were shot down before they could reach a launching position. *Hiryu's* flight officer testified after the war that their torpedoes "didn't seem to have any speed at all"; one that porpoised was hit and exploded by machine-gun fire.[11] One torpedo plane, hit by anti-aircraft fire, crashed *Akagi's* flight deck and bounced off into the sea; two or three more were shot down by anti-aircraft fire; and out of six TBFs only one returned, badly shot up; no brilliant debut for the Avenger, which was to accomplish so much good later in the war. One of the two B–26s that returned to Midway and crash-landed was repaired so that it could proceed next day to Pearl Harbor, where the pilot's story lost nothing in the telling and an Air Force colonel went on the air with a tall tale of torpedoing a Japanese carrier.[12] This was the first news that the American public had of the battle. The Army claimed three torpedo hits on the carriers and the Navy admitted one; actually there were none, not even a near-miss.

At this point came a bit of good luck for the United States. Admiral Nagumo when sending his first strike against Midway at break of day, had reserved 93 planes armed with bombs and torpedoes to deal with enemy ships, in case any were discovered in the vicinity. But the search mission that he sent out, consisting of seven cruiser float planes, was late in starting and almost perfunctory.[13] The first three float planes, launched between 0435 and 0442, found nothing. The fourth, from cruiser *Tone*, got off at 0500, half an hour late — luckily for us! Two hours passed, and no contact report reached the Admiral. At 0700 he received a mes-

---

[11] USSBS 530 p. 12, confirmed by Capt. Ohara (exec. of *Soryu*) in *Inter. Jap. Off.* I 168.
[12] Gilbert Cant *America's Navy in World War II* (1943) pp. 226–8; Fletcher Pratt in *Harper's* July 1943 p. 250.
[13] The Japanese seldom used carrier planes for searching, but Nagumo did so use one dive-bomber each from *Akagi* and *Kaga*, on the southerly sectors.

sage from Lieutenant Tomonaga, commanding the planes that had just finished striking Midway: "There is need for a second attack wave." Ten minutes later came in the bomber attack from Midway, which proved that Tomonaga was right. So, at 0715, the Japanese Admiral made a fatal decision. He "broke the spot" (discontinued the stand-by condition of readiness) of the 93 planes prepared for instant launching against surface forces, ordered them struck below to clear his flight decks for the recovery of the Midway strike, and ordered the torpedo planes' armament to be changed to bombs for a second attack on the atoll — a job that required a good hour's hard work.

Then, at 0728, came a message from the belated *Tone* plane that shifted the scenery. On his return flight this pilot sighted "what appears to be ten enemy surface ships in position bearing 10°, distance 240 miles, from Midway. Course 150°, speed over 20 knots." For the first time Nagumo knew he had to deal with enemy ships. But the report was so vague, with no hint of enemy carriers, that the Admiral did not see fit to cancel the scrambling of his attack group. Besides, he had to keep his flight decks clear to recover the Midway strike. Perhaps the reported enemy force did not amount to much anyway. Ten ships — he could take care of them at his leisure.

Nagumo deliberated for fifteen minutes, and at 0745 changed his mind. He signaled his own force, "Prepare to carry out attacks on enemy fleet units. Leave torpedoes on those attack planes which have not as yet been changed to bombs." Perhaps he then recalled Hara's major error at Coral Sea — wasting a major air effort on an oiler. For, two minutes later, the Admiral radioed the *Tone* search plane "Ascertain ship types and maintain contact." The pilot replied at 0809, "Enemy is composed of 5 cruisers and 5 destroyers," an estimate that he augmented at 0820, "The enemy is accompanied by what appears to be a carrier." [14] A conservative fellow, that pilot!

[14] *O.N.I. Review* May 1947 pp. 18, 19, 44 and 45, where Nagumo complains that the 0728 message was not delivered to him until about 0800, which his own 0745 message belies.

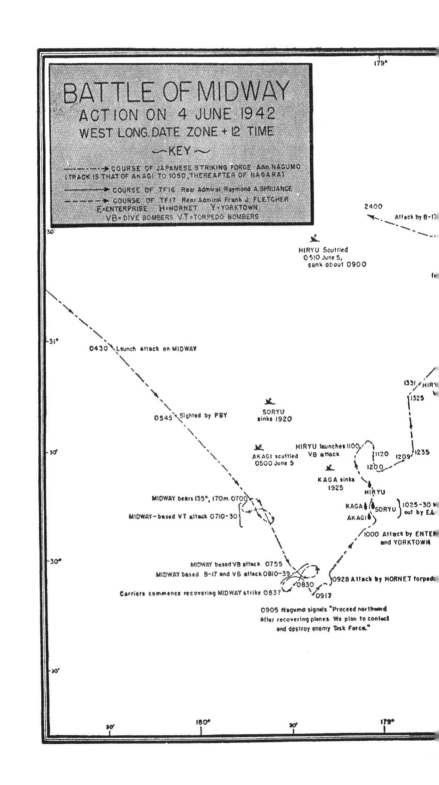

BATTLE OF MIDWAY

ACTION ON 4 JUNE 1942

WEST LONG. DATE ZONE + 12 TIME

~KEY~

→ COURSE OF JAPANESE STRIKING FORCE Adm. NAGUMO
(TRACK IS THAT OF AKAGI TO 1050, THEREAFTER OF NAGARA)

→ COURSE OF TF16 Rear Admiral Raymond A. SPRUANCE

----→ COURSE OF TF17 Rear Admiral Frank J. FLETCHER
E=ENTERPRISE H=HORNET Y=YORKTOWN
VB=DIVE BOMBERS VT=TORPEDO BOMBERS

179°

2400

Attack by B-17

HIRYU Scuttled
0510 June 5,
sank about 0900

0430 Launch attack on MIDWAY

1331 HIR
1325

0545 Sighted by PBY

SORYU
sinks 1920

HIRYU launches 1100
VB attack

1120 1209 1235
1200

AKAGI scuttled
0500 June 5

KAGA sinks
1925

HIRYU

MIDWAY bears 135°, 170m. 0700

KAGA SORYU
AKAGI

1025-30
out by E.

MIDWAY-based VT attack 0710-30

1000 Attack by ENTE
and YORKTOWN

MIDWAY based VB attack 0755
MIDWAY based B-17 and VB attack 0810-39

0830

0928 Attack by HORNET torped

Carriers commence recovering MIDWAY strike 0837

0917

0905 Nagumo signals "Proceed northward
after recovering planes. We plan to contact
and destroy enemy Task Force."

180° 30' 179°

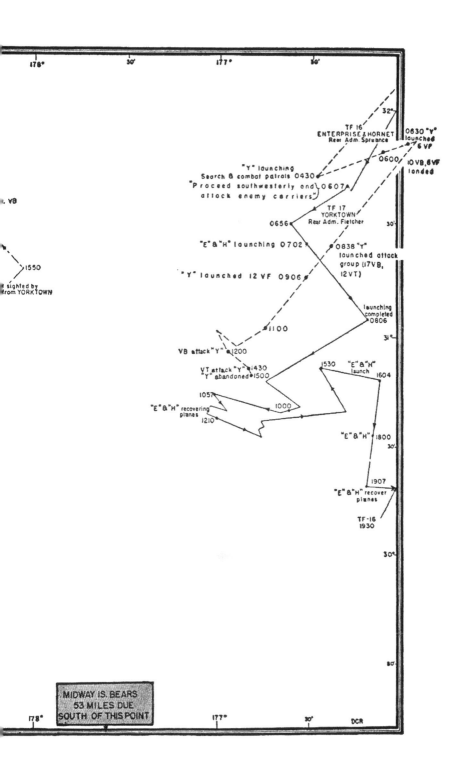

178°   30'   177°   30'   32°

TF 16
ENTERPRISE & HORNET
Rear Adm. Spruance

0830 "Y"
launched
6 VF

0600

10 VB, 6 VF
landed

"Y" launching
Search & combat patrols 0430
"Proceed southwesterly and 0607A
attack enemy carriers"

VB

TF 17
YORKTOWN
Rear Adm. Fletcher

0656

30'

0838 "Y"
launched attack
group (17 VB,
12 VT)

1550

"E" & "H" launching 0702

"Y" launched 12 VF 0906

sighted by
from YORKTOWN

launching
completed
0806

31°

1100

VB attack "Y" 1200

1530   "E" & "H"
launch   1604

VT attack "Y" 1430
"Y" abandoned 1500

1057

"E" & "H" recovering
planes

1000

1210

"E" & "H" 1800

30'

1907
"E" & "H" recover
planes

TF-16
1930

30°

80°

MIDWAY IS. BEARS
53 MILES DUE
SOUTH OF THIS POINT

178°   177°   30'   DCR

Thus, at 0820, Nagumo learned for the first time that he would have to deal with at least one American carrier. But he was now even less capable of doing anything about it than he had been half an hour earlier. His planned attack group was already broken down. His flight decks must be kept clear for the planes expected momentarily from Midway. He had to be on the receiving not the giving end of a carrier battle. What a break of luck!

In the meantime, the Japanese carriers had been beating off more land-based air attacks, a process not conducive to tactical thinking by the staff. At 0755 sixteen Marine Corps dive-bombers, which had taken off from Midway an hour earlier, came in. Owing to the inexperience of the pilots,[15] the flight commander, Major Lofton Henderson, decided to make a glide-bombing attack. "Zekes" jumped his planes and shot down several, including his own. Captain Elmer G. ("Ironman") Glidden USMC then took over the lead and dropped nine or ten bombs, all of which missed *Hiryu*, but one plane machine-gunned the carrier's deck and killed four sailors.[16] Only eight of these SBDs returned, and six of them were damaged beyond repair. On one, 259 hits were actually counted; but the pilot, Lieutenant Daniel Iverson USMC, who even had the throat microphone shot off his neck, survived.

Fifteen Flying Fortresses, commanded by Lieutenant Colonel Walter C. Sweeney USA, had cleared Midway before dawn to attack the Occupation Force, but were diverted to the carriers by Captain Simard, and found them at 0810. They dropped 8500 pounds of bombs per plane from 20,000 feet altitude and returned safely, claiming four hits on two carriers. But none were better than near-misses.[17]

[15] They had never flown SBDs before coming to Midway and had had no chance to fly them there because of the accidental blowing up of the aviation gas storage tank.

[16] The strafing plane may however have been a stray Wildcat. For evidence that *Hiryu* was the carrier attacked, see her damage report in *O.N.I. Review* May 1947 p. 57. The story that Maj. Henderson crashed his plane against a carrier is a myth.

[17] The combined Japanese log in *O.N.I. Review* May 1947 p. 18 states that at 0510 (0810 plus 12 time) "Bomb hits on *Akagi* and *Hiryu* were noted" — obviously

Immediately after the B–17s pulled away, at 0820, eleven Marine Corps Vindicators, which had taken off with the SBDs, came in on the carrier force. "Zekes," scenting easy meat, swarmed over these slow and almost defenseless bombers in such numbers that the flight leader, Major Benjamin W. Norris USMC, shifted to the nearest target, battleship *Haruna* — already alleged to have been sunk by Colin Kelly off Luzon. Ten of them dove on her at 0830 and dropped bombs. All missed;[18] but nine of the planes returned safely.

Thus these seaplane and land-based air attacks on the morning of 4 June resulted only in severe losses to the Midway-based groups, and some dearly-bought experience. An examination of Japanese records and the interrogations of Japanese officers by United States Army officers after the war will convince the most optimistic that no damage and only a few casualties were inflicted on enemy ships by land-based planes, whether Army, Navy or Marine Corps, on the Fourth of June.[19]

In the midst of these Flying Fortress and Vindicator attacks, or just between the two, the enemy formation ran foul of U. S. submarine *Nautilus*. She had intercepted the early search-plane report

---

by other ships in the formation. These were evidently near-misses mistaken for hits, as all Japanese officers in the Striking Force, when questioned after the war, denied that any hits were made in this or in other land-based air attacks. Nor can claims that the B–17 attack "broke up the enemy's formation and flight operations" be sustained. Formation was resumed as soon as evasive action was completed, and the first planes of the Midway strike did not return until 0837.

[18] A near-miss that buckled some of her stern plates, but did not affect her fighting efficiency, was inflicted by *Enterprise* dive-bombers later in the day, as is evident from the sequence of events related by her exec. in USSBS 530 p. 26. See also testimony of the assistant gunnery officer of *Kirishima* in USSBS 138 (Navy No. 33). The Japanese log (*O.N.I. Review* May 1947 p. 19) indicates that at 0839, nine minutes after the attack on *Haruna,* one or two Vindicators went for *Akagi* but were evaded.

[19] See especially USSBS 530, in which Maj. Gen. O. A. Anderson USA and other Army officers put ten important Japanese officers, who had served at Midway, to very adroit cross-questioning in order to make them admit that their ships had sustained hits by land-based planes, but obtained no satisfaction whatever. The official *Army Air Forces in World War II* Vol. I 457–8 admits with obvious reluctance that no hits were made by A.A.F. planes except by B–17s on *Hiryu* late in the afternoon.

of contact with the carriers and promptly hastened north, looking for trouble. At 0800 she found it, in the shape of a depth-charge attack (the first of four that day), but managed to come up for a look-see at 0820. "The picture presented on raising the periscope was one never experienced in peacetime practice," reported her skipper, Lieutenant Commander W. H. Brockman Jr. "Ships were on all sides moving across the field at high speed and circling away to avoid the submarine's position. Ranges were above 1000 yards. The . . . cruiser had passed over and was now astern. The battleship was on our port bow and firing her whole starboard broadside battery at the periscope. Flag hoists were being made, searchlights were trained at the periscope." At 0825 *Nautilus* fired one torpedo at the battleship at a range of 4500 yards and missed; then submerged to 150 feet. She survived undamaged the intensive depth-charge attack that followed.[20]

This first phase of the battle ended in the enemy's favor. In exchange for perhaps 40 planes he had destroyed over half the aircraft based on Midway and inflicted severe damage on the installations. All his fighting ships were intact and his "Zekes" and anti-aircraft fire had mowed down almost every good bomber that Simard had sent out. At 0835, when the Japanese planes began to return, Midway appeared to need but one more strike to soften it up for the landing forces. But there was never to be a second strike on Midway. Birds of death and destruction were already winging their way to the Japanese carriers from *Enterprise* and *Hornet.*

4. *Forenoon Battle of the Carrier Planes*

a. Launching and Tactics

We left *Enterprise* and *Hornet* early on the morning of 4 June when Admiral Spruance received his order from Admiral Fletcher,

---

[20] *Nautilus* Patrol Report for 4 June. This torpedo attack is not noted in the Japanese logs summarized in *O.N.I. Review* May 1947. At 0910 *Nautilus* fired a torpedo at destroyer *Arashi* and missed.

"Proceed southwesterly and attack enemy carriers when definitely located. I will follow as soon as planes recovered."

It was 0607, about an hour and ten minutes after sunrise. A gentle breeze — about 6 or 7 knots — was blowing from the SSE, the sea was calm and visibility good. All ships went to general quarters. Within a few minutes the two carriers, six cruisers and nine destroyers of Task Force 16 had changed course to 240° and bent on 25 knots. The aviators, who had breakfasted as early as 0130 and twice manned their planes and twice been ordered back to the ready room,[21] began warming up for a real strike.

Spruance had originally intended to launch his planes at 0900 when there would be less than a hundred miles of ocean for them to cover, provided the Japanese carriers maintained course toward the atoll. But, as reports came in of the strike on Midway, he decided, on the advice of his chief of staff, to launch two hours earlier in the hope of catching the carriers in the act of refueling planes on deck for a second strike on the atoll. That was a tough decision for Spruance to make. He knew that the greater distance to cover hazarded a loss of many planes and pilots through running out of gas; his torpedo planes had a combat radius of only 175 miles. But the "commensurate risk" seemed worth accepting. And he made his choice at just the right moment: about twenty minutes before Nagumo decided — so fortunately for us and disastrously for him — to break down his attack group that had been readied for bombing ships and to rearm the planes for a second strike on Midway.

Planes started taking off from *Enterprise* and *Hornet* at 0702.[22] Within half an hour, before launching was half complete, Admiral

---

[21] This precaution annoyed the aviators, but it was a proper one in view of the danger that the Task Force might be jumped by enemy carrier planes coming out of the weather front.

[22] Cdr. R. M. Lindsey (*Enterprise* Landing Signal Officer) Report "Battle of Midway." Just before launching, TF 16 separated into two task groups: *Enterprise* took cruisers *Northampton*, *Vincennes* and *Pensacola* and destroyers *Balch*, *Benham*, *Aylwin*, *Monaghan* and *Phelps*; *Hornet* took cruisers *Minneapolis*, *New Orleans* and *Atlanta* and destroyers *Ellet*, *Worden* and *Conyngham*. This was carrier doctrine at the time; but within a year it was abandoned in favor of sticking together, which made for a more effective CAP and AA defense.

Spruance knew that his force had been snooped by an enemy float plane. That was the one from cruiser *Tone*, whose belated and inaccurate contact report gave Nagumo his first hint of what to expect. Spruance feared that he had lost that precious tactical asset, surprise; but there was no question of canceling the strike. Moreover, Captain Browning estimated that the Japanese planes which had attacked Midway Island could not return to their carriers before 0900; hence Nagumo, even if he knew where the American carriers were, must maintain course toward Midway for some time in order to recover. And so he did, although recovery was completed earlier than Browning had calculated.

A second important decision by Spruance was to make an all-out attack; to launch a "full load" — every operational plane except those needed for patrol around the task force. That again proved to be the correct decision, although it required over an hour to complete the launching (since about half the planes had to be brought up from the hangar deck), and in the meantime the planes first launched were eating up gas. The strike comprised 20 Wildcat fighters, 67 Dauntless dive-bombers and 29 Devastator torpedo-bombers,[23] fairly evenly divided between *Enterprise* and *Hornet* air groups, in addition to 18 Wildcats which swooped around Task Force 16 as combat air patrol, and the same number to relieve them. After launching, the ships resumed base course 240° with 25-knot speed.

Fletcher promptly adopted the same course and speed as Spruance. He delayed launching, however, for over two hours, thinking that there might be other Japanese carriers than those already reported, against which he could more profitably direct his attack. At 0838, having received no additional contact reports, he decided to launch half his dive-bombers and all his torpedo planes, with fighter escort. By 0906 *Yorktown's* strike group of 17 SBDs, 12 TBDs and 6 F4F–3s was in the air; another deckload was readied to take off if needed. The Admiral's caution in saving planes

[23] This represented all SBDs but 8 reserved for anti-submarine patrol and all the TBDs.

for an emergency was natural and proper; it was less than a month since he had been misled by poor contact reports into going all out for little *Shoho* at the Battle of the Coral Sea.

This Fourth of June was a cool and beautiful day, perfect for carrier war if the wind had only been stronger and from the enemy's direction. At 19,000 feet pilots could see all around a circle of 50 miles' radius. Only a few fluffy cumulus clouds were between them and an ocean that looked like a dish of wrinkled blue Persian porcelain. Small consolation, to be sure, for these young men who were to fall that day in flames or drown in the broad ocean whose mastery they were to win for their country. Yet, if a sailor must die, the air way is the fairest. The tense, crisp briefing in the ready room; the warming up of planes which the devoted "ground crews" have been checking, arming, fueling and servicing; the ritual of the take-off, as precise and ordered as a ballet . . . Planes swooping in graceful curves over the ships while the group assembles; hand-signaling and waving to your wing-man, whom you may never see again; a long flight over the superb ocean; first sight of your target and the sudden catch at the heart when you know that they see you, from the black puffs of anti-aircraft bursts that suddenly appear in the clear air; the wriggling and squirming of the ships, followed by wakes like the tails of white horses; the dreaded "Zekes" of combat air patrol swooping down on you apparently out of nothing; and finally the tight, incredibly swift attack, when you forget everything but the target so rapidly enlarging, and the desperate necessity of choosing the exact moment — the right tenth of a second — to release and pull out.

While these bright ministers of death were on their way, Nagumo's Striking Force continued for over an hour, as Spruance had hoped, to steam toward Midway. The four carriers were grouped in a box-like formation in the center of a protecting screen of two battleships, three cruisers and eleven destroyers. *Akagi*, flagship here as in the Pearl Harbor strike, had the flank position to starboard. Two thousand meters astern steamed her sister ship *Kaga;* five thousand meters to port steamed the other carrier division, *Hiryu* and *Soryu*.[24] They had come through these repeated strikes by land-based bombers without suffering a single hit, and, after shooting down half the planes that attacked them had straightened out again on the southeasterly course. Their crews were feeling very proud and confident. But Admiral Nagumo, fearing the worst, was nervous and apprehensive.

At 0837 the four Japanese carriers commenced recovering planes returning from Midway. The belated attack of a "tail-end Charley" among the Marine Corps Vindicators did not bother them. The air was now full of messages from reconnaissance planes about the approach of American carrier-based aircraft. At 0905, before the last of his planes were recovered, Admiral Nagumo could wait no longer. He ordered Striking Force to turn to the ENE — a 90-degree change of course. "We plan to contact and destroy the enemy Task Force," he signaled to the vessels under his command.[25] Plane recovery completed, the formation executed the change of course at 0917. The Japanese carriers were in exactly the condition Spruance wanted to find them — all bomber planes on board, rearming and refueling going on feverishly.

b. Slaughter of the Torpedo-bombers

Now came a break for Nagumo. By his change of course to 70° he evaded the dive-bombers of one American carrier. Commander Stanhope C. Ring, *Hornet's* attack group commander, leading 35 SBDs with fighter cover, missed the enemy at his anticipated position on the southeasterly course, followed that bearing toward Midway, and so drew a blank. Thirteen of his bombers had to land at Midway for refueling, two splashed in the lagoon, all his Wildcats had to ditch for lack of gas, and the entire group missed the battle.

Lieutenant Commander John C. Waldron, leading *Hornet's*

[24] *Inter. Jap. Off.* I 4, 13, 58, 167; USSBS 530 p. 7.
[25] *O.N.I. Review* May 1947 p. 20.

torpedo squadron, knew that he had small chance to survive. In his last message to the squadron, appended to his attack plan the evening before, he had written: —

I feel we are all ready. . . . I actually believe that under these conditions we are the best in the world. My greatest hope is that we encounter a favorable tactical situation, but if we don't, and the worst comes to the worst, I want each of us to do his utmost to destroy our enemies. If there is only one plane left to make a final run-in, I want that man to go in and get a hit. May God be with us all.[26]

Just before launching he reported to Captain Marc Mitscher for final instructions and "promised he would press through against all obstacles, well knowing his squadron was doomed to destruction with no chance whatever of returning safely to the carrier." [27] Waldron's low-flying TBDs became separated en route from Ring's high-flying planes, owing to intervening cloud layers; but Waldron turned northward when he missed the Japanese carriers where they were supposed to be. At about 0925 he sighted two columns of smoke rising over the horizon, and changed course for them. That was the enemy. Within a few minutes the Japanese combat air patrol found Waldron, naked of fighter-plane protection. Anti-aircraft fire, too, began to reach the TBDs when they still had eight miles to go. Waldron wiggled his wings as a signal to follow, opened up the throttle and pressed home an attack at low altitude. "Beset on all sides by the deadly Zero fighters, which were doggedly attacking them in force, and faced with a seemingly impenetrable screen of cruisers and destroyers, the squadron drove in valiantly at short range. Plane after plane was shot down by fighters, anti-aircraft bursts were searing faces and tearing out chunks of fuselage, and still the squadron bored in. Those who were left dropped their torpedoes at short range." [28]

[26] Quoted in Sidney L. James "Torpedo Squadron 8 — as Told by Ensign Gay, the Only One Who Came Back" *Life* Magazine 31 Aug. 1942 p. 72.
[27] Capt. Mitscher's *Hornet* Action Report, Appendix on recommended awards. Waldron knew he was doomed because if the enemy were found at the anticipated position the TBDs would not have sufficient fuel to return.
[28] Mitscher's Appendix.

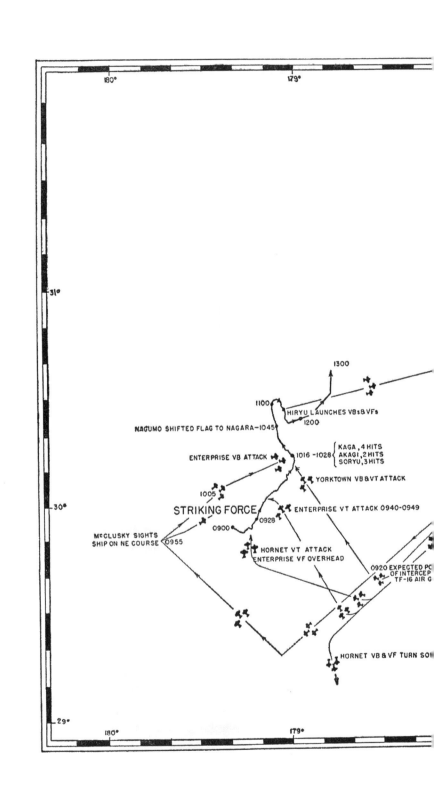

180° 179°

31°

1300

1100

HIRYU LAUNCHES VBs & VFs

1200

NAGUMO SHIFTED FLAG TO NAGARA-1045

{ KAGA, 4 HITS
AKAGI, 2 HITS
SORYU, 3 HITS }

ENTERPRISE VB ATTACK

1016 -1028

YORKTOWN VB & VT ATTACK

1005

STRIKING FORCE

ENTERPRISE VT ATTACK 0940-0949

0928

0900

McCLUSKY SIGHTS
SHIP ON NE COURSE 0955

HORNET VT ATTACK
ENTERPRISE VF OVERHEAD

0920 EXPECTED PO
OF INTERCEP
TF-16 AIR G

HORNET VB & VF TURN SOU

30°

29°

180° 179°

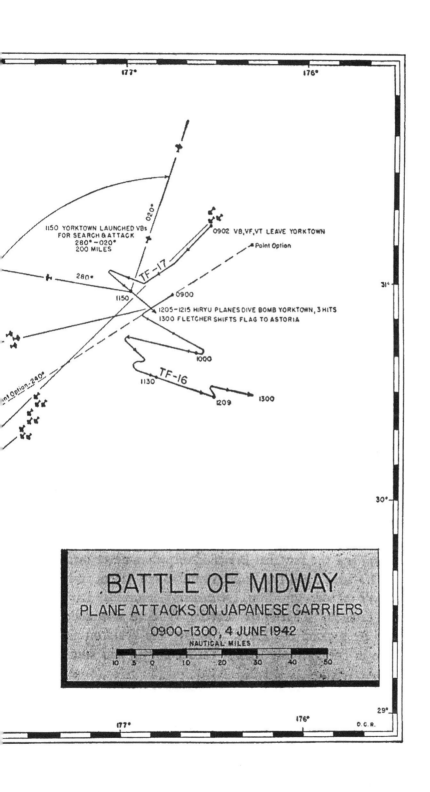

BATTLE OF MIDWAY
PLANE ATTACKS ON JAPANESE CARRIERS
0900-1300, 4 JUNE 1942
NAUTICAL MILES

Then they, too, were shot down, every one. And for a plane to splash when flying at high speed close to the water was like hitting a stone wall.

Out of thirty pilots and crewmen in the fifteen planes, Ensign George H. Gay alone survived. He launched his torpedo and pulled out ten feet above the carrier's deck. Then his left rudder pedal was knocked out by an explosive bullet and the plane splashed. His radioman was already dead. Gay, only slightly wounded, managed to reach the surface as the plane sank, and hid under a rubber seat cushion to escape the notice of strafing "Zekes." From that low and precarious vantage point he observed the next attack, inflated his life raft at dusk, climbed aboard and was rescued by a Catalina the following afternoon.[29]

The *Enterprise* torpedo squadron, Lieutenant Commander Eugene E. Lindsey, which departed on its mission at 0806 simultaneously with *Hornet's*, never had fighter protection because its Wildcat escort (Lieutenant Gray's Squadron 6) inadvertently accompanied Waldron instead. By changing course in time, Lindsey sighted the carriers shortly after 0930. Because of the short combat radius of his planes, he decided to attack immediately without waiting for the dive-bombers. Clever maneuvering by the Japanese forced the TBDs to circle widely in order to make a beam attack on carrier *Kaga*, over which the "Zekes" were as thick as flies around a garbage can. Down they flew to attack the lumbering Devastators. Ten of the 14, including Lindsey's, were shot down; and the few that launched torpedoes never made a hit.[30]

This attack had barely been snuffed out when, at 1000, *Yorktown's* torpedo squadron, Lieutenant Commander Lance E. Massey, came in.[31] Thach's six escorting Wildcats were soon overpowered by a cloud of "Zekes." Massey, like Waldron and Lindsey, bore in courageously against carrier *Soryu*, and another slaugh-

[29] *Life* 31 Aug. 1942 pp. 78, 80.
[30] Report by Lt. (jg) R. E. Laub, senior survivor of the squadron, to McClusky. Time of attack was between 0940 and 0958.
[31] VT-3, as this squadron was designated, was flying in company with VB-3, Lt. Cdr. M. F. Leslie, whose attack will be mentioned shortly.

ter ensued. Seven Devastators, including Massey's, fell in flames; only five were able to launch torpedoes and three of these were shot down. Again, no hits.

Thus, out of 41 torpedo planes from the three carriers, only six returned, and not a single torpedo reached the enemy ships. Yet it was the stark courage and relentless drive of these young pilots of the obsolete torpedo planes that made possible the victory that followed. The radical maneuvering that they imposed on the Japanese carriers prevented them from launching more planes. And the TBDs, by acting as magnets for the enemy's combat air patrol and pulling "Zekes'" down to near water level, enabled the dive-bombing squadrons that followed a few minutes later to attack virtually unopposed by fighter planes, and to drop bombs on full deckloads in the process of being refueled.[32]

c. Dive-bombers Sink Three

The Japanese were given no time to glory in their victory over the Devastators, for the Dauntless dive-bombers from *Enterprise* and *Yorktown* appeared immediately after. Lieutenant Commander Clarence McClusky of *Enterprise* had launched early and at 0745 had been ordered by Admiral Spruance "to proceed on mission assigned" without the torpedo-bombers, which were the last to be launched and for which, as the more vulnerable, the Wildcat escort was reserved.[33] So McClusky got going at 0752 with no fighter-plane protection. An hour and a half later, when he reached the point of anticipated contact with the Japanese carriers, only empty ocean met the group commander's eye. He decided to search beyond the safe limit of fuel endurance, and continued for 35 miles in the same direction, thinking the enemy might

---

[32] "There is a marked tendency for our fighters to over-concentrate on enemy torpedo planes" is one of the few self-criticisms in the "East Pacific Combat Report of *Soryu*" made by a surviving pilot.

[33] The torpedo-bombers, as we have seen, got there first — two minutes before the *Enterprise* dive-bombers — because although slower they had flown a shorter route.

have changed course to the southwestward. At 0935 he turned northward, and at 0955, from 19,000 feet altitude, sighted a Japanese destroyer high-tailing to the northeastward and throwing spray. This was *Arashi*, which had dropped behind to deliver a depth-charge attack on *Nautilus*. Correctly assuming that she was trying to catch up with Nagumo's Striking Force, McClusky took his course from her.

Lieutenant Gray's fighter squadron from *Enterprise* made the mistake of attaching itself to Waldron's *Hornet* torpedo squadron, and never knew it. Gray sighted the Japanese carriers as early as 0910, and almost at the same moment saw Waldron's VT-8, flying about 19,000 feet below him, fly into a low-hanging cloud in the direction of the enemy. He assumed they were about to attack and awaited the signal prearranged with Lindsey, which of course never came, to come down and cover them. So Gray's Wildcats passed the time of the disastrous torpedo-plane attack uselessly orbiting at high altitude where there were no "Zekes" to fight. At 0952 Gray broke radio silence to inform McClusky that he was running short of gas and would have to return soon, and at 1000, somewhat belatedly it would seem, he reported the presence and course of half the Striking Force. That was the first word to reach Fletcher or Spruance that any of their planes had found the enemy. A few minutes later McClusky heard the unmistakable voice of Miles Browning over the radio telephone shouting. "Attack! Attack!" to which the group commander replied, "Wilco as soon as I find the bastards!" or words to that effect.[34]

Within a few moments he found them. He could see all four carriers rapidly maneuvering to escape the torpedo-plane attacks,

[34] Gray's and McClusky's reports and letters; details from Admiral Spruance and Cdr. John Foster, operations officer of *Hornet* who heard Gray's message at 1000. McClusky believed that *Enterprise* had the information about the Japanese reversal of course, but failed to inform him owing to overanxiety to preserve radio silence. That is not correct. McClusky is apparently borne out by a statement in *Hornet* Action Report p. 3, but the officer who wrote this report has explained to me that he did not intend to convey that impression. It seems strange that neither Gray nor Waldron, who had sighted the carriers at 0910 and 0925, broke radio silence to announce their position.

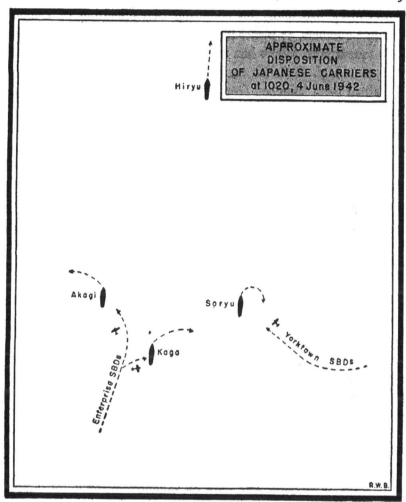

APPROXIMATE
DISPOSITION
OF JAPANESE CARRIERS
at 1020, 4 June 1942

Hiryu

Akagi

Soryu

Kaga

Enterprise SBDs

Yorktown SBDs

R. W. B.

not yet over. The diameter of their circular disposition was roughly eight miles. *Akagi* was the westernmost carrier, with *Soryu* on her starboard beam; *Kaga* steamed astern on *Akagi's* starboard quarter, and *Hiryu* was well ahead — a position which afforded her a few hours' grace.[35]

[35] Comparing this disposition with the regular formation given in *Inter. Jap. Off.* I 4, it is evident that the formation had been reversed at the change of course and that *Hiryu* was out of position.

McClusky had under his command two squadrons of Daunt-less dive-bombers, 37 planes including his own. He ordered Galla-her's squadron to follow him in attacking *Kaga*, and Best's to take care of *Akagi*. Gallaher carried 500-pound bombs because his SBDs had been launched from the carrier so early that less than half the flight deck had been available, not enough take-off for a heavily armed plane; but Best's, which had taken off later, carried 1000-pound bombs. By great good luck Best's second division of three planes attacked *Kaga* by mistake, so that each carrier got its share of the half-ton bombs. Both squadrons made 70-degree dives at about 280 knots, encountering no interference from fighter planes and very little from anti-aircraft fire. For the Japanese com-bat air patrol had come down low to get the torpedo planes a few minutes earlier and there was no time to climb back.

This dive-bombing attack knocked out two carriers. *Akagi* had 40 planes on her flight deck being fueled and serviced. At 1026, only two minutes after she had evaded the last of the torpedo-bombers, she received three bomb hits. "We were unable to avoid the dive-bombers because we were so occupied in avoiding the torpedo attacks," said Captain Aoki.[36] Her log thus describes the attack: "Three bombers dive on *Akagi* from positions bearing 80 degrees to port . . . At about 500 meters altitude, bombs were loosed. First was a near-miss about 10 meters abeam of bridge; second hit near the elevator amidships (fatal hit); third hit the flight deck on the port side, aft." [37]

These were enough. The third hit exploded in the midst of air-planes on the flight deck that were just changing their armament from bombs for Midway to torpedoes for Fletcher and Spruance. The second bomb exploded in the hangar, detonating the stored torpedoes. "There was a terrific fire aboard ship which was just like hell!" said Nagumo's chief of staff, an unusually outspoken Japanese: —

[36] *Inter. Jap. Off.* I 13; USSBS 530 p. 8.
[37] *O.N.I. Review* May 1947 p. 23.

Admiral Nagumo thought the situation was under control and refused to come down from the bridge, but the captain of the ship
advised him that the ship was out of control and that it should be
abandoned, and wanted him to abandon ship, but he refused; Admiral
Nagumo was an extremely hot-tempered person, and consequently
insisted on remaining on the bridge. I myself as chief of staff tried to
convince him that it was his duty as C. in C. to abandon ship and
transfer to some other ship where he could control the actions of the
fleet, because it was no longer possible to communicate with other
ships by wireless from *Akagi*, and the signal flags and semaphore
weren't sufficient to direct the battle. Although Admiral Nagumo refused to come down, I finally had the others drag him by the hand
and talk him into leaving the ship, but couldn't find a way down,
everything was so covered with smoke and flame; there was no way
of getting down from the bridge except by a rope which we hung
from the bridge. . . . When I got down, the deck was on fire and
anti-aircraft and machine guns were firing automatically, having been
set off by the fire aboard ship. Bodies were all over the place, and it
wasn't possible to tell what would be shot up next. . . . I had my hands
and feet burned — a pretty serious burn on one foot. That is eventually
the way we abandoned the *Akagi* — helter-skelter, no order of any
kind.[38]

According to the log, it was at 1047 that Nagumo and staff left
in this manner, which must have been a sore trial to Japanese dig-
nity. They were taken off by a destroyer and transferred to light
cruiser *Nagara* of the screen, where Nagumo flew his flag during
the remainder of the battle. En route to the cruiser the Admiral
could see fires raging on *Soryu* and *Kaga;* but he decided to continue the battle with the yet undamaged *Hiryu.* The ritual of transferring the Emperor's portrait from *Akagi* to a destroyer was completed at 1715. Damage control labored two hours longer — very
inefficiently according to the chief of staff [39] — trying to control
fires and rig enough power to work her into port; but at 1915 the
engineer officer reported that there was no hope, and Captain

[38] USSBS 530 p. 39; Rear Adm. R. Kusaka.
[39] Kusaka's statement appended to "Full Translation of Japanese Fleet Organization at Midway" ATIS 16647 B.

Aoki ordered all hands to abandon ship. She drifted northward and before sunrise 5 June was sunk by a torpedo from a Japanese destroyer.[40]

Kaga means "increased joy," but whatever luck the name had brought to that ship ran out fast when McClusky, Gallaher and Best began working her over.[41] Four hits they scored. One bomb, landing just forward of the "island," blew it to bits and killed everyone on the bridge, including the Captain. The other three set fire to planes that were being refueled, penetrated the hangar and induced explosions in the gasoline or bomb-stowage room below. In a few moments *Kaga* was a mass of flames, and the Emperor's portrait was hurriedly transferred to a destroyer. A considerable number of officers and men abandoned ship forthwith, but others remained on board to fight the fires.[42]

Commander Amagai, flight officer of *Kaga*, swimming near the burning carrier, saw a periscope rise above the surface. The submarine, which has never been identified,[43] fired a torpedo at *Kaga* which hit. "But," said Amagai, "it was such a glancing blow fired at such an angle that the torpedo bounced off the side of the ship and circled slightly, after which the warhead dropped off and sank, although the body of the torpedo remained floating near me. . . . Several of our sailors clung to the floating after part of the torpedo" — a use of American torpedoes not anticipated by the Bureau of Ordnance. Amagai from his fish-eye view observed the

---

[40] *O.N.I. Review* May 1947 pp. 12, 23, 32, 35, 41; both here and in damage report on p. 55, the position is given as lat. 30°30′ N, long. 178°40′ W. The chart on p. 38, however, as well as the chart prepared for us at Tokyo, places *Akagi*'s sinking about 35 miles W of this position, which seems more likely in view of the prevailing wind. 178° is probably a mistake for 179°.

[41] The synthetic Striking Force log in *O.N.I. Review* May 1947 pp. 22–3 notes "*Akagi* sees *Kaga* being dive-bombed" at 1022, and "Fires break out aboard *Kaga*" at 1024; Nagumo's report on p. 12 says it was all over by 1025, but the damage report on p. 56 gives the time as 1030 as does the chart, p. 38. What probably happened is that McClusky and Gallaher attacked a few minutes before the last division of VB-6.

[42] USSBS 530 pp. 57–62; *O.N.I. Review* p. 12.

[43] Suspected to be *Nautilus;* but see note to sinking of *Soryu,* below. Of the other boats of the Midway Patrol that were ordered by Admiral English from Pearl early on the 4th to pursue the enemy, *Grouper* and *Gudgeon* made contacts but failed to develop them.

carrier "burning fiercely from stem to stern, and the anti-aircraft batteries were firing from induced explosion of their magazines." Even the paint on her topsides was aflame. After floating about for three hours, this officer was picked up by a destroyer from whose deck he saw one tremendous explosion in *Kaga;* and shortly after, at 1925, she sank hissing into a 2600-fathom deep.[44]

One or two minutes before *Akagi* and *Kaga* received their lethal bomb hits from McClusky's SBDs, Leslie's squadron of 17 SBDs from *Yorktown* struck *Soryu.* The attack group to which these planes belonged [45] had begun its flight at 0906, more than an hour and a quarter after that of *Enterprise* and *Hornet,* but the *Yorktown* air group commander was a little smarter than his opposite numbers in figuring out the shortest way to the enemy carriers. *Yorktown's* planes were directed to fly straight to the line that connected the last reported position of the enemy force with Midway; and, if nothing was sighted there, to fly up the reverse bearing, away from Midway. Leslie, on approaching that line at an altitude of 20,000 feet, saw smoke over the horizon which he rightly guessed came from Japanese ships making high speed. He promptly turned north and so caught up with McClusky.[46] He also caught up with *Yorktown's* torpedo planes, which had started twelve minutes earlier. The operation plan called for the dive-bombers to attack first, but Massey went in impetuously with his Devastators and, as we have seen, was slaughtered. Not so Leslie, who by a fortunate coincidence had arrived over the target at the same moment as McClusky and selected *Soryu* for attack while McClusky was concentrating on *Akagi* and *Kaga.* Leslie commenced his attack from 14,500 feet.

[44] USSBS No. 530 p. 61. The Japanese damage report in *O.N.I. Review* p. 56 says it was the bomb hits at 1030 which, by inducing "explosions in gasoline (or bomb-stowage room) caused sinking." Position, lat. 30°23'18" N, long. 179° 17'12" W.

[45] The whole group consisted of 17 SBD, 12 TBD and 6 F4F–4; but the torpedo-bombers became separated en route and attacked independently, as already related.

[46] Information from Capt. Leslie and Capt. M. E. Arnold (junior flight officer of *Yorktown*). McClusky missed the same long view of Japanese smoke because there were clouds between him and the enemy carriers, but by the time Leslie came along the sky had cleared somewhat.

Soryu had just armed and fueled an attack group for a second sortie. Planes were lined up on the flight deck ready to take off, others in the hangar were being refueled and rearmed, and she was turning south into the wind to launch.[47] Leslie's squadron dove down-sun along her fore-and-aft axis at intervals of thirty seconds to one minute, in three waves. The first approached the carrier from the starboard bow, the second from the starboard quarter, and the third from the port quarter. Although release altitudes averaged 2500 feet, three lethal hits with 1000-pound bombs were scored between 1025 and 1028. The first penetrated the flight deck forward of the superstructure, exploded in the hangar below and folded the forward elevator back against the bridge. The second struck amidships in the midst of spotted planes, turning the after part of the flight deck into a sheet of flame and blowing a "Zeke" over the side just as it was being launched. The third hit near the after elevator.[48] The entire ship burst into flames, and within twenty minutes the crew were ordered to abandon by Captain Yanagimoto, whom they last saw bellowing "Banzai!" on the bridge.[49] And not one of Leslie's planes was shot down.

United States submarine *Nautilus* now lent a hand. Commander Brockman, since his unsuccessful attack on the cruiser screen at 0825, had been making best surface speed to get back into the fight. At 1145 he sighted on the horizon, eight miles distant, smoke which he suspected came from a burning carrier. An hour later, after making a periscope-depth approach, he identified the flattop as of *Soryu* class. Escorted by two destroyers, she was making about two knots on an even keel; and although the after part of her flight deck was demolished all fires appeared to be under control. The executive officer of *Soryu* had sent a damage-control party back on board, and as *Nautilus* closed they could be seen trying

---

[47] These and other details are in part from the interrogation of Capt. Ohara (exec. of *Soryu*) in USSBS 530 pp. 72–74, and *Inter. Jap. Off.* I 168.

[48] H. Ohara in *Inter. Jap. Off.* I 168; Cdr. Amagai of *Kaga* in USSBS 530 p. 62.

[49] *O.N.I. Review* May 1947 p. 13. Four SBDs which were to have been the last to dive, seeing that *Soryu* was already burning furiously, shifted their attack to a nearby battleship and light cruiser but scored only a near-miss on that most near-missed ship of the Japanese Navy, *Haruna*.

to pass a towline to small boats under the carrier's bow. Brockman took his time to reach a good firing position undetected, and between 1359 and 1405 fired three torpedoes from a distance of 2700 yards. All three hit and exploded — Captain Komura of cruiser *Chikuma* saw them.[50] A prolonged depth-charge attack now began on *Nautilus*, and a long death agony for *Soryu*. When the submarine came up for another look at 1610 the carrier was burning along her entire length, recalling (to the submariners' great satisfaction) the spectacle of *Arizona* at Pearl Harbor. Finally the gasoline stowage aft exploded, whipsawing the ship; the after part sank first and then the forward half blew up and sank around 1920.[51]

The American dive-bombers had eventful flights back to their carriers. As McClusky pulled away from the burning *Akagi* his plane was pursued by two "Zekes" for about 35 miles. He kept his SBD skimming the water, only 20 feet above the surface, which baffled the "Zekes." They used 7.7-mm tracers to get his range, and then opened up with their 20-mm, but fortunately had only a small supply of this caliber. At that they put 55 small and three big holes in the plane — one of them through No. 9 cylinder, which continued nevertheless to function — besides peppering the pilot's left shoulder with fragments. As McClusky wove the plane this way and that, his radio mechanic W. G. Chochalousek did wonders with a .30-caliber Browning; he shot down one "Zeke" and discouraged the other so that it pulled away. On another SBD a twin-mounted machine gun broke loose during the dive. Al-

[50] *Inter. Jap. Off.* II 460.
[51] Position given in Nagumo's report and damage report, *O.N.I. Review* pp. 13 and 56, is lat. 30°42′30″ N, long. 178°37′30″ W; the meridian was probably 179° W, as she could hardly have drifted eastward in an easterly wind, and *Nautilus* position at first sighting was lat. 30°13′ N, long. 179°17′ W. This account of the sinking is from *Nautilus* Patrol Report, *Soryu's* exec. Ohara in USSBS 530 p. 74 and *Inter. Jap. Off.* I 168. In view of Cdr. Amagai's story related above, it may be suspected that *Nautilus's* victim was *Kaga;* but the Japanese evidence and Brockman's positive identification as "*Soryu* class," which had a very different appearance from *Kaga,* seem conclusive. After the depth-charging of *Nautilus* — the fourth she had undergone that day — a mess boy remarked to the skipper, "Captain, I certainly got religion!" And for some time he wrote out a daily sermon which he posted on the bulletin board for the benefit of all hands.

though these guns are so heavy that it normally takes two men to lift them into the cockpit, gunner Floyd D. Adkins managed to prevent his from being snatched away by the powerful slip-stream, and on the pull-out laid it on the plane's fuselage and shot down an attacking "Zeke." [52]

Admiral Spruance's staff had miscalculated Point "Option." That is a moving point whose initial position is set in advance of a carrier-plane mission. It moves, theoretically, with the carriers; pilots are informed of the course and speed the carrier expects to make good, and that becomes the course and speed of Point "Option." The plane's navigator or pilot draws the line on his chart with 15- to 30-minute intervals pricked off, calculates before starting home-ward at what place on the line Point "Option" will be, and sets his course accordingly. In this instance the O.T.C. had set Point "Option's" course as 240° and speed at 24 knots. The carriers were unable to make good more than 12 knots on that course, as they frequently had to head at 27 knots into the light and diminish-ing easterly airs to launch and recover combat or anti-submarine air patrol, and every such operation lost ground. And nobody let the planes know that *Enterprise* and *Hornet* were behind sched-ule. Consequently, when McClusky's squadron reached the place where Point "Option" should have been, no ships were in sight. *Enterprise* was a good 60 miles to the northeastward. After mak-ing a circular search, McClusky spotted a carrier and was just about to land when he saw it was *Yorktown;* just then he sighted *Enterprise* beyond. With only two gallons of gasoline left he con-tinued to her and landed wobbly but safe. Others were not so lucky as their group leader; several splashed for want of gas. [53]

Commander Leslie, having avenged on *Soryu* the loss of *York-town's* torpedo-bombers, withdrew close to the water through

[52] Cdr. R. M. Lindsey "Battle of Midway" p. 17; Lt. W. E. Gallaher's Report.
[53] *War College Analysis* says between 4 and 7 were so lost out of the total of 14 in that attack. Our carriers were equipped with automatic homing equip-ment and several of McClusky's planes used it successfully to locate *Enterprise*. but others had had their radio equipment shot up and had to depend on Point "Option."

heavy anti-aircraft fire from cruisers and destroyers. Fortunately he had figured out that Point "Option" would move at a speed nearer 12 than 24 knots, so every one of his 17 SBDs found their carrier promptly. They were held in the air circling *Yorktown*, waiting for Lieutenant Commander Thach's fighter planes to turn up, because the Wildcats were certain to be low on gas and might be wanted again in a hurry. Thach had been an interested if somewhat preoccupied spectator of the attack on the Japanese carriers for a good half hour. After losing one of his Wildcats and seeing two more chased out of the area by "Zekes," he and the two others climbed to 3000 feet where, by employing the famous "Thach weave" that he had invented, they managed to beat off 15 or 20 more "Zekes." Every so often a TBD would come limping out of the mêlée when Thach and his wing men would escort her clear and return for more. He and four others of his squadron returned to their carrier safely (although two planes were badly shot up) and he brought Admiral Fletcher the first visual evidence that three Japanese carriers were burning and exploding.

While Thach was making his oral report, word came from the radar room that *Yorktown* was about to be attacked, and Leslie's SBDs, whose turn had come to land, were ordered to clear out. After the attack was over, all but two, which ditched for want of gas, landed on the deck of *Enterprise*.

Shortly after noon, when this crucial phase of the Battle of Midway ended, three Japanese carriers were in a sinking condition and the American Carrier Force was intact. But *Enterprise* had lost 14 out of 37 dive-bombers, 10 out of 14 torpedo-bombers and one Wildcat; *Hornet* had lost all her torpedo-bombers and 11 or 12 Wildcats; *Yorktown* had lost all but one of her torpedo-bombers, two dive-bombers and three Wildcats. This was no excessive price for what had been accomplished, but it was a frightful blow to the carrier air groups, whose aviators had given everything they had.

5. *Attacks on* YORKTOWN; *Sinking of* HIRYU

Admiral Nagumo, when he saw that he would have to abandon *Akagi*, transferred the tactical command of the Striking Force to Rear Admiral Abe, commanding his cruiser and battleship screen. Abe had one undamaged carrier with a full air group left; and from scout plane contacts he gathered that Fletcher had no more than two carriers, possibly but one; if so, she or they must already have expended most of their planes. At 0847 Nagumo radioed Yamamoto, "Sighted enemy composed of one carrier, five cruisers and six destroyers at position bearing 10° 240 miles from Midway. We are heading for it." [54] That carrier was *Yorktown*, and Abe had placed the Indian sign on her, at 1050.

He passed the word to Admiral Yamaguchi in *Hiryu*, "Attack the enemy carrier," and *Hiryu* blinked back, "All our planes are taking off now." Launching of the first attack group — 18 dive-bombers and six fighters — was completed by 1100; the second attack group of ten torpedo-bombers and six fighters took off at 1331.[55] Two reconnaissance planes from cruiser *Chikuma*, which had located Admiral Fletcher's force, were ordered to lead the dive-bombers to it.

Help was coming, too, for the hard-pressed Striking Force. Precisely at noon, two heartening messages reached Nagumo, who by then had shifted his flag to *Nagara* and taken back the tactical command. The air commander of *Hiryu's* attack group radioed, "We are bombing the enemy carrier." Admiral Kondo, commander in chief of the Second Fleet that had been supporting the Occupation Force to the southwestward, radioed that he was bringing his powerful force of battleships, cruisers and destroyers up north at 28 knots in support.[56] And, twenty minutes later,

---

[54] *O.N.I. Review* May 1947 p. 23. By "sighted" he meant reported by one of his planes.

[55] These numbers included one VT from *Akagi* and two VF from *Kaga* that had joined *Hiryu* when unable to land on their own carriers. Same, pp. 48–9.

[56] Same, pp. 24, 25. His position was then lat. 28° N, long. 175° E (*War College Analysis*).

Yamamoto ordered carriers *Ryujo* and *Junyo*, of the force that had attacked Dutch Harbor, to come south and join *Hiryu*. At the same time the Aleutian Screening Force was ordered to rendez-vous with Yamamoto at 0900 June 5 in preparation for a fleet action.

Things were beginning to look up for the enemy. The Samurai clans were gathering, and their swords were sharp.

By noon *Yorktown* had a combat air patrol of twelve Wildcats in the air and was refueling the patrol just relieved, as well as three others that had returned from the strike on Nagumo's force. Leslie's dive-bombers that had sunk *Soryu* were orbiting, ready to land, when *Yorktown's* radar reported 30 to 40 planes approaching from the WSW, 40 miles out. The returning victors were waved away, fuel lines were drained and filled with CO_2, combat air patrol was sent out to intercept, *Yorktown* bent on 30.5 knots and maneuvered violently.

It was now a few minutes before noon. "The attack is coming in, sir," said Admiral Fletcher's aide. Frank Jack, bending over a chart to figure out his next move, merely looked up a minute and said, "Well, I've got on my tin hat. I can't do anything else now!" [57]

The Wildcat pilots of the combat air patrol, part of Thach's "Fighting 3," did themselves proud, shooting down or sending home minus their bombs over half of the 18 "Vals" that were approaching; but eight got through. Cruisers *Astoria* and *Portland* and the destroyers between them knocked down two.[58] The other six made three hits, of which two were serious. From one "Val," as it disintegrated under anti-aircraft fire, a bomb tumbled out on *Yorktown's* flight deck; its explosion killed many men, started fires below and spread black smoke over the ship. The officer of the hangar deck, Lieutenant A. C. Emerson, released the sprinkler system and water curtains, which quickly extinguished the fires. The next bomb came in from the port side and exploded in the smokestack, firing the soot and paint, which flaked off and started

[57] Foster Hailey in *N. Y. Times* 23 June 1942.
[58] The official Japanese report lists 13 bombers and 3 fighters "self-exploded," a euphemism for "shot down." *O.N.I. Review* May 1947 p. 48.

fires elsewhere, ruptured the uptakes from three boilers, disabled two of them, and snuffed out fires in five out of six boilers. Her speed dropped to 6 knots and by 1220, twenty minutes after the hit, to zero. A third bomb exploded on the fourth deck, starting a fire in a rag-stowage compartment adjacent to the forward gasoline tanks and magazines. Her magazines were promptly flooded, and CO_2 prevented the gas from exploding.

As the fire on the "island" had knocked out the ship's radar, rendering flag plot and communications untenable, Admiral Fletcher shifted his flag to cruiser *Astoria*. At about 1315, when the transfer was completed, he directed cruiser *Portland* to take the carrier in tow. She never passed the towline because *Yorktown's* damage-control parties worked to such good purpose that by 1340 four boilers were back on the line. Down came her breakdown flag — blue St. Andrew's cross on yellow field — and to everyone's joy she began turning up 18 to 20 knots; but that was not enough. She was beginning to refuel fighter planes when a cruiser's radar picked up *Hiryu's* second attack wave, distant 40 miles. And within an hour this gallant carrier was a useless derelict.

Spruance, who had seen the smoke of the dive-bombings from over the horizon, had already detached cruisers *Pensacola* and *Vincennes* and destroyers *Benham* and *Balch* from his force to augment Fletcher's. They were cruising in disposition "Victor," one mile out, so disposed as to afford the carrier ample anti-aircraft protection on her vulnerable bows and quarters. But they were not enough.

Yorktown had time to launch eight Wildcats — with an average of only 23 gallons in each tank — which joined the four planes already in the air in an attempt to intercept. They were unable to cope with the ten fast Japanese torpedo-bombers and six escorting "Zekes," which were visible at nine miles' distance approaching from the westward at 7000 feet. The time was 1430. Anti-aircraft fire was not opened immediately because of recognition difficulties; but after seeing a Wildcat shoot down a "Zeke" all the task force guns, large and small, gave tongue. *Yorktown* turned hard left, the cruisers keeping station as best they could; this placed *Portland* a little ahead of *Yorktown* on her port bow, and *Astoria* another ship's length or two farther ahead, on the carrier's starboard bow; *Pensacola* and *Vincennes* were on her quarters. The torpedo planes separated to attack from four different angles at masthead height or lower. When they closed to 3000 yards, the heavy cruisers tried tactics that their divisional commander, "Poco" Smith, had worked out. With their main batteries, their 5-inch 25s, and everything that would bear, they fired right into the sea across the planes' path. The shells exploded on impact, sending up a veritable Niagara of water ahead of each group of planes. It seemed impossible that any winged craft could penetrate the shimmering, watery curtains; but four "Kates" did and released torpedoes within 500 yards of the now slowly moving carrier. One of their pilots, on his pull-out, passed so close aboard that he could be seen shaking his fist.[59] At about 1442, *Yorktown* dodged two torpedoes but two others hit and exploded, breaching most of the fuel tanks on her port side, jamming the rudder, severing all power connections and causing an immediate list of 17 degrees, which increased to about 26 degrees in the next 20 minutes.

Captain Buckmaster, advised by his damage control officer that counterflooding was impossible without power, and that their watertight integrity had been only half restored by the repairs at Pearl,[60] feared the *Yorktown* was about to capsize. A few minutes before 1500 he ordered Abandon Ship. Four destroyers closed to take off the crew or pick them up from the water. The others screened, expecting a third air attack. The sea was smooth and, although the water was much colder than that of the Coral Sea, it is believed that nobody drowned. Floating bluejackets amused each other by calling, "Taxi! Taxi!" and thumbing imagi-

[59] Story of Jule Bodenschatz in *Chicago Tribune* 5 Aug. 1942. The Japanese lost 5 out of 10 torpedo-bombers and 3 out of 6 fighters in this attack. *War College Analysis.*

[60] The latter supposition was incorrect; after the Pearl Harbor Navy Yard repairs her watertight integrity was better than it had been before Coral Sea. See Buships War Damage Report No. 23 on *Yorktown,* 28 Nov. 1942, p. 12.

nary rides at drifting debris; strains of the "Beer Barrel Polka" floated from one raft full of officers and men.[61]

Admiral Fletcher, estimating before the first attack on *Yorktown* that one enemy carrier was intact, had had the foresight to send out a search mission of ten scout bombers commanded by Lieutenant Wallace C. Short. After searching far and wide for over three hours[62] they were on their way back to *Yorktown*, happily ignorant of her disaster, when at 1445 pilot Samuel Adams made what his commanding officer stoutly maintains to have been "the best, clearest and most accurate" carrier-plane-contact report of the entire war. He saw *Hiryu*, two battleships, three cruisers and four destroyers steaming north, about 110 miles W by N of where *Yorktown* then was.[63] A few minutes later *Yorktown* was abandoned, but, on the basis of Lieutenant Adams's report, she was amply avenged.

At 1530, as Admiral Spruance ordered, *Enterprise* turned into the wind and launched an attack mission of 24 SBDs, ten of them refugees from *Yorktown*, and all veterans of the morning attack on the other three carriers.[64] No fighter escort was provided, as all surviving Wildcats were needed for combat air patrol. The dive-bombers, led by the redoubtable Gallaher, jumped *Hiryu* and her attendant cruisers at 1700. The same dive-bombing tactics that had proved successful in the morning were employed. *Hiryu*, making 30 knots, received four direct hits, of which one blew off the forward elevator platform so that it crashed against the "island," knocking out all facilities there; the others started uncontrollable fires.[65] Among those who went down with her was the

---

[61] Story by petty officer Harvey Wilder in *Atlanta Journal* 16 Sept. 1942.

[62] Assigned sector was 280° to 20° clockwise, radius 200 miles.

[63] Lt. Short's report of this mission to C.O. *Enterprise*, 7 June; recent conversations with old *Yorktown* men. Lt. Adams was shot down 6 June in the attack on *Mikuma*. The *War College Analysis* states that the contact as reported was 42 miles, 276° from *Hiryu's* actual position, but fortunately the carrier took a course that brought her right in the way of the attack group.

[64] *Hornet* also launched an attack group of 16 dive-bombers at 1603 but they arrived too late for *Hiryu* and dove at the cruisers, making only near-misses.

[65] Damage report in *O.N.I. Review*, May 1947 p. 57; interrogations of flight officer Kawaguchi and navigation officer M. Cho of *Hiryu* in USSBS 530 pp. 12-15

division commander, Rear Admiral Yamaguchi, an outstanding flag officer who, it is said, was slated to be Yamamoto's successor.

Enterprise and *Yorktown* lost three more SBDs with their crews in this attack.

Within an hour the already defeated Japanese Striking Force was attacked by a number of Flying Fortresses from Molokai and Midway; but the usual ill fortune attended them. Every one of their bombs missed. One Fort strafed *Hiryu*, already on fire but steaming, knocked out an anti-aircraft gun and killed several men.[66] This was the only damage which B-17s inflicted on the enemy in the Battle of Midway, despite their valiant efforts to supplement the deadly work of the carrier planes. From Midway, Major Benjamin W. Norris USMC, who had succeeded Major Henderson as commander of the decimated Marine bomber squadron, took off at 1900 with the squadron's few operational planes — five Vindicators and six SBDs — to make a night attack on the burning *Hiryu*. They failed to find her, and Major Norris never returned.[67]

Fire gradually ate into *Hiryu's* vitals. All hands, including the Emperor's portrait, were ordered to abandon ship at 0315 June 5 by Captain Kaku, who stayed on board. At 0510 two destroyers tried to sink her with torpedoes. She floated, burning fiercely, until 0900,[68] and when she went down Nagumo had lost the last of his four fleet carriers.

Now let us see what was happening on board Combined Fleet flagship *Yamato*, several hundred miles to the rear. Messages from

___

and 46–51; of Kawaguchi in ATIS Report No. 1 and *Inter. Jap. Off.* I 5 (he says 6 hits and 2 near-misses out of 14 drops); Capt. Watanabe in same, I 66.

[66] Same Interrogations. A squadron of 6 B-17s led by Maj. G. A. Blakey was diverted to this attack when en route Molokai–Midway. Six of Lt. Col. Sweeney's B-17s also participated.

[67] Heinl *Marines at Midway* p. 39.

[68] *O.N.I. Review* p. 57 gives position of torpedoing as lat. 31°27′30″ N, long. 179°23′30″ E; on p. 13 long. is given as W, which is probably correct. Position of sinking not stated. The chief engineer and about 35 members of *Hiryu's* black gang, who had been left to their fate when the carrier was abandoned, cut their way out, dived overboard and picked up a lifeboat just as she was going down. Sighted 18 June by a PBY and rescued by seaplane tender *Ballard*, ordered to the spot by Capt. Simard, they made an interesting survivors' report which is Enclosure B to Cincpac's Report on Battle of Midway.

Nagumo, announcing the hits on three carriers, "aroused the utmost consternation," recalled Yamamoto's yeoman. But news of the first attack on *Yorktown* cheered the Admiral considerably. He had lost three of his four big carriers; but if, as Nagumo informed him, the enemy had never had but one carrier he now had none; and in any case Yamamoto had overwhelming gunfire superiority. Acting promptly, he broke radio silence at 1220 June 4 to order the Aleutian Screening Group and Kondo's Second Fleet to join his Main Body by noon next day, while the Midway Occupation Force retired temporarily to the northwestward.

No sooner was this order given than both Yamamoto and Nagumo received for the first time an accurate statement of the United States Task Force, from two different sources: *Hiryu's* returning aviators, who had seen all three carriers, and an American pilot rescued from the water, who had the information extorted from him.[69] At 1330, as we have seen, *Hiryu* launched her second attack on *Yorktown*, and at 1700 *Hiryu* in turn was knocked out.

"The game is up, thought everybody on *Yamato's* bridge," recalled the loquacious yeoman. "The members of the staff, their mouths tight shut, looked at one another . . . indescribable emptiness, cheerlessness and chagrin . . ." Yamamoto could only say "Is Genda all right?" He was the one officer essential to recovery of air power. He had been saved when *Akagi* was abandoned.[70]

As Yamamoto hastened with his Main Body to support the decimated Striking Force, he exchanged an interesting series of dispatches with Nagumo. At 1915 he radioed a stouthearted message to all division and force commanders: —

1. The enemy fleet, which has practically been destroyed, is retiring to the East. 2. Combined Fleet units in the vicinity are preparing to pursue the remnants and at the same time to occupy Midway. 3. The Main Body is scheduled to reach lat. 32° 10' N, long. 175° 43' E, on course 90°, speed 20 knots, by midnight. 4. The Mobile Force, Oc-

[69] *O.N.I. Review* pp. 26–27.
[70] "Yamamoto's Yeoman's Story."

cupation Force (less Crudiv 7) [71] and Advance Force (submarines) will immediately contact and attack the enemy.[72]

Nagumo had no stomach for these heroics. Midway was no fun like Pearl Harbor and Trincomalee! On the strength of a highly inaccurate sighting report from one of *Chikuma's* planes, which confirmed his own fears, he radioed to Yamamoto at 1130, "The total strength of the enemy is 5 carriers, 6 cruisers and 15 destroyers. These are steaming westward. . . . We are offering protection to *Hiryu* and retiring to the northwest at 18 knots." And again, at 2250, "There still exist 4 enemy carriers . . . 6 cruisers and 16 destroyers. These are steaming westward. None of our carriers are operational." [73]

Yamamoto promptly answered these fainthearted messages by ordering Kondo, already hastening northeastward, to relieve Nagumo, who was peremptorily told to take charge of the sinking carriers and such ships as were standing by them. Kondo at 2340 ordered all ships under him to prepare for a night engagement, but, before the dispositions had been made, the Commander in Chief changed his mind.

As more intelligence came in, showing that his four splendid carriers were sunk or burning derelicts and that two American carriers were probably still operating, Yamamoto realized that, if he persisted in pushing forces eastward in search of a night battle, he was likely to get a dawn air attack instead. Everyone on his staff felt the same, and finally at 0255 June 5 Yamamoto bowed to the logic of events and ordered a general retirement.[74] He was destined never to have the big fleet engagement which he so ardently desired; some four-score American aviators had seen to that. He had lost all his fast carriers together with their entire

---

[71] These cruisers had been ordered to go ahead and bombard Midway.
[72] *O.N.I. Review* p. 35. At about the same time Yamamoto ordered the Aleutian occupation to proceed.
[73] Same, pp. 13, 37.
[74] Same, p. 41. Kondo joined Yamamoto at 0815 June 5, when both retired to the northwestward, Nagumo trailing. The Aleutian Screening Force joined later in the day.

complement of planes, about 250 in number.[75] Never was there a sharper turn in the fortunes of war than on that June day when McClusky's and Leslie's dive-bombers snatched the palm from Nagumo's masthead, where he had nailed it on 7 December.

Deep gloom settled over the entire Combined Fleet. "I wonder what are the feelings of the ones who planned this," confided an officer of the Landing Force to his diary. "We are retreating. . . . It is utterly discouraging. . . . The Marines, who were showing off, have not even courage to drink beer." [76] Could one say more?

[75] The killed and missing figures given by the Japanese (*O.N.I. Review* p. 71) are: *Akagi*, 221; *Kaga*, about 800; *Hiryu*, 416; *Soryu*, 718. This does not necessarily include the aviators. Capt. Kawaguchi, air officer of *Hiryu*, states in *Inter. Jap. Off.* I 4 that his carrier lost about 60 pilots and about 500 crew; in ATIS Report No. 1 he says only 20 of 150 flying personnel survived. Capt. Ohara, exec. of *Soryu*, states in *Inter.* I 168, that his ship lost "about 700," including "about 30 pilots." He also is authority for 250 planes being lost, which was exactly what Cincpac estimated at the time.

[76] Diary of officer of "Kure" S.N.L.F., communicated by Capt. Layton.

CHAPTER VIII

Midway: The Pursuit Phase

5–7 June

1. Contact Lost, 5 June

THE FOURTH of June — day that should live forever glorious in our history — decided the Battle of Midway. By destroying the four Japanese carriers and their air groups, the American aviators had extracted the sting from the Combined Fleet. Everything that followed now appears as anti-climax; but the situation during the night of 4–5 June was far from clear to the people at Midway, to Fletcher and Spruance, or, for that matter, to Nimitz and Yamamoto.

Spruance, whose freedom of movement was confirmed by Fletcher after the abandonment of *Yorktown*,[1] could not be certain that the four enemy carriers attacked by his force and *Yorktown* were out for keeps. A disturbing bit of news came in from Major Blakey's B–17s. When attacking the burning *Hiryu* late in the afternoon they had encountered a number of "Zekes." These must have flown off *Hiryu* before she was abandoned, and were simply doing what they could before ditching; but, for aught he knew, they might have come from a fifth carrier. Spruance knew that the Japanese supporting naval forces, which nobody had yet found, included carriers. With *Yorktown* disabled, the

---

[1] Spruance radioed to Fletcher shortly after 1300 June 4: "TF 16 air groups are now striking the carrier which your search planes reported . . . Have you any instructions for me?" To which Fletcher replied: "None. Will conform to your movements." Fletcher was steaming to the eastward in *Astoria* with *Portland* and four destroyers, carrying survivors.

air groups of his own carriers decimated, and no support in sight, he had to calculate the possible damage he could inflict against the risks involved.

As he explained in his report, "I did not feel justified in risking a night encounter with possibly superior enemy forces, but on the other hand I did not want to be too far away from Midway the next morning. I wished to have a position from which either to follow up retreating enemy forces or to break up a landing attack on Midway."[2] Consequently he withdrew *Enterprise* and *Hornet* to the eastward, and did not reverse course until midnight.

Spruance was subjected to much criticism after the action for not having given chase immediately after 1907 June 4 when he had recovered planes from his strike on *Hiryu.* By steaming eastward for five hours, it was claimed, he had given the enemy time to escape. This criticism was based on ignorance of what Yamamoto was doing. Now that we have ample data of Japanese ship movements, it is clear that Spruance's judgment was sound and his decision correct. A glance at our chart for 5 June will show why. Vice Admiral Kondo, when he received news of the first serious attack on the Striking Force, around noon 4 June, decided on his own responsibility to come to Nagumo's assistance. Leaving the transports almost unprotected, Commander in Chief Second Fleet, in heavy cruiser *Atago* with three other heavies, two *Kongo*-class battleships, light carrier *Zuiho* and a destroyer squadron, commenced at 1400 June 4 a high-speed run to the northeastward. By midnight most of Kondo's force was about 125 miles from the battleships and cruisers formerly under Nagumo's command, and Rear Admiral Tanaka in *Jintsu* with ten destroyers was not far behind. If *Enterprise* and *Hornet* had steamed westward instead of eastward after 1900, they would have run smack into this heavy concentration shortly after midnight, which was exactly what the Japanese wanted. Their ships were better trained for night action than ours; there was a last-quarter moon which to some extent

[2] CTF 16 Action Report 16 June p. 3. Planes of carrier *Zuiho* of the Occupation Force attacked a Midway patrol plane at 1845 June 5, 350 miles 313° from Midway.

would have neutralized the advantage of radar; and carriers without night-flying, radar-equipped planes are exceedingly vulnerable after dark. Furthermore, even if Kondo could do no more than hold Spruance, the Japanese Main Body was fast approaching from the northwest. Yamamoto would have been handed the fleet action he so ardently desired, on a silver platter.

At Pearl Harbor and in Washington, too, the situation was far from clear. Nimitz and King were very cautious in their releases. On 5 June Cincpac announced, "It is too early to claim a major Japanese disaster. . . . The enemy appear to be withdrawing but we are continuing the battle." On the 6th he went so far as to say, "A momentous victory is in the making," but "the battle is not over. . . . The following enemy losses are claimed: two or three carriers and all their aircraft destroyed, in addition to one or two carriers badly damaged." Next day, the 7th, Admiral King held his first press conference since he had become Chief of Naval Operations. "Although the enemy's forces have taken some hard knocks," he said, "I would not say they have been defeated yet; they have 'withdrawn.'" And, in answer to a journalist who expressed the hope that the Pacific Fleet would chase the Nips all the way to Japan, he remarked that such action "might not be well advised."[3] Certainly, if we had been in Yamamoto's place we would have tried another throw of the dice before going home; and Yamamoto almost did so.

Exactly when did the Japanese Commander in Chief realize he was not going to take Midway? Our guess is, shortly after midnight between 4 and 5 June.

At 2030 June 4 he had ordered submarine *I-168* to close Midway and shell the air base until 0200 June 5, when Admiral Kurita's Close Support Group would take over and complete destruction of the installations, preparatory to landing. Kurita's four cruisers, *Kumano, Suzuya, Mikuma* and *Mogami*, equal in size and strength to our later *Baltimore* class and about three knots faster, were the most powerful then afloat. They had fought all through the South-

[3] *N. Y. Times*, 6, 7 and 8 June 1942.

west Pacific campaign and were victors of several engagements. There is no doubt that the combined fire power of their forty 8-inch 50-caliber guns would have inflicted great damage on Midway. But, at 0020 June 5, Yamamoto canceled the scheduled bombardment and ordered Kurita to join the Main Body. Then, as we have already seen, at 0255 he ordered a general retirement. The fueling rendezvous that he then set for 7 June was so far to the northwestward as to prove that he had definitely abandoned the landing on Midway.

The 5th of June was a glum day on board *Yamato*, as the Admiral's yeoman recalled the scene. The Admiral's air officer, with sunken eyes and two days' growth of beard, seemed in a daze. Yamamoto "sat sipping rice gruel helplessly on the forward bridge"; his face was ashen, his eyes glittered.[4] He was furiously thinking. Perhaps there was still a chance to bait Spruance into a surface engagement.

2. *Pursuit of* MOGAMI *and* MIKUMA, *5–6 June*

Fortunately, three United States submarines of the Midway Patrol Group had been left at their stations west of the atoll when the rest went north to chase Japanese carriers. At about 0215 June 5, Admiral Kurita's column of four Japanese cruisers and two destroyers was sighted in the moonlight by submarine *Tambor* at a position 90 miles due west of Midway. The boat observed this force commence its retirement (Kurita having received Yamamoto's 0020 order), and at 0342 was herself sighted. Kurita ordered an emergency turn. Cruiser *Mogami*, last in the column, failed to get the word promptly and rammed the port quarter of *Mikuma*, next ahead. Both were damaged, *Mogami* catching fire and smashing so much of her bow that she was unable to make more than 12 knots, and *Mikuma* trailing oil. The Admiral continued full-speed retirement with his two untouched cruisers, leaving both destroyers

---

[4] "Yamamoto's Yeoman's Story."

to screen the damaged ones.[5] *Tambor's* skipper, Lieutenant Commander Murphy, was unable to get in position to shoot, but he tracked the enemy ships and identified them at break of day, around 0412.

In the meantime, all hands at Midway passed a sleepless night hard at work, repairing damage and fueling planes by hand pumps from 55-gallon drums.[6] Japanese submarine *I-168*, after prowling about the atoll for over three hours, began its scheduled bombardment at 0130; but the shells dropped in the lagoon and the boat was soon driven off by return fire from the Marines' coast-defense batteries. Shortly before dawn 5 June all available PBYs were sent out to search the sector 250° to 20° for 250 miles out, and twelve B-17s followed them at 0430. A Catalina sighted *Mogami* and *Mikuma*, which it took to be battleships, and on receipt of this report Captain Simard ordered the Forts to attack. At 0615 they reported inability to find the targets.[7] Simard then sent out his Marine bombing squadron, which had lost two commanding officers the day before. Only six SBDs and six Vindicators were fit for the mission. They took off promptly in clear weather, picked up an oil slick at 0745, followed it to the westward, found the two cruisers and attacked at 0805, the SBDs dive-bombing and the Vindicators glide-bombing. *Mogami* and *Mikuma* threw up such heavy and accurate anti-aircraft fire that the planes were badly bounced about and their aim spoiled. The final score was six near-misses and one plane crash on an after turret of *Mikuma*, a brave sacrifice hit by Captain Richard E. Fleming USMC of the SB2U formation.[8]

[5] Interrogation of Capt. A. Soji of *Mogami*, *Inter. Jap. Off.* II 361.

[6] Some 45,000 gals. of gas were hand-pumped night of 4-5 June, and 75,000 gals. night of 5-6 June.

[7] Eight of Maj. Blakey's B-17s, which had been orbiting over Kure since early dawn awaiting better target information, attacked at 0830, after the Marines' planes; but all their bombs missed (Soji Interrogation) and two, the only B-17s lost at Midway, failed to return.

[8] Soji said: "I saw a dive-bomber dive into the last turret and start fires. He was very brave." This was not known until after the war. Capt. Fleming's plane was probably hit lethally close to the bomb-dropping point, when he directed it so that it crashed on the cruiser instead of in the sea. The wreckage of his plane can

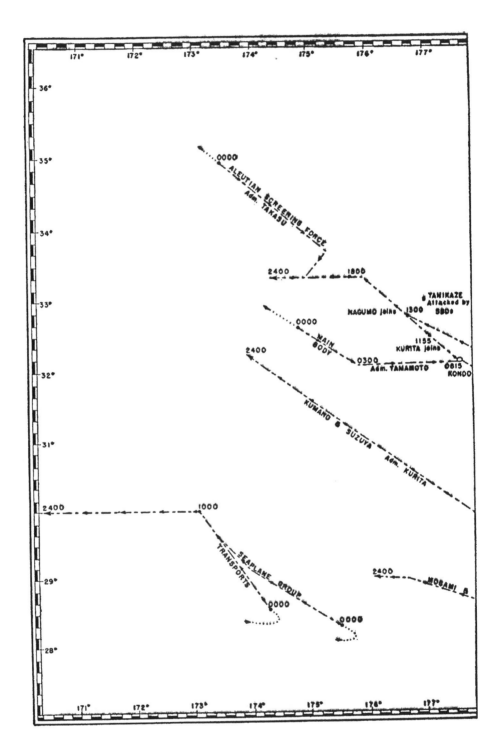

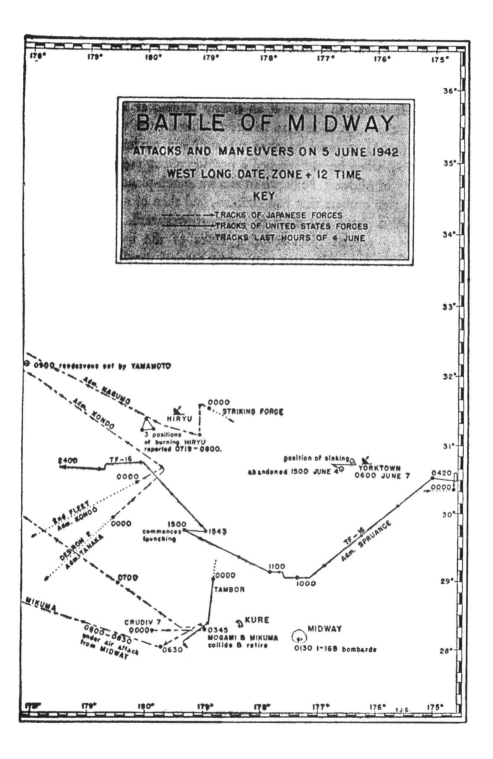

BATTLE OF MIDWAY

ATTACKS AND MANEUVERS ON 5 JUNE 1942

WEST LONG. DATE, ZONE + 12 TIME

KEY

— — — — → TRACKS OF JAPANESE FORCES
——————→ TRACKS OF UNITED STATES FORCES
· · · · · · · · · · TRACKS LAST HOURS OF 4 JUNE

Tambor's original contact report of Kurita's group as "many unidentified ships" at 0215 June 5 was relayed to Admiral Spruance. It looked to him as if an enemy landing at Midway were still on the cards, so at 0420 he altered course from west to southwest (230°) in order to close the atoll and render air support. At 0600, when he had reached a position about 130 miles northeasterly of Midway, he began to receive search-plane reports, first of the two cruisers that had collided, and then of a large enemy disposition about 200 miles to the northwestward. Delayed and confusing reports from scouting PBYs of the burning *Hiryu* created the impression that two enemy carriers were afloat though damaged.

Here was a situation that required clear thinking. At about 0930 Spruance altered course to due west and passed about 50 miles north of Midway.[9] After considering which group of targets to choose for his next plane attack, he selected the one to the northwestward for its promise of one or more carriers still afloat, changed course to NW by W (300°) at 1125 and began a stern chase. At 1500 he turned into the gentle east wind to launch a search and attack group.

Launching of 32 SBDs from *Enterprise* and 26 from *Hornet* was completed at 1543, June 5. There was a heavy overcast, and poor visibility. The two groups searched respectively 315 and 265 miles out on a 30-mile front to the northwestward but found no target of any importance. On the return flight they encountered destroyer *Tanikaze*, detached by Nagumo to ascertain whether *Hiryu* was still afloat. The Japanese destroyer skipper, who had already dodged bombs dropped in two separate attacks by Midway-based B-17s that afternoon, was equally successful in evading the 50-odd SBDs that made dive-bombing attacks, and shot down one of them. The others returned safely after nightfall and made one

---

be seen on top of the conspicuous 8-inch turret in our photograph of *Mikuma*. Heinl *Marines at Midway* pp. 40–41.

[9] His advance was slowed by reversals of course to launch CAP, and he was also delayed by rescuing the crew of a ditched plane. But for these two delays, his search on 5 June might have been successful.

of the first successful night landings in our carrier combat history. Thus the 5th of June passed without any further damage being inflicted on the retiring enemy, except the crash on *Mikuma* which cost Captain Fleming his life.

Admiral Spruance had once more proved the truth of the old naval maxim, "a stern chase is a long chase." Deciding it was no use trying to catch Kondo, he changed course to the westward at 2040 in search of the two damaged cruisers.

As may be seen by our chart, Yamamoto had collected four of his scattered groups — Kondo's Second Fleet, Tanaka's destroyer squadron, Takasu's Aleutian Screening Force, and the battleship and cruiser components of Nagumo's Striking Force — and had retired well beyond the range of Spruance's planes, though not of those based on Midway.[10] Eleven battleships, eight heavy cruisers, several destroyer divisions and two light carriers were under his immediate command; and, except for those under Nagumo and Kurita, no ship of this great fleet had yet fired a shot or sighted an enemy plane.

Mogami and *Mikuma* saw plenty. Before the sun rose on 6 June to a clear, hot day, *Enterprise* launched a reconnaissance flight which picked up the two crippled cruisers making best speed to the westward.[11] By 0800 the first attack group of 26 SBDs and 8 F4Fs took off from *Hornet;* the second of 31 SBDs, 3 TBDs and 12 F4Fs from *Enterprise* followed at 1045; and a third of 24 SBDs and 8 F4Fs was launched at 1330 from *Hornet.* The wind was light from the southwest, blowing straight from the enemy, so that the carriers closed distance rapidly between strikes. By the time of the third strike they were within 90 miles of him and pilots

[10] Because their main object was to rescue surviving aviators afloat, Capt. Simard's plane searches from Midway on 5 June were sent out only 250 miles, and so fell far short of finding the main enemy Fleet. The delays incident to fueling B-17s by hand from drums prevented the "Forts" from going out until the afternoon. Letter from Capt. Simard.

[11] *Hornet* SBDs which had landed on "Big E" the night before made separate contacts, evaluating the enemy as two groups 40 miles apart, one containing battleships; but in reality there was only one, the two heavy cruisers and two destroyers.

flying high could see both forces at the same time in the clear air.

The two damaged cruisers, with no air defense — even their float planes had been jettisoned — were neat targets. *Mogami* in the first attack received two bomb hits, one of which penetrated No. 5 turret and killed everyone within; two more hits in the second attack started fires and a third sealed up one burning engine room and killed over 90 men. *Mogami*, apparently, had a charmed life. She managed to make Truk for temporary repairs,[12] but it was over a year before she was able to rejoin the fleet.

Mikuma was less fortunate. After the second attack the captain ordered her abandoned. Destroyer *Arashio*, after an attempt to close which was ineffectual owing to the fires, recovered hundreds of men from the water. When *Hornet's* final dive-bomber attack came in about 1445, most of the survivors on the deck of this destroyer were killed by a bomb. Another bomb hit on *Mikuma* detonated the cruiser's torpedoes. Both screening destroyers left the cruiser to her fate, and she went down that night.[13]

At 1553 *Enterprise* launched two camera-equipped SBDs to photograph the damaged ships. They failed to locate *Mogami* but took the photographs of *Mikuma* in her death agonies that are among the most remarkable of the Pacific War. Promptly released, these photographs told the public better than any words that the air age had arrived in naval warfare. If they could have known what we now know, that *Mogami* and *Mikuma* were the cruisers that had sunk *Houston* and *Perth*, they would have enjoyed the photographs even more.

Two incidents, one comic and one tragic, concluded this busy day. Midway Island had been reinforced by so many Flying Fortresses from Oahu since the 4th that 26 of the big 4-engine bombers were now available. One hour after he had received Spruance's reports of contacts on the cruisers, Captain Simard dispatched these

---

[12] Capt. Soji in *Inter. Jap. Off.* II 363.

[13] Same, and statement by two survivors in Enclosure B, Cincpac Report. These were the last of 19 who secured a life raft. Capt. Watanabe in *Inter. Jap. Off.* I 66 says about 1000 men were lost with *Mikuma*.

B–17s to help put *Mogami* and *Mikuma* under. Owing to lack of training in navigation their pilots were unable to locate the enemy; but during the afternoon one group of six sighted a vessel, identified it as a Japanese cruiser, and dropped a pattern of twenty 1000-pound bombs from an altitude of over 10,000 feet. On their return to Midway, these B–17 pilots declared they had sunk this vessel in the unprecedented time of fifteen seconds. A few days later, United States submarine *Grayling* came into port, her crew inquiring angrily why they had been bombed by B–17s and forced to crash-dive — at the exact position where the "Japanese cruiser" had been "sunk." [14]

The tragic incident was a gallant attempt by Major General Clarence L. Tinker USA to knock out the Japanese bomber base at Wake. In command of four new Army Liberators that reached Midway from the West Coast on 6 June, General Tinker took off that very night. Each plane carried extra gas tanks and four 500-pound bombs. Overcast prevented the navigators from checking their long course by star sights; they were unable to find the little atoll by the time there was just enough gas left to get back; General Tinker's plane disappeared early in the flight. No trace of it or of him was ever found.

Admiral Spruance, after recovering the two photographic planes around sundown 6 June, reëstimated the situation with his usual clarity. His pilots were exhausted after three days' flying and fighting; he had only four destroyers [15] to screen his two carriers and six cruisers and they had not been fueled from a tanker since 31 May; his task force had now reached long. 174°30′ E, over 400 miles west of Midway. There was little prospect of gain in con-

---

[14] Comsubspac War Diary 7 June; Cincpac *Report of Actions and Campaigns, 1942–43* section 60.

[15] The two he had sent to stand by *Yorktown* stayed with her, and then joined Fletcher; another had to be detached to destroy a ditched PBY and could not catch up; *Maury* and *Worden* got so low on fuel that Spruance had to detach them at 1240 June 6 to fuel at lat. 32° N, long. 178° W. *Maury* had only 21,002 gals. left — about 15 per cent of capacity — and *Worden* had 37,083 gals. left — about 24 per cent of capacity — at end of 6 June. The other DDs left with CTF 16, with amount of fuel at end of 6 June, were *Phelps* (58,555), *Aylwin* (57,574), *Conyngham* (44,707) and *Ellet* (42,865).

tinuing the stern chase, and much risk of trouble through running into a concentration of enemy submarines or within the range of Wake-based bombers. Spruance, feeling that he had pushed his luck far enough, turned the prows of his ships eastward, to where *Cimarron* and *Guadalupe* were waiting to give them a big drink of oil.

The Battle of Midway was over.

Yamamoto did not yet know it. When he received word by radio of the first attack on *Mogami* and *Mikuma* on 6 June, together with a poor search-plane contact report to the effect that *Enterprise* and *Hornet* were operating due east of the two cruisers, he thought he saw a chance to reverse the verdict of battle. Forming a new task force out of six heavy cruisers and the *Jintsu* destroyer squadron, he ordered them at noon to make best speed south, rendezvous with *Mogami* and *Mikuma*, and attack Spruance. More than that, hoping that Task Force 16 in its pursuit of the cruisers would work south to within bomber distance (600 miles) of Wake Atoll (which, as we have seen, Spruance was too smart to do), Yamamoto called up air reinforcements from the Marshalls; and at 1550 June 6 he ordered his Main Body and Second Fleet to steam south and engage, when and if Spruance took the bait. Yamamoto actually commenced this southward movement in search of a fight and so continued until 0700 June 7, when he turned west to a fueling rendezvous. His cruiser-destroyer force, however, found crippled *Mogami* and gave her escort to Truk.

By the afternoon of the 7th Yamamoto had dropped his last plan for an offensive. After spending most of the 8th fueling he started for home, this time for keeps. Yet even then he sent two heavy cruisers and a destroyer division to cruise in the vicinity of Wake and send out heavy radio traffic designed to bait Spruance within air-bombing radius of the atoll.[16]

[16] *War College Analysis* pp. 170–71, 183–84; Toyama in *Inter. Jap. Off.* I 252.

3. *Last of* YORKTOWN, *5–7 June* [17]

The abandonment and subsequent loss of the carrier *Yorktown*, so quickly repaired and so gallantly fought, is the one blot on an otherwise golden scroll of victory.

That she should not have been abandoned after the torpedo-plane attack on 4 June is proved by the fact that she reached equilibrium when she had listed 25 degrees, and floated for twenty-four hours without any human hand to help. To aviators who flew over her on 5 June she appeared to be intact, not burning, and not heeling too badly.[18] The abandonment was orderly if incomplete; within a couple of hours 2,270 survivors, almost her entire crew, were on board the seven destroyers of the screen.[19]

Shortly after the abandonment Admiral Fletcher in *Astoria*, with *Portland* and all destroyers of his task force, started eastward, intending to transfer survivors to the cruisers. At 1800 he detached *Hughes* to stand by the empty carrier with orders to sink her if there were danger of capture by the enemy. *Hughes* located *Yorktown* shortly after dark on 4 June and stood by all night.[20] At dawn the destroyer's commanding officer notified Cincpac that in his opinion *Yorktown* could be saved. Just before the end of the morning watch, his lookouts observed the splash of machine-gun bullets in the water on the port side of the derelict carrier and saw a man on deck waving. A boarding party from *Hughes* returned with two seamen, one with a serious abdominal wound and the other suffering from a fractured skull and other injuries. Both had been left for dead in the sick bay; the former — who died shortly after his rescue — had managed to crawl topside and fire

[17] Memo. of Cdr. W. G. Shindler of *Yorktown* to Cincpac, "made up from notes approved by Admiral Fletcher" 8 June 1942, enclosed in Cincpac's *Advance Report on Midway* to Cominch, 15 June; Lt. Cdr. D. J. Ramsey (C.O. *Hughes*) "Operations in Connection with U.S.S. *Yorktown* from Time of Abandonment . . . until Sinking" 11 June 1942.

[18] No fires were burning except the one smoldering in rag stowage.

[19] Comdesron 6 (Capt. E. P. Sauer) Action Report; *Morris* Action Report.

[20] Cruisers *Vincennes* and *Pensacola* rejoined Admiral Spruance's task force, to which they belonged; but *Balch* and *Benham*, also on "loan" from TF 16, stayed with Fletcher.

machine guns to attract attention. A thorough inspection found no more men alive, but three coding machines intact and numerous secret publications lying about.[21] Lieutenant Commander Ramsey also sent a small salvage party — all he could spare — on board the carrier.

If only there had been a fleet tug with the Task Force, *Yorktown* might have been towed to safety. Or, lacking a tug, she might have been taken in tow by a cruiser as Admiral Fletcher originally intended, and as was done with other damaged carriers later in the war. Admiral Nimitz ordered to *Yorktown's* assistance fleet tug *Navajo*, then patrolling south of French Frigate Shoals; minesweeper *Vireo*, then patrolling off Pearl and Hermes Reef; and destroyer *Gwin* which was hurrying out to join Spruance.[22] *Vireo*, the nearest, arrived first, found *Yorktown* with *Hughes* standing by shortly before noon 5 June [23] and by 1426 had passed her a towline. But she was barely able to make headway with the heavy carrier against the tradewind. A little over an hour later, destroyer *Gwin* arrived and found *Yorktown* "listing to port about 25 degrees and slightly down by the head." Commander Holcomb [24] sent on board a small salvage party which, in coöperation with the one from *Hughes*, had time before nightfall to jettison anchors and various loose gear. But nothing could be accomplished after dark, when the men returned to *Gwin*.[25]

During most of the 5th, while *Vireo* struggled with the carrier against a rising sea, *Astoria* and *Portland* were about 150 miles to the eastward fueling destroyers and taking over survivors. At about noon Admiral Fletcher and Captain Buckmaster decided to do what they should have done the previous evening, to send

---

[21] *Hughes* Report. She also picked up a fighter pilot from *Yorktown* who had splashed eighteen hours earlier and rowed 6 miles in his rubber raft toward his carrier.

[22] Cincpac *Report on Midway. Gwin* left Pearl 2 or 3 June to augment Spruance's screen; Nimitz diverted her on the evening of the 4th to *Yorktown.*

[23] Position lat. 30°43′ N, long. 176°50′ W, from *Vireo* Action Report.

[24] The division commander who became senior officer present and directed operations from *Gwin.*

[25] *Gwin* War Diary.

a proper salvage party on board the carrier and attempt to bring her into port. The Captain, 29 selected officers and 141 men who volunteered for the job were transferred to destroyer *Hammann* which, escorted by destroyers *Balch* and *Benham*, set a course for *Yorktown* — over twenty-four hours after she had been abandoned.[26] They sighted her, still being towed at snail's pace by little *Vireo* and guarded by destroyers *Hughes*, *Gwin* and *Monaghan*,[27] at 0200 June 6. Before daybreak *Hammann* secured to *Yorktown's* starboard side, transferred the salvage party and provided power, pumps and water for their work.[28] A careful plan of action had been laid out beforehand, and Captain Buckmaster and his men worked like beavers. They quenched the one remaining fire, corrected the list by counterflooding with the aid of *Hammann's* power pumps, jettisoned planes and removable weights from the port side and had made considerable progress by midafternoon. Four or five destroyers circled the carrier unit 2000 yards out, operating their echo-ranging sound gear; sufficient anti-submarine screen by any standard, and these destroyers were veterans of anti-submarine warfare in the Atlantic. But sound conditions were poor, owing to oil and flotsam from the carrier, and visibility was perfect.

Yorktown might still have been saved, but for smart work by the enemy. At dawn 5 June Admiral Nagumo had sent two cruiser float planes to search eastward. One of them, about 0700, reported *Yorktown* abandoned and drifting. Shortly after receiving this word Yamamoto ordered submarine *I-168*, which had shelled Midway early that morning, to go get the carrier. As the plane had given the position wrong, *I-168* spent over twenty-four hours searching, but in the early afternoon of June 6 pertinacity was rewarded by sight of the *Yorktown* group. The submarine skillfully penetrated the screen undetected, reached a perfect po-

[26] The rest of TF 17 then headed easterly to rendezvous with oiler *Platte* and sub tender *Fulton;* the latter had been sent out from Pearl to take over *Yorktown* survivors.
[27] Sent to augment the screen by Admiral Fletcher after transferring survivors.
[28] *Hammann* and CTF 17 Action Reports; Cincpac Report, Enclosure C.

sition for a one-two shot, and at about 1330 fired four torpedoes. One missed, two went under *Hammann's* keel and exploded on *Yorktown*, and one hit the destroyer amidships, breaking her in two so that she sank within four minutes with great loss of life.[29]

While three destroyers hunted the submarine in vain until almost midnight and two picked up survivors, *Vireo* cut the towline and transferred the salvage party to destroyer *Benham*. Captain Buckmaster intended to resume salvage operations at first light, 7 June. During the night the carrier's list suddenly increased and at dawn it was evident she was doomed. The escorting destroyers half-masted their colors, all hands came to attention, uncovered; and at 0600, with her loose gear making a horrible death rattle, *Yorktown* rolled over and sank in a two thousand-fathom deep.[30]

The best comment on this unfortunate loss, which the Navy could ill afford at that juncture, is an order issued by Admiral Nimitz before the end of the month: "In the event a ship receives such severe battle damage that abandonment may be a possibility, a skeletonized crew to effect rescue of the ship shall be ready either to remain on board or to be placed in an attendant vessel."[31]

4. *Conclusion*

At this time the Aleutian situation was still obscure, and Admiral Nimitz believed that there was more work for his carriers up north. *Saratoga*, flying the flag of Rear Admiral Aubrey W. Fitch, es-

---

[29] Nine out of 13 officers, 72 out of 228 men were killed and several more died of wounds. Many of these were killed, when already floating, by an underwater explosion, probably caused by a torpedo which was observed to be running hot in its tube as she went down. One hero of *Hammann* was Berlyn M. Kimbrell, who rechecked all the depth charges on "safe" after the torpedo hit, made men on the fantail put on life jackets, shoved them overboard, and was the last to leave. He was killed by the underwater explosion. Cdr. A. E. True, the skipper, was picked up by *Balch* more dead than alive four hours after the explosion. He had been supporting in the water two seamen who were already dead when recovered, and all three were heavily covered with fuel oil.

[30] *Benham* Action Report. Position lat. 30°46′ N, long. 176°24′ W (erroneously given as long. 167° in Action Report).

[31] Pacific Fleet Letter 25 I–42, 30 June 1942, quoted in *War College Analysis* p. 142.

corted by light cruiser *San Diego* and four destroyers, had been making best speed from the West Coast while the Battle of Midway was going on, and arrived at Pearl Harbor on the morning of 6 June. Within twenty-four hours she had fueled, collected another destroyer and oiler *Kaskaskia* and departed. Fitch's orders were to rendezvous with Spruance at a point about 200 miles north of Niihau, turn over as many replacement planes to *Enterprise* and *Hornet* as they required, and return to Pearl. Spruance was then to take his carriers up north to engage enemy forces in the Aleutians. The rendezvous was made as planned and the two carriers took on 34 replacement planes from *Saratoga*. But all hands were relieved when, early on 11 June, Cincpac suspected that Yamamoto was setting up a trap for our carriers south of Kiska and ordered the victorious Task Force 16 back to Pearl Harbor.[32]

On Midway Atoll the principal business on the days following the battle was repair and air-sea rescue. Commander Massie Hughes sent his Catalinas out on daily rescue missions, flying as low as 100 feet above the water in the cold front to the northwestward. In ten days they rescued 27 aviators who were floating on life rafts, including Lieutenant (jg) Gaylord Probst who had made the initial hit of the battle.[33]

Midway was the second of five great battles in the Pacific in which aircraft did all the hitting, with some assistance from submarines but none from ships' gunfire (except of course the antiaircraft batteries). Even more than Coral Sea it emphasized the vital rôle of carrier-borne air power in modern naval warfare. Yamamoto had to abandon his mission despite the possession of vastly superior gun power and without firing a shot, because Fletcher and Spruance, with one well-directed carrier thrust, had destroyed the Japanese air component while preserving most of

---

[32] Yamamoto was even attempting deception by plain-language simulation of a disabled battleship calling for help, to bait Spruance within reach.

[33] Story by Foster Hailey in *New York Times* 17 June 1942. From Pearl Harbor, early on 5 June, Admiral English ordered submarines *Narwhal*, *Plunger* and *Trigger* to comb the waters north and west of Midway, but their patrol reports mention no survivors.

their own. The tactical performance of the three American carrier air groups would have been considered ragged later in the war. Yet they had won, through courage, determination and the quick seizure of opportunities. The performance of land-based air, on the contrary, had been most disappointing, both in bombing and in searching. Two squadrons of well-trained scout planes based on Midway, engaged only in finding and tracking enemy ships, might have accomplished more for the cause than all the Army, Navy and Marine Corps bombers together.

Midway was a victory of intelligence, bravely and wisely applied. "Had we lacked early information of the Japanese movements, and had we been caught with carrier forces dispersed, . . . the Battle of Midway would have ended differently," commented Admiral Nimitz.[34] So, too, it might have ended differently but for the chance which gave Spruance command over two of the three flattops. Fletcher did well, but Spruance's performance was superb. "Lord of himself"[35] yet receptive to advice; keeping in his mind the picture of widely disparate forces yet boldly seizing every opening — Raymond A. Spruance emerged from this battle one of the greatest fighting and thinking admirals in American naval history.

The Japanese knew very well that they were beaten. "I felt bitter," remembered Nagumo's chief of staff; "I felt like swearing."[36] Before the ships reached home "Tokyo Rose" and other official broadcasters began making the usual claims that an incredible number of United States planes and ships had been shot down, sunk or damaged;[37] but these loud-speakers were soon muzzled, and word

[34] Cincpac Report 28 June 1942.

[35]   . . . *Ille potens sui*
          Laetusque deget, cui licet in diem
          Dixisse, Vixi. — HORACE *Odes* iii, 29

[36] Kusaka's statement appended to "Full Translation" (ATIS 16647 B).

[37] The diary of a man in the "Kure" landing force, 9 June, comments bitterly on the official communiqué, claiming the sinking of two American carriers and 135 planes, and admitting only the loss of one carrier, one cruiser and 35 planes. "What a big difference from what we know! . . . It is a great tragedy. . . . How and when can we take revenge?"

went out from Imperial Headquarters that Midway was taboo. It thrust the Japanese war lords back on their heels, caused their ambitious plans for the conquest of Fiji, New Caledonia and New Zealand to be canceled, and forced on them the unexpected and unwelcome rôle of the defensive.

Midway was the first really smashing defeat inflicted on the Japanese Navy in modern times. Yet there were two consolations for Yamamoto. The Japanese Fleet was intact, except for the carriers; and the Northern Area Force had occupied Kiska and Attu.[38]

[38] The manner in which the story of Midway was given out at Pearl Harbor and Washington, creating a first impression that all the damage on the enemy had been inflicted by B-17s and other land-based bombers, was very discouraging to naval aviators then, and to this day has not been wholly eradicated from the public mind. The first story, as we have seen (chap. vii footnote 12) was broadcast by a B-26 pilot. On 9 June the *N. Y. Times* ran an editorial to the effect that Midway showed "what land-based air power can do to naval and air power attacking from the open sea." On 12 June it ran a streamer headline, ARMY FLIERS BLASTED TWO FLEETS OFF MIDWAY, followed by a front-page dispatch from Robert Trumbull at Pearl Harbor, stating, "The Army fliers who actually dropped the bombs reported personally" hits on 3 carriers, 1 cruiser, 1 battleship or cruiser, 1 destroyer and 1 large transport. General Hale was also quoted as expressing his belief that the battle was primarily won by B-17s, and on page 9 is a play-by-play account of these mythical hits by Lt. Col. Sweeney, who concluded, "I am sold on the effectiveness of high-level bombing" of ships. Admiral Nimitz declined to allow any contradiction to be made, but on 12 June he permitted Cdr. Murr E. Arnold, air officer of *Yorktown*, to be interviewed about the Navy's part, and the *N. Y. Times* 13 June carried an article by Trumbull quoting him. Yet even then, Arnold did not know of the loss of *Hiryu* and modestly claimed for the Navy only a share in the damage. The A.A.F. pilots, of course, believed what they said, since it is almost impossible for a high-level bomber to distinguish between a hit and a near-miss.

CHAPTER IX

The Aleutians[1]

January–June 1942

West Longitude dates, Zone plus 10 time

1. Background and Preparations

ON A GLOBE the Aleutian chain resembles the Malay Barrier that the Japanese made such efforts to secure, but there the likeness stops; the Aleutians are one of the earth's poorest regions in natural resources. A Nisei translation of a Japanese Army report puts it neatly: "As for useful resources available such as food, there are only two or three types of birds, fox, marine animals and few seaweeds, besides the comparatively plentiful fishes." That is what the Aleuts live on, but few others can. All the islands are very mountainous, with no trees, few places level enough for an airfield and few harbors affording shelter to large ships. They are covered by tundra, a spongy mat of dead grass from one to four

---

[1] Aleutians operations through 12 June 1942 are included in *War College Analysis* of Midway. Admiral Theobald issued no overall Action Report but his War Diary is useful; those of N.A.S. Dutch Harbor and Patwing 4, more so. Vol. I of *Army Air Forces in World War II* deals with the A.A.F. adequately. For background I have depended on a manuscript "Preliminaries to Alaskan Campaign" prepared for this work by the former Commander Alaskan Sector, Capt. Ralph C. Parker, to whose conversations I am greatly indebted for sundry facts and slants. Japanese sources, besides those mentioned in chap. viii footnote 1, are the interrogation of Cdr. M. Okumiya of Admiral Kakuta's staff in *Inter. Jap. Off.* I 92, Desron 1 Action Report, translated by Central Intelligence Group, and two excellent reports compiled in 1946 by Japanese Army officers for General MacArthur; titles of the official translations are "First Demobilization Unit, 'Vol. XV Operations in Aleutian Islands,' Special Staff U. S. Army Historical Division, No. 851–90" (referred to here as Japanese Army Report); and Same, "Aleutian Islands Campaign – Operation Record," No. 851–50; but this contains few naval data.

Illustrations

Vice Admiral Frank Jack Fletcher

Rear Admiral Aubrey W. Fitch

Coral Sea — The Bombing and Sinking of Carrier Shoho

The Bombing of Shokaku

Lexington hit and abandoned; destroyer *Morris* alongside

The Loss of Lexington, Coral Sea

Lexington *Exploding and Burning*

Rear Admiral Raymond A. Spruance

Enterprise

Admiral Halsey and staff — identical with Admiral Spruance's at Midway

Front double row, left to right: Lt. Col. Julian P. Brown USMC, Lt. Cdr. S. E
Burroughs, Capt. Miles R. Browning (dark jacket), Lt. Cdr. G. E. Grigg
Admiral Halsey, Capt. B. Groesbeck, Cdr. W. H. Ashford, Cdr. W. H. Buracke

Enterprise and Flag Staff

A Marine Corps SB2U-3 (Vindicator)

Hornet

At Midway

Admiral Nagumo

From Jane's Fighting Ships

Cruiser *Ashigara*

Cruiser *New Orleans*

Fighting Ships

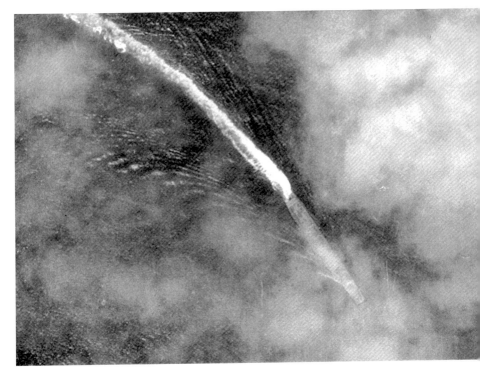

Akagi

Soryu

Air Bombing Attacks, 4 June

Mikuma *after Carrier Plane Attacks, Midway*

Yorktown *Hit and Abandoned*

Rear Admiral Robert A. Theobald and Chief of Staff,
Captain Frank G. Fahrion

Catalina on patrol

S.S. *Northwestern* on beach, Dutch Harbor

Aleutians

S–27

Cuttlefish

Submarines

Thresher

Gun crew

Submarines

A *Maru* sunk by *Guardfish*

A *Maru* sunk by *Seawolf*, Davao Gulf, Mindanao

Periscope Views from United States Submarines

The raiders on board *Nautilus*

Lieutenant Colonel Evans F. Carlson and Major James Roosevelt with Japanese flag captured at Makin

The Marine Corps and Nautilus *Raid on Makin*

Avengers over Espiritu Santo

Landing craft at Beach "Red," Guadalcanal

Cape Esperance and Savo Island

Florida Island; destroyer *Ellet* or *Wilson* passing

Views in Ironbottom Sound, 7 August 1942

Vice Admiral Robert L. Ghormley

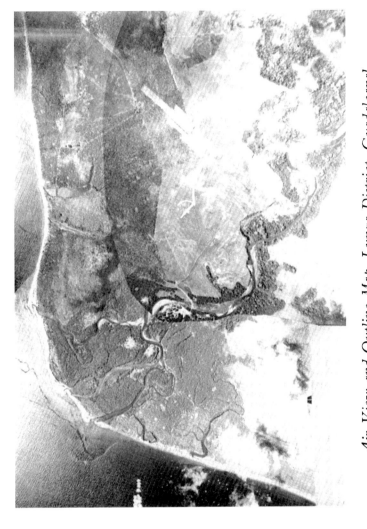

Air View and Outline Map, Lunga District, Guadalcanal

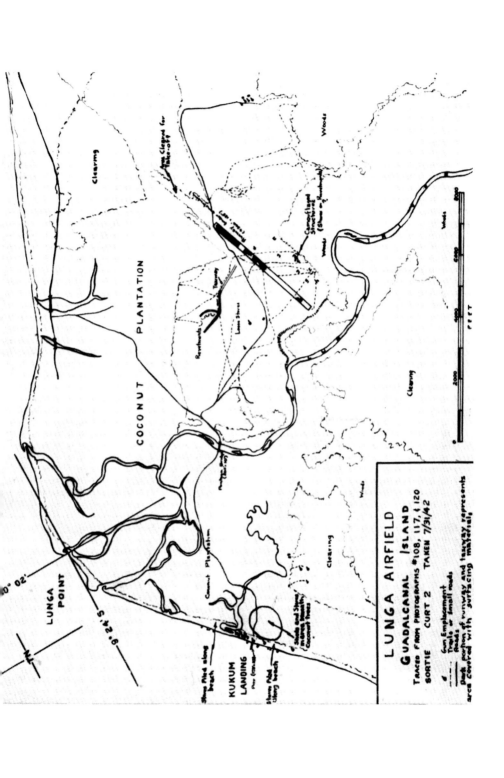

LUNGA AIRFIELD
GUADALCANAL ISLAND
TRACED FROM PHOTOGRAPHS #108, 117, & 120
SORTIE CURT 2   TAKEN 7/31/42

Gun Emplacement
Trails or small roads
Dark portion of runway and taxiway represents
area covered with surfacing material;

COCONUT PLANTATION

Clearing

LUNGA POINT

KUKUM LANDING

Woods

Clearing

Clearing

Woods

FEET
0   2000   4000   6000   8000

Rear Admiral McCain and Major General Vandegrift

Beach Blue →

1-A/A Reported

2-A/A Positions reported

Benzene and Kerosene stored along road

under constr

2-Heavy A/A po

Air View of Tulagi

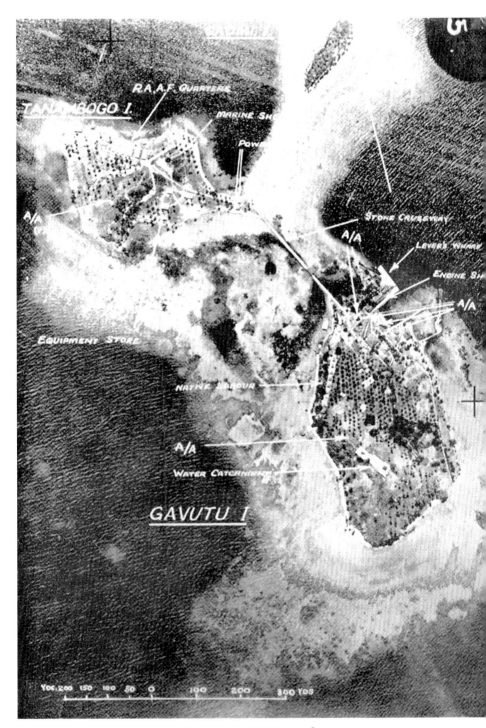

Gavutu and Tanambogo

Tulagi

Gavutu-Tanambogo

Air Views during the Attack, 7 August 1942

Japanese torpedo-bombers

Transport burning in background

Enemy Air Attack on Transports, 8 August 1942

feet thick, difficult to walk on and impossible to drive over; and under the tundra is a black volcanic ash that turns to mud when it rains, as it generally does. In 1941 the islands were uninhabited except for the Army and Navy establishments at Dutch Harbor and small Aleut settlements in that vicinity and on Atka and Attu.

Although operations in the Aleutians were something more than a sideshow to the Midway affair, they might be called the fifth and least important ring in Yamamoto's Greatest Show on Earth: the one where the less graceful acrobats, the not-quite-trained animals and the second-string clowns catered to the fifty-cent seats. Kiska, to be sure, was cast for a rôle in the new defensive perimeter against which the United States Navy was expected to beat out its brains; but Yamamoto would doubtless have traded the whole Aleutian chain, if he had it, for one little thousand-acre lot called Midway.

Naturally the President of the United States, the Joint Chiefs of Staff, Cominch and Cincpac could take no such frivolous view of the Aleutians. These islands belonged to Alaska Territory, and there is always a strong public sentiment against relinquishing a portion of one's "sacred soil," no matter how worthless, to the enemy. And on the globe the Aleutians looked like a natural Japanese invasion route to the United States, by the island-hopping technique so successful in the East Indies. The great-circle course from Tokyo to Seattle and San Francisco skirts their southern shores; Attu, westernmost of the chain, is only 650 miles from Paramushiro in the Kuriles where the enemy had a naval and air base. From Attu it is only 725 miles by air to Dutch Harbor, Unalaska, the westernmost United States base there before the war; and from Dutch Harbor to Juneau, the capital of Alaska, is but another 1158 miles by airline along the coast. Major prophets like Homer Lea and Billy Mitchell had long ago predicted that the Japanese would invade the United States that way, and the possibility could not be overlooked.

The Japanese did many foolish things during the war, but never, so far as we know, did they seriously contemplate anything so idiotic as invading the United States via the Aleutians — yet they thought we were foolish enough to try the reverse! The short distances that we have cited are less significant than the air distance from Attu to Japanese industrial centers — roughly 2000 miles — or from Paramushiro to the nearest American industrial center, Seattle — 3150 miles. Any invading force would have to be transported by air or sea; the Alaskan terrain precludes all possibility of motorized ground invasion. Ships and planes would have to cope with Aleutian weather, chronically unsettled and often bursting out in violent and unpredictable tempests — the famous williwaws, a major menace to navigation — owing to a continual conflict between the warm Japanese current and the bitterly cold air masses flowing down over the Bering Sea. Rain, snow, mist or a low, thick overcast may be expected 365 days a year in the Aleutians; flying weather is the exception rather than the rule; and about 1 June begins the foggy season when (says our Japanese informant) "activity of planes and warships are restrained considerably." But, he adds cheerfully, "There is no fear of icebergs."[2]

The same weather and terrain conditions made this invasion route equally unattractive to American strategists, although in the speculation of sundry amateurs it appeared to be the "natural" route for attacking Japan. Build a few bomber strips in the islands, send hundreds of Superfortresses every day to bomb Japanese industrial centers, and the war would be won. Eventually, when we developed an airfield at Attu, it became a useful base for attacking Paramushiro, pinning down Japanese forces in the Kuriles and keeping their high command guessing; but any large-scale bombing offensive along that line would have expended B–29s faster than they could be built.

General Buckner made a witty and true estimate of the possibility of a Japanese invasion of the United States by the Aleutians–Alaska route: "They might make it, but it would be their grand-

---

[2] Japanese Operation Record (see note 1), p. 20.

children who finally got there; and by then they would all be American citizens anyway!"

Yet, impracticable as this invasion route was, the United States Army and Navy could not afford to assume that the enemy was too intelligent to attempt it; nor could the Japanese war lords risk the chance that American air fanatics might prevail over sound strategic sense.

Five years before the war, Alaska was virtually undefended. In 1937 Rear Admiral Ernest J. King, then Commander Fleet Aircraft, obtained a few thousand dollars for the development of a seaplane base at Sitka. The Hepburn Board recommended an expenditure of nineteen millions to improve the Sitka base and to develop others for seaplanes and submarines on Kodiak (the large island southeast of the Alaskan Peninsula) and at Dutch Harbor at the eastern extremity of the Aleutians. Congress made the appropriation, the work began under civilian contractors, Seabees and Army engineers continued it throughout the war. By September 1941, Sitka, Kodiak and Dutch Harbor had been commissioned as naval air stations, and the last two were ready to service submarines. In the light of later events it would have been better to have started with Dutch Harbor and placed the other two bases well out on the Aleutians chain; but the Hepburn Board rejected this suggestion for the "good" reason that weather conditions would have made the building and maintenance of such far-flung bases unduly hazardous and expensive, and the unspoken but no less "real" reason that any such action would probably have been viewed by Japan as an invasion threat and touched off the war.

Naval efforts were supplemented by those of the Civil Aeronautics Authority and Army engineers who, in the face of many obstacles, built a series of staging fields north from Puget Sound, inland, and out to Cold Bay on the Alaskan Peninsula.[3] Finally, in the early months of 1942, Army engineers commanded by

---

[3] The others, south to north, were at Metlakahtla, Yakutat, Cordova, Naknek, Port Heiden and Sand Point.

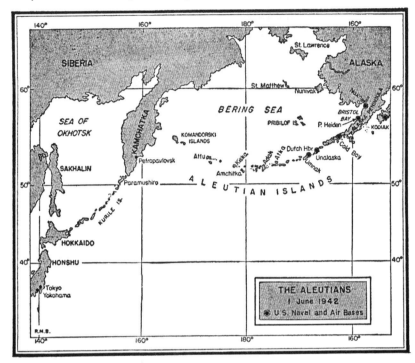

Colonel Benjamin B. Talley, overcoming unheard-of conditions with notable enterprise and energy, built a 5000-foot runway on Otter Point, the northern end of the island of Umnak, within supporting distance of Dutch Harbor. This airstrip was so unstable that fighter planes bounced thirty feet into the air on impact. Aviators said it was like landing on an inner-spring mattress, and every bomber that landed gave the field a sort of permanent wave.[4] The XI Army Air Force, commanded by Brigadier General William O. Butler, garrisoned these airfields. But only two Army aircraft-warning radar sets were in operation in the whole of Alaska.[5]

In mid-1940 the Army had established the Alaskan Defense Command under Brigadier General Simon Bolivar Buckner. The Navy followed suit by creating an Alaskan Sector under the 13th Naval

[4] *Army Air Forces in World War II* I 166–70, 303–8, 464 describes the difficulties of construction.
[5] Same, p. 308.

District whose headquarters were at Seattle, and appointing Captain Ralph C. Parker to the command. Gunboat *Charleston* was assigned to him as a headquarters-flagship. Three small fishing vessels were purchased, converted to patrol craft, as the nucleus of the "Alaskan Navy." These were controlled by a local character of infinite resource, energy and cunning — Commander Charles E. ("Squeaky") Anderson USNR. By May 1942 Captain Parker had under his command, in order to defend Alaska and its coastwise commerce from enemy submarines or whatever else they might send thither, two old destroyers, one 240-foot and two 165-foot Coast Guard cutters, a few more converted fishing vessels and ten Catalinas — one each at Dutch Harbor and Kodiak, the others farther south.[6] Flagship *Charleston* was the only one of these vessels equipped with sonar or with guns larger than 3-inch; both she and the cutters and destroyers were in constant use escorting freighters bringing construction workers and material to the new bases and airfields, none of which were complete.[7] The set-up offered unusual opportunities for enemy submarines; but, as if in answer to prayer, the big Japanese I-boats confined themselves to reconnaissance.[8]

Such was the situation — air base developments under way, and the most meager of ground force, air or naval protection to Alaska — when word reached Cincpac in early May that a thrust by the

[6] Capt. R. C. Parker to C.N.O. 1 June 1942; quoted from his "Preliminaries to Alaskan Campaign" pp. 22, 23.

[7] The Royal Canadian Navy Pacific Command, which included three 7000-ton auxiliary cruisers armed with 6-inch guns, seven 1170-ton corvettes, 12 minesweepers and numerous "Fairmiles" and other patrol craft, had about all it could do to patrol and convoy along the Canadian coast between Alaska and Washington; but it was in close communication with the Alaskan Sector Command and would have been brought into the defense picture in June if necessary. The same is true of the Royal Canadian Air Force, which was ready to move a considerable number of planes up to Kodiak if called upon.

[8] I believe that the following were the only submarine attacks on the West Coast during the first seven months of 1942, and their sinkings of merchant ships were few and far between: *I–17* fired about 20 shells in the general direction of an oil refinery near Ellwood, Cal., on 23 Feb. Another shelled a Canadian telegraph station on Estevan Pt., Vancouver I., on 20 June. The same or another sub shelled Ft. Stevens, Ore., about 25 miles south of the Columbia, on the 24th. *O.N.I. Weekly* 25 Feb. and 24 June 1942.

Japanese into Alaskan waters would form part of their Midway operation in early June. Admiral Nimitz reacted, as we have seen, by allocating five cruisers, fourteen destroyers, six submarines and suitable auxiliaries to deal with this northern menace, and by placing them, as well as Captain Parker's "Alaskan Navy," under the command of Rear Admiral Robert A. Theobald,[9] one of the most able and energetic flag officers in the Navy. Task Force 8 was activated 21 May 1942, but its components had to be collected from various parts of the Pacific and the main body, five cruisers and four destroyers, did not get together until a few hours after the Japanese first struck Dutch Harbor.

This is not to say that the Alaskan Sector was unprepared. Admiral Theobald was unable to reach Kodiak until 27 May; but Captain Parker and General Buckner had been alerted almost two weeks earlier and had done everything possible to send civilians and merchant shipping out and bring ships, planes and fighting men in. As Cincpac, on orders of the Joint Chiefs of Staff, had declared a state of "fleet opposed invasion" in the Alaskan Sector, Admiral Theobald commanded all defense forces, including the Army Air Force; but as a newcomer in Alaska he chose to assert his prerogative discreetly and to obtain Army coöperation by persuasion rather than command. In a four-day conference with General Butler, Captain Parker, Captain Gehres and other key officers, he worked out a task organization and an operation plan for his surface, submarine, tender-based naval air and Army air components. The details of the task organization will be found in the next section; suffice it here to mention the six principal groups, with what they were called upon to accomplish.

   1. *Main Body:* Five cruisers and four destroyers under Admiral

[9] Robert A. Theobald, born San Francisco 1884, graduated 9th in class of 1907 Naval Academy. First command, destroyer *Walke* in 1915. During World War I, gunnery officer of *New York*; 1924-27, head of the postgraduate school at Annapolis. After completing the senior course at the Naval War College he served in War Plans at Washington. Chief of staff Commander Destroyers Battle Force, 1932; C.O. *Nevada* 1937; chief of staff to Admiral Bloch 1939; two divisional commands with rank of Rear Admiral; Commander Destroyers Pacific Fleet, Dec. 1941.

Theobald's personal command. To patrol south of Kodiak and "exploit opportunities"; that is, look for a chance to fight.

2. *Surface Search Group:* The old "Alaskan Navy," largely composed of patrol craft. To act as pickets to signal the enemy's approach.

3. *Air Search Group:* Twenty Catalinas and one B–17 based on tenders at Cold Bay, Sand Point and Dutch Harbor. To fly daily searches, locate and track Japanese forces.

4. *Air Striking Group:* About 65 Army pursuit planes and 20 medium and heavy bombers, at Kodiak, Cold Bay and Umnak, together with reinforcements at Anchorage. To attack enemy ships when located.

5. *Destroyer Striking Group:* Nine destroyers stationed at Makushin Bay, Unalaska. To strike enemy forces approaching Dutch Harbor or Cold Bay.

6. *Submarine Group:* Six boats, disposed in the hope of intercepting the enemy.

This North Pacific Force (as Task Force 8 was subsequently designated) had much less information of enemy movements or intentions than had Fletcher and Spruance of what the Japanese were after farther south. Admiral Nimitz knew fairly accurately, and let Admiral Theobald know, the composition of the Second Mobile Force, whose first mission was to strike Dutch Harbor; and he suspected that one or more amphibious groups were moving up behind it. But he had no intelligence of where the carrier planes intended to strike, nor, until 28 May, of where the amphibious groups proposed to land. The general expectation was that the Second Mobile Force would beat up the three American bases at Umnak, Dutch Harbor and Cold Bay, after which ground forces would attempt to seize these bases or positions near them. What the ultimate intentions of the enemy were, in this quarter, nobody knew; possibly only to establish a sort of road block against the United States' using this northern route to attack Japan,[10] but

[10] In some quarters in Washington it was believed, despite Molotov's assurance in May that Russia had no such apprehension, that Japan intended shortly to de-

not improbably to seize vantage points for an invasion of the Canadian and American Northwest. Washington had not yet recovered from the "anything can happen now" feeling that followed Pearl Harbor. Many important people believed that there would be an invasion of or strike on the West Coast, rather than on Midway or the Aleutians. Consequently, hundreds of Army planes which might have been useful in the Aleutians were retained on West Coast fields.[11]

Now that Japanese sources are available, it becomes humorously evident that their globe-gazers, too, had been impressed with these deceptively short distances and that the Halsey-Doolittle raid on Tokyo had given Imperial Headquarters a bad case of the jitters. Yet, despite all the Japanese fishermen and sealers who infested Aleutian waters before the war, the enemy knew very little about Aleutian topography and still less of American activities there since the war's beginning.[12] The Japanese planners thought that Dutch Harbor was garrisoned by a whole army division instead of, as was the case, by 4748 troops and 639 bluejackets and Marines (including the aviation ground crews); that Kiska, where we had a total of ten unarmed men in a weather-reporting station, was defended by two or three hundred Marines; and that Attu, where Mr. and Mrs. Charles Jones ministered to the needs of a small Aleut village, supported "a wireless station, observatory and garrison unit of unknown strength." Enemy plane reconnaissance of these western islands was thwarted by weather; submarine reconnaissance of them and of Dutch Harbor was more successful but came too late to change the operation plan.[13] Imperial

---

clare war on Russia, and wanted Aleutian bases from which to break up lend-lease shipments by the West Coast — Vladivostok or Petropavlovsk route. See Vol. I of this History, p. 159; III pp. 36-7, 40, 48, 61.

[11] This expectation was furthered by the sightings of enemy submarines off the coast of British Columbia on May 4, 6, 8, 12 and 13, and off the Oregon coast on May 12, 14, 17 and 21; another was sighted 477 miles west of Columbia River mouth on the 31st. Northwestern Sea Frontier War Diary May 1942.

[12] "No true intelligence was available concerning the enemy's situation in the Aleutians." Japanese Army Report p. 2.

[13] *I-9* on the Western Is. 25/26 May; Dutch Harbor by *I-19* 28/29 May and Kodiak by *I-25* on 26/27 May (report in Desron 1 Action Report); *I-19* report

Headquarters had toyed with the idea of capturing Dutch Harbor — which was what many high-ranking Americans expected them to do — but decided against it because insufficient shipping was available; the main show of Midway and the multitude of other commitments in the South and Southwest took almost everything afloat that flew the Rising Sun.

However, Vice Admiral Hosogaya, who was given the command[14] and the responsibility, could deploy in the Aleutians fairly strong forces: —[16]

1. *Second Mobile Force:* Built around two light carriers, whose objective was to strike Dutch Harbor 3 June in order (*a*) to deceive Nimitz into the belief that the main Japanese attack was coming there and so deflect his forces from Midway; (*b*) destroy installations that might be intended for mounting an air invasion of Japan; (*c*) cover and support the two following: —

2. *Kiska Occupation Force:* 500 Special Naval Landing Troops and 700 or more construction men, to capture that island and make it the northern anchor of the new ribbon defense.

3. *Adak-Attu Occupation Force:* 1200 Army troops in two transports, the first to take Adak and the second, Attu; mainly in order to deny them to United States forces.

That was all. The Japanese had no intention of capturing anything east of Adak. They had no plan for invading the Alaskan mainland, Canada or the United States. The Aleutian section of the Midway operation, apart from its diversionary aspect, was essentially defensive. Its object was to prevent the United States' invading Japan. The high command even suspected that American invasion forces were already concentrating along the Seattle-Dutch Harbor axis. Accordingly, in May, there was a careful reconnaissance of these possible invasion ports by submarines. *I–26,*

caused Admiral Omori to suggest his force be switched to Dutch Harbor, but even *I–19* reported no airfield on Umnak.
[14] He was Commander Fifth Fleet (see Vol. III p. 26), entrusted with the defense of the Japanese Northern islands; but for this operation, in which the Fifth Fleet was augmented, he was designated Commander Northern Area Force.
[16] See next section for details.

a plane-carrying submarine, even steamed to the outer coast of the State of Washington where it launched a plane to reconnoiter Seattle. The plane reported, much to the relief of the high command, that no heavy ships were there.[16]

Cincpac staff finally smelt out these modest designs of the enemy on the Aleutians, and Nimitz so informed Theobald on 28 May, in a dispatch which said that his Intelligence believed that the Japanese Aleutian forces included one task group destined for Kiska and another which might well be for Attu. Theobald, however, feared that the information upon which this was based might be a ruse to draw him westward and get behind him. He still believed that the enemy would try to land somewhere between Umnak and Cold Bay in order to seize Dutch Harbor. The danger to us if he did was so much greater than any possible damage he could do in the Western Aleutians that the Admiral decided to deploy his Main Body in waters about 400 miles due south of Kodiak, whence he could defend the Eastern Aleutians and Alaska. After all, if a small and inadequate police force is warned of an impending bank robbery, but receives an eleventh-hour tip-off that the gang is only going to rifle a rural mailbox, it would be unwise to relax vigilance at the bank.

Admiral Theobald's situation was very difficult. He felt that he had not the force to cope with Admiral Kakuta's two carriers. Army planes could not follow him out to sea and provide air cover; the fat Navy Catalinas were suitable only for patrol and search. If Theobald should lead his Main Body boldly westward, seeking a gunfire engagement, he might wake up to find Kakuta between him and his base; or, if Kakuta decided to gratify him, it would only be after inflicting serious attrition by carrier-plane strikes. A night destroyer attack on Kakuta would be a farce because there is no night in 55° north latitude in June; but the nine destroyers based near Dutch Harbor should manage to break up an enemy landing. It all came down to this. Initial reliance had to be placed on the two air forces to perform the functions for which

---

[16] *Inter. Jap. Off.* I 93. I have seen no evidence that this plane was sighted.

they were designed — Navy Catalinas and Army pursuit planes to locate and track the enemy ships; and Army bombers to hit them. After that, Theobald might find an opportunity to use his guns.

The PBYs were well deployed when Theobald arrived at Kodiak — 12 of the 20 at Dutch Harbor — but the Army planes were not. General Butler, to the Admiral's consternation, proposed to base the bulk of them at Kodiak and Anchorage, and to leave unoccupied the two westernmost Army airfields (Cold Bay and Otter Point), because of their unfinished condition. Admiral Theobald, who has been described as having one of the best brains and worst dispositions in the Navy, exhibited at this crisis a sweet reasonableness that brought the Army Air Force around to his point of view. He persuaded the General to send sixty per cent of his planes to the two western bases where they could support the naval forces in the defense of Dutch Harbor. So, 21 P-40s and 14 bombers were flown up to Cold Bay; 12 P-40s to Otter Point, Umnak. These were radar-equipped, which made operation in fog practicable; but the pilots were not well trained in flying over water and they had no time to become familiar with Aleutian terrain and weather before being called upon to fight.

Daily overnight search flights were begun about 28 May from the three westernmost airfields and tenders to a distance of 400 miles, and from Kodiak to a distance of 700 miles. Admiral Theobald's effort to have more PBYs sent up from the West Coast were unavailing until 7 June, when the operation was practically over. The twenty small cutters and converted fishing vessels were to be deployed as picket ships both on the Pacific and Bering Sea approaches to Dutch Harbor, and our chart shows where they should have been on 3 June; but several were too far away to get there in time and others were too weak to hold station long enough to intercept the enemy. All these arrangements were worked out and decided by Admiral Theobald at Kodiak during the last four days of May.

On the First of June the Admiral departed Kodiak in cruiser *Nashville*, and made rendezvous with the rest of his Main Body, approaching from different angles, about 400 miles south of the Kodiak anchorage, at 0700 June 3. In view of his expectation of enemy landings near Dutch Harbor, this operating area was well chosen. Nevertheless, because he guessed wrong, this decision took the Main Body out of any possible action. And the rule of radio silence prevented the Admiral from directing his air and light surface groups except by making high-speed trips to Kodiak in his flagship.

Kakuta had already made his first air strike on Dutch Harbor before Theobald reached his rendezvous hundreds of miles to the eastward.

2. *Task Organizations*

a. Japanese [17]

NORTHERN AREA FORCE

Vice Admiral Boshiro Hosogaya (C. in C. Fifth Fleet) in *Nachi*

Heavy Cruiser NACHI; destroyers IKAZUCHI, INAZUMA
Supply Group: 3 Cargo Ships, Oilers FUJISAN MARU, * NISSAN MARU

  * Sunk 18 June by A.A.F. bombers.

SECOND MOBILE FORCE, Rear Admiral Kakuji Kakuta [18] (Comcardiv 4)

Light Carriers RYUJO (16 VF, 21 VT), JUNYO (22 VF, 10 VT, 21 VB)
Heavy Cruisers TAKAO, MAYA
Destroyers AKEBONO, USHIO, SAZANAMI; Oiler TEIYO MARU

ADAK-ATTU OCCUPATION FORCE, Rear Admiral Sentaro Omori
in CL *Abukuma*

Destroyers WAKABA, NENOHI, HATSUHARU, HATSUSHIMO
Transports MAGANE MARU and KINUGASA MARU carrying "Northern Sea" (Hokkaido) Army Detachment, 1200 men, Major M. Hozumi
Seaplane carrier KIMIKAWA MARU (6 float planes), destroyer SHIOKAZE, small minesweepers

KISKA OCCUPATION FORCE, Captain Takeji Ono

Light Cruisers KISO, TAMA; Auxiliary Cruiser ASAKA MARU
Destroyers HIBIKI, AKATSUKI, HOKAZE

---

[17] See also Midway Task Organization, this Volume, for the Aleutian Screening Force — which did not actually support the Aleutians operation.
[18] Surname incorrectly given in some translations as Tsunoda. Plane numbers from WDC Nos. 161,733 and 161,709 (latter for *Junyo* in July), which I believe to be more authentic than those in Japanese Army Report p. 17 and *Inter. Jap. Off.* I 93.

Transport HAKUSAN MARU carrying Maizuru Special Naval Landing Force, 550 men, Lt. Cdr. N. Mukai

Transport TAMAGAWA MARU carrying 700 labor troops and construction equipment

3 Subchasers; Minesweepers

PATROL AND RECONNAISSANCE GROUP
Rear Admiral Shigeaki Yamasaki

Submarines I-9, I-15, I-17, I-19, I-25, I-26

b. United States

TASK FORCE 8
Rear Admiral Robert A. Theobald [19] in *Nashville*

TG 8.6 MAIN BODY, Admiral Theobald

CA	INDIANAPOLIS	Capt. Edward W. Hanson
CA	LOUISVILLE	Capt. Elliott B. Nixon
CL	NASHVILLE	Capt. Francis S. Craven
CL	ST. LOUIS	Capt. George A. Rood
CL	HONOLULU	Capt. Harold Dodd

Desdiv 11, Commander Frederick Moosbrugger

GRIDLEY	Lt. Cdr. Fred R. Stickney
MCCALL	Lt. Cdr. William S. Veeder
GILMER	Lt. Cdr. Herman O. Parish
HUMPHREYS	Lt. Cdr. John K. Wells

TG 8.1 AIR SEARCH GROUP, Captain Leslie E. Gehres [20]

20 PBY of Patwing 4, and one B-17 of A.A.F., based on tenders:

WILLIAMSON	Lt. Cdr. Frederick N. Kivette, at Sand Point
GILLIS	Lt. Cdr. Norman F. Garton, at Dutch Harbor
CASCO	Cdr. Thomas S. Combs, at Cold Bay

TG 8.2 SURFACE SEARCH OR SCOUTING GROUP
Captain Ralph C. Parker, at Kodiak

Gunboat CHARLESTON	Cdr. Gordon B. Sherwood
Oiler ORIOLE	Lt. Cdr. Mellish M. Lindsay Jr.

14 YPs and 5 Coast Guard Cutters:

HAIDA	Cdr. Norman H. Leslie USCG
ONONDAGA	Lt. Cdr. Stewart P. Mehlman USCG
CYANE	Lt. Cdr. Leslie B. Tollaksen USCG
AURORA	Lt. (jg) Frank M. McCabe USCG
BONHAM	Lt. (jg) William C. Gill USCG

[19] Later called North Pacific Force. Admiral Theobald's Op Plan 1-42, May 27; other sources for air components.

[20] Also 3 VSO, 1 B-17 and 2 LB-30 at Kodiak. The LB-30 was a B-24 built to British Specifications.

TG 8.3 AIR STRIKING GROUP, Brigadier General William O. Butler USA

	Initial Deployment [21]	*At Close of 4 June*
At Ft. Randall, Cold Bay	21 P-40, 12 B-26, 2 B-18	25 P-40, 12 B-26, 5 B-17, 1 LB-30
At Ft. Glenn, Umnak	12 P-40	7 P-40, 8 B-26
At Kodiak	15 P-39, 17 P-40, 5 B-17, 2 LB-30	?
At Anchorage	25 P-38, 15 P-39, 4 P-36, 7 B-17, 5 B-18, 12 B-26, 2 LB-30	?

TG 8.4 DESTROYER STRIKING GROUP, Commander Wyatt Craig
(Comdesdiv 6)

CASE	Cdr. Robert W. Bedilion
REID	Cdr. Harold F. Pullen
BROOKS	Lt. Cdr. Charles T. Singleton Jr.
SANDS	Lt. Cdr. John T. Bowers Jr.
KANE	Lt. Cdr. John J. Greytak
DENT	Lt. Cdr. Paul H. Tobelman
TALBOT	Lt. Cdr. Edward A. McFall
KING	Lt. Cdr. Kenneth M. Gentry
WATERS	Lt. Cdr. Henry J. Armstrong

TG 8.5 SUBMARINE GROUP, Commander Burton G. Lake

S-18	Lt. James H. Newsome
S-23	Lt. Harold E. Duryea
S-27	Lt. Herbert L. Jukes
S-28	Lt. John D. Crowley
S-34	Lt. Cdr. Thomas L. Wogan
S-35	Lt. James E. Stevens

TG 8.9 TANKER GROUP, Captain Houston L. Maples

AO SABINE	Capt. Maples
AO BRAZOS [22]	Cdr. Thomas J. Kelly
S.S. *Comet*	Irvin E. Larkin, master

Naval Air Station Commanders, under Captain Parker

Commander William N. Updegraff, Dutch Harbor
Commander John Perry, Kodiak
Commander Jackson R. Tate, Sitka

---

[21] For deployment of fields more remote from the action see *Army Air Forces World War II* I 464–5. There was one fighter squadron and one reconnaissance squadron of the Royal Canadian Air Force at Yakutat. 4 June figures for Kodiak and Anchorage are not available.

[22] Sent from Seattle to supply oil, ammunition, torpedoes and blood plasma to the Alaskan Sector. It was this supply of fuel oil, 22,000 barrels delivered to the four new tanks at Dutch Harbor, that was destroyed on 4 June.

3. *Strikes on Dutch Harbor, 3–4 June* [23]

The Japanese Northern Area Force, consisting of the old Fifth Fleet reinforced by every ship that Admiral Hosogaya could beg or borrow from Yamamoto,[24] was organized at Ominato, the naval base on the northern bight of Honshu. The two amphibious forces were trained and rehearsed on Mutsukai Bay and the near-by shores of Hokkaido. Admiral Kakuta's carrier force left first on 25 May and steered due east; the Kiska force sortied next, on the 27th, but refueled at Paramushiro in the Kuriles before heading for its destination; the more formidable Adak-Attu force left a day later and steamed very slowly, in order to keep roughly parallel to the Kiska invaders.[25] The Commander in Chief, Admiral Hosogaya in *Nachi*, accompanied a supply unit that proceeded from Ominato to Paramushiro, departed thence 2 June and made for a fueling rendezvous and stand-by area south of the Western Aleutians. Planes, patrol craft and flying boats were readied at Paramushiro to be rushed into Kiska after the landing.[26]

During the small hours of 3 June, under a fog-dimmed summer twilight, Admiral Kakuta's Second Mobile Force — two light carriers, two heavy cruisers and a destroyer screen — made its fast run-in toward Dutch Harbor. By good luck, aided by Aleutian weather, Kakuta eluded the search planes that had been out all night looking for him, and also penetrated the line of picket boats without being detected. His launching position, 165 miles south of Dutch Harbor,[27] was reached around 0250. But, by the same

[23] The data for this attack given in *Army Air Forces World War II* I 462–70 have been corrected from the Japanese Army Report, which shows that the A.A.F. did rather better than its historians estimated.

[24] He expected two more CAs and another carrier division that had participated in the Ceylon strikes, but they could not be got ready in time, and the destroyers in Kakuta's force arrived from the Coral Sea only the day before his sortie. Army Report p. 13.

[25] See chart.

[26] Army Report, p. 14; "Record of Activities Jap Cruisers" (WDC No. 160, 623).

[27] *War College Analysis* p. 23, quoting *Ryujo* Action Report (WDC No. 161, 733).

token, the Japanese carrier planes had difficulty with their navigation. Many straggled and *Junyo's* attack group turned back halfway to the target. *Ryujo's*, which got through — nine bombers and three fighter planes — found fine weather with a 10,000-foot cloud ceiling over Dutch Harbor.

The radar of seaplane tender *Gillis* detected their approach at 0540. She and the other ships present [28] went to general quarters and made haste to get underway and stand out to sea, but none were able to clear the harbor until the attack was over. Owing to fair weather over Dutch Harbor, *Ryujo* planes had no difficulty in finding targets — the tank farm, radio station, Army barracks at Fort Mears, and moored Catalinas. In a period of twenty minutes, starting shortly after 0807, they inflicted considerable damage and killed about 25 soldiers and sailors, but lost one of their number [29] to anti-aircraft fire which they described as "powerful."

One of the attacking planes sighted five destroyers of Commander Craig's Striking Group in Makushin Bay and radioed the information to Admiral Kakuta. This gave the Admiral a new target for the second strike, launched about 0900. Weather now favored the defense and not one plane found the destroyers at Makushin Bay. Moreover, one group had an unpleasant surprise when it flew over Otter Point, Umnak. Two Army P-40s attacked, shot down two Japanese planes and damaged two more irreparably. The new Otter Point airfield was concealed by overcast, and Kakuta's intelligence officers could not imagine where they were based.

Carriers and cruisers closed to a distance of 130 miles south of Dutch Harbor to recover, and around noon commenced retirement on a southwesterly course. As yet only one American plane, a PBY, had sighted them, although many had been searching assiduously; and the PBY contact report, made on 2 June, was

[28] *Talbot, S-27,* U.S.C.G.C. *Onondaga,* Army transports *President Fillmore* and *Morlen. King* Action Report.
[29] Claimed by *Gillis,* but other ships and Army shore installations were firing too. *Fillmore* brought into action a battery of 37-mm guns on her deck. Japanese credit ground fire. A bomber was lost at take-off.

inaccurate.[30] Captain Gehres, commander of the naval planes at Dutch Harbor, believed that the carriers were operating in the Bering Sea.[31]

Admiral Theobald's Main Body in the meantime was about 500 miles SSE of Kakuta's position. The Admiral was becoming more and more restive and angry. He was receiving radio news, most of it bad; but the rule of radio silence precluded his giving any orders outside visual signaling distance. The enemy had two strikes on him, yet nobody could find the enemy. During the evening of 4 June, after receiving word of the second day's strike on Dutch Harbor, he could stand it no longer, peeled off from his Main Body in *Nashville* and headed for Kodiak.[32]

Admiral Kakuta fueled his destroyers during the night and changed course for Adak, which Yamamoto had ordered him to soften up. Day brought a fog mull so thick that he had to cut speed to 9 knots. His meteorologists predicted worse weather to the westward, but promised good visibility over Dutch Harbor. So the Admiral decided to cancel the Adak strike and pay a second visit to Dutch Harbor. Thick weather again enabled him to elude all search planes and picket boats. At 1600 June 4, *Ryujo* and *Junyo* commenced launching an attack group of eleven dive-bombers, six "Kates" for high-level bombing, and 15 fighters. During their absence the Second Mobile Force was at last detected by American search planes, and several Army bombers were sent out to grope for it in the fog and mist. They found the carriers but got nothing better than near-misses; a B-26 and a B-17 were shot down. The Japanese carrier planes, moreover, enjoyed their previous good luck in finding fair weather over the target. Four new 6,666-barrel fuel tanks and their contents were destroyed, one wing of the hospital was demolished, an uncompleted hangar damaged, the beached barracks ship *Northwestern* partially destroyed, and

---

[30] *Army Air Forces World War II* I 466.

[31] *War College Analysis* p. 196, quoting Patwing 4 War Diary.

[32] *Nashville* arrived Kodiak at 0531 June 5 and left at 1606 same day, rejoining the Main Body at sea at 0700 June 6.

the death list raised to 43.[33] But only repeated bombings could have knocked out Dutch Harbor as an operating base, and this was the last.

Before returning to their carrier, the *Junyo* pilots rendezvoused over the western cape of Unalaska, whence their startled gaze beheld the new landing field at Otter Point, Umnak. This was the first that any Japanese knew of an American airfield in the Aleutians. Eight of Major John Chennault's P-40s, based there, shot down three planes from *Junyo*.[34] But by the end of this day the Navy had lost six of its 20 PBYs and the A.A.F. contingent was minus three bombers and two P-40s.

More disturbing to Admiral Kakuta than the discovery of the Umnak airfield were the radio dispatches he received from Admiral Yamamoto while his planes were still in the air. In quick succession, around 1600, Kakuta's force was ordered south to rendezvous with Nagumo, and the occupation of the Western Aleutians as well as of Midway was "temporarily postponed." [35] It was not difficult for Kakuta to infer that Nagumo had taken a beating off Midway and wanted his light carriers. At the same time Yamamoto ordered the powerful Aleutian Screening Force,[36] which had been detached 3 June to support Kakuta, back to his Main Body.

Yamamoto's vacillation did not last long. At 1930 June 4, less than four hours after the "temporarily postponed" order, he informed Commander Northern Area Force by radio that the occupation of the Western Aleutians must go on as planned.[37] The

[33] O.N.I. Narrative *Aleutians Campaign* pp. 7–8, and *War College Analysis* p. 368 quoting N.A.S. Dutch Harbor Action Report 6 July 1942.

[34] Two bombers and 1 "Zeke"; 2 more bombers were lost on the return flight. *Ryujo* lost only one fighter plane.

[35] These are C. in C. Combined Fleet's dispatch op. orders Nos. 115, sent at 1420, and 156, sent at 1510 (plus 10 time) *O.N.I. Review* May 1947 pp. 26, 27. The designator for "Aleutians" is there wrongly translated "Kiska."

[36] See Midway Task Organization for composition of this force.

[37] *O.N.I. Review* May 1947 p. 33, No. 157. The Army Report on the Aleutians states that the orders first to cancel and then to go on with Kiska and Attu came from Imperial Headquarters and were only relayed by Yamamoto. The record in *O.N.I. Review* does not bear this out. It is puzzling to find in Desron 1 Action Report a "postpone temporarily" despatch from Hosogaya at 1810 June 5 (plus 10 time) countermanded at 0210 June 6.

Kiska and Adak-Attu occupation forces, which had cheerfully turned back toward Japan after a week of very rough, foul and "bitterly cold" weather,[38] now reversed course. And before Kakuta had gone more than halfway to the southern rendezvous he too was turned around; at 1500 June 5 Second Mobile Force was ordered "returned to the Northern Force."[39] For, even though the big game off Midway had been lost, there was no reason why the junior team up north should not win a consolation prize.

Instead of going north again Kakuta's force, to the great relief of its members, was directed to a "stand-by area" some 600 miles SSW of Kiska, where it rendezvoused with Admiral Hosogaya in *Nachi*. With the Northern Area Force commander was an oiler group, and some of the capital ships originally destined for Midway were transferred to his command by Yamamoto in the expectation that a United States force might come that way.[40] Although Hosogaya's Northern Area Force had become far stronger than heretofore, it was now as much out of the picture as Theobald's Main Body. Kakuta was ordered to move north on 12 June to try to intercept American planes attacking Kiska, but Aleutian weather muffled both ships and planes. And a few days later all Japanese forces retired.

The American sailors would have been very much pleased to have had this information. Patrol planes out of Dutch Harbor were being run ragged. Captain Parker, who represented Admiral Theobald ashore, sent a dispatch on 7 June to Admiral Nimitz that continuous operation of the Catalinas was resulting in losses "without being followed by successful attacks and compensating damage to the enemy" who appeared to be operating "with impunity" both in and out of bombing range. He believed that the islands were in grave danger unless more planes, whether land-based or

---

[38] Japanese Operation Record (see chap. ix footnote 1) p. 19.

[39] *O.N.I. Review* May 1947 p. 42.

[40] Battleships *Kongo* and *Hiei*, light carrier *Zuiho*, heavy cruisers *Tone* and *Chikuma*, were the principal ships so detached, and on 12/13 June Hosogaya was also sent CV *Zuikaku* and CAs *Myoko* and *Haguro*. The dispatch is in Desron 1 Report p. 23.

carrier-based, were sent up immediately. This dispatch produced a prompt reinforcement of the air forces in the Aleutians,[41] but not in time to affect the result.

4. *Occupation of Attu and Kiska, 7–14 June*

The discovery by *Junyo* pilots of the new Otter Point airfield on Umnak may have had some influence on Japanese movements, although not nearly so much as most Americans supposed at the time. Several popular commentators, assuming that the enemy intended to take Dutch Harbor and proceed to the Alaskan mainland, credited the Umnak-based P–40s with frustrating the entire operation. A writer in *Reader's Digest* even declared that "by that slim chance we saved Alaska"; that but for the P–40s, the Japanese would have been "running Alaska from the governor's house in Juneau," by 1943.[42]

That comforting theory was excellent for the morale of the Army Air Force in the Aleutians, which, not for want of gallantry or zeal but for lack of appropriate training and fair weather, made not a single hit on an enemy ship during the nine days of the campaign. But it had no basis in fact. Admiral Hosogaya, who was responsible for the decision to give up taking Adak, may have thought that Umnak was too close — 350 miles — to Adak for safety. Since, in any event, Adak was only to be occupied by an advance detachment in the smaller transport,[43] and a possible cancellation had been anticipated in Hosogaya's operation plan, this change was unimportant.

Rear Admiral Omori, commander of the Adak-Attu Occupation Force, was ordered by Hosogaya early on 5 June, when about 225

---

[41] Besides Army planes, 12 F4Fs were flown up from escort carrier *Copahee* at Seattle to Kodiak.
[42] W. Clemens "Report on the Aleutians," *Reader's Digest* March 1943 p. 96. Another current view of copy-room strategists was that the Japanese, balked at Midway, had occupied Kiska to "save face."
[43] "Aleutians Campaign Fuel Sheet" in captured *Nachi* documents makes this clear.

miles southwest of Adak, to turn back and proceed to Attu. That he did, and landed his 1200 troops on the morning of 7 June, after some unnecessary minesweeping and a beach reconnaissance at dawn in thick fog. They landed on Holtz Bay and marched overland through snow to Chichagof. The main part of the detachment got lost and made Massacre Bay by mistake. Although the Japanese blamed this on poor maps,[44] their performance was lamentable; a few hundred Marines could have thrown them back easily. Chichagof was "assaulted" and the entire population – 39 Aleuts (15 of them children) and Mr. and Mrs. Jones – was taken prisoner.[45] According to the Japanese, their transports when unloading in the morning of 8 June were attacked without success by a United States submarine.[46] Unloading of all equipment was completed on the 10th.

The Kiska Occupation Force, augmented by a seaplane carrier and destroyer from Omori's group, proceeded according to plan. That landing, too, was made on 7 June without opposition from the ten members of the temporary United States weather station. This was not the last time that a fully equipped amphibious force landed on Kiska and found no enemy to fight.

Kiska, as we have seen, was to have been the northern anchor of the new defense chain. Lacking Midway, it was now useless for that purpose. The high command nevertheless decided to keep Kiska and develop it as an air base, partly as a block to invasion, partly for nuisance and morale value. The Japanese people, who heard few facts about Midway, were gratified to learn that the Rising Sun was flying over two more American islands; and, by the same token, the occupation of Kiska and Attu took some of the relish out of the news of Midway in the United States.

The American planes based at Umnak, Dutch Harbor and Cold Bay lost touch with Kakuta's force after its retirement on 4 June.

[44] Japanese Operation Record p. 21; dispatch of 7/8 June from Maj. Hozumi to Admiral Omori, in Desron 1 Action Report.
[45] Mrs. Jones's story of mistreatment by her captors was printed in *Honolulu Star Bulletin*, and other papers, 12 Sept. 1945.
[46] Army Report, p. 22.

Persistent efforts were made during the next few days to regain contact, but the Japanese ships were no longer within air range. Early
on 5 June a completely false contact report by a patrol plane misled everyone on the American side. Two large carriers, two heavy
cruisers and three destroyers were reported to be steaming toward
Dutch Harbor from a point in the Bering Sea.[47] Every available
plane was sent out to search and attack, but without result; no
wonder, since no such force existed outside the pilot's imagination.
This false contact was doubly unfortunate because Admiral Theobald, already beginning to suspect the truth — that the Dutch Harbor strikes had been diversionary and that no landing in that area
was intended [48] — now felt that his earlier estimate of enemy intentions was confirmed. This was it! Admiral Nimitz, too, was affected
by the false contact report into making the plan we have already
noted to send *Enterprise* and *Hornet* to rendezvous with *Saratoga*,
take on replacement planes and proceed north to engage the Japanese carriers. Admiral Theobald came ashore again at Kodiak early
on June 8 to confer with his group commanders and make plans
for the destruction of both Kakuta's force and the hypothetical
one. He then returned to his usual operating area south of Kodiak
where, on the 10th, he learned that *Enterprise* and *Hornet* were
not coming north after all, and that the enemy had occupied Kiska
and Attu. Words fail us (though they did not fail the Admiral)
for expressing the exasperation that he felt at this juncture. Now
convinced that he could not control events from a ship at sea, he
came ashore for keeps a few days later, setting up his headquarters
at Kodiak.

Captain Gehres at Dutch Harbor, fearing the worst when reports from American weather observers in Kiska and Attu ceased
to come in on 8 and 9 June, moved tender *Gillis* up to Atka Island,
halfway to Kiska, in order to place his patrol planes within shorter
range of the western islands.[49] On the afternoon of the 10th, one of

---

[47] Position lat. 53°20′ N, long. 173°10′ W. *War College Analysis* pp. 198, 205–06.
[48] Dispatch of 1627 June 5 to Cominch and Cincpac, in War Diary.
[49] B–17s had been searching the Kiska area daily since 5 or 6 June but had
flown so high that they observed no enemy activity whatsoever.

his Catalinas reported four ships in Kiska Harbor and a tent colony on Attu. This was the first news received on the American side of the Japanese landings that had taken place three days earlier.

Admiral Nimitz, promptly notified, ordered the submarine group, which as yet had made no significant contacts, to move into the Western Aleutians, and ordered Captain Gehres to bomb the Japanese out of Kiska. For forty-eight hours, beginning 11 June, the PBYs did their best. They used tender *Gillis* at Nazan Bay, Atka, as a staging point and worked their crews to the point of exhaustion. General Butler's heavy Army bombers based at Cold Bay staged through Otter Point and attacked too, but none of these strikes had any deterrent effects on enemy activities in Kiska. On the contrary, they stimulated a counterattack on Gazan Bay, 14 June, by the Japanese flying boats that had been moved from Paramushiro to Kiska. Captain Gehres, warned in time by Intelligence, pulled *Gillis* out before the planes came in.[50]

Thus, the Aleutians part of the great Midway operation may be said to have ended in mid-June with a minor Japanese victory, the occupation of two islands of little except nuisance value. A new phase may be said to have begun on 11 June; the Japanese trying to hold what they had,[51] and the Americans trying to blast them out. And in this new phase, which we shall deal with later, the Army Air Force drew first blood, bombing and sinking transport *Nissan Maru* off Kiska on 18 June.[52]

The Aleutians battle, like Midway, was a contest of air power, in which weather consistently aided the offensive by shrouding ships in a protective mist, while sweeping land targets clear. One naturally speculates what might have happened if Admiral Theobald had believed the Intelligence report received on 28 May, which gave the real Japanese objectives, and if he had moved

---

[50] Destroyer *Hulbert*, sent up from Cold Bay to support *Gillis*, evacuated the 62 Aleut inhabitants of Atka.

[51] "Attu and Kiska shall be securely occupied, and the capture of Adak shall not be carried out." Order No. 106 of Naval General Staff, 23 June 1942, quoted in Army Report p. 23.

[52] JANAC p. 32; Japanese Army Report p. 27. For the U. S. submarine offensive of the summer, see pp. 215–19, below.

west. The outcome of a battle between his cruiser force, supported only by land-based air, and Kakuta's carrier and cruiser force would have been largely a matter of luck, depending on the weather. If land-based planes could have neutralized *Junyo* and *Ryujo*, Theobald's superior gunpower might have won; but, considering that during the entire course of the war no Japanese carrier (so far as I can discover) was hit by a PBY, a B–26 or a B–17, the chance of such a hit in the Alaskan weather of June 1942 was negligible. It was probably fortunate that Theobald operated well out of harm's way and that his five cruisers were saved for distinguished fighting careers later in the war. It is certainly fortunate that Admiral Nimitz recalled *Enterprise* and *Hornet* instead of sending them westward; for by 12 June Hosogaya, operating south of Kiska, had been reinforced by the big carrier *Zuikaku*, light carrier *Zuiho*, two battleships and four heavy cruisers. That deployment was Yamamoto's last effort to trap Spruance and reverse the fortunes of Midway.

Admiral Theobald, however, deserved a better fate than to have his reputation smothered in northern mists.

PART II
Submarine Actions

CHAPTER X

Submarine Patrols[1]

1 April 1942–8 February 1943

Dates and times are those of the Zone in which
the boat was operating.

1. *The Silent Service*

a. American Submarines

MECHANICALLY-minded Americans early conceived the
idea of a ship traveling under the water. In the nation's
infancy Bushnell and Fulton produced workable submarine boats,[2]
and during the Civil War various submersible contraptions were
used by both sides. The invention of the diesel engine and the
storage battery enabled inventors Holland and Lake, with Navy
encouragement, to transform the submarine from the experimental gadget of a weak sea power to the practical weapon of a major

---

[1] Our principal sources are the submarine commanding officers' Patrol Reports,
which in general are more detailed and carefully prepared than the Action Reports
of surface ships. Two ms. compilations have been consulted: the "Submarine
Operational History World War II" prepared under the direction of Comsubpac's
operations officer, Capt. Richard G. Voge; and "Submarine Commands" in the
Administrative Series prepared by the Office of Naval History. A number of personal interviews also are on file in the Office of Naval Records. For statistics
compiled at the end of the war, JANAC and Comsubpac's *U. S. Submarine Losses
World War II* have been relied upon. Capt. J. H. Willingham Jr. read the first
draft and offered many valuable suggestions. Rear Admiral R. W. Christie resolved several questions which could not be answered from the records. This
Part has been extended to include submarine patrols and actions in the Pacific
until 8 Feb. 1943, the conclusion of the Guadalcanal campaign.

[2] It is probably because the original submarines were boat-size that American
submariners have always referred to their vessels, even when they have attained
tonnages close to 3000, as "boats."

sea power. Despite an uninspiring record in World War I, when not a single sinking was credited to an American submarine, the United States Navy went right on experimenting and building, confident that undersea warships would be wanted if the nation ever went to war again.[3]

By 7 December 1941 there were 55 large and 18 medium-sized submarines in the Asiatic and Pacific Fleets, out of a total of 111 in the entire Navy; not counting 73 under construction. These were to be one of the most decisive weapons of the Pacific war. Nearly one third of all Japanese combat ships destroyed were their victims, and no less than 63 per cent of Japanese merchant tonnage sunk was accounted for by the American underseas boats. As the "silent service" operated under conditions of highest secrecy, few stories of its exploits were given out and no correspondent was taken to sea before 1945. This policy of secrecy was both wise and necessary; the contrary German policy of publicizing U-boats hurt them in the end. But to this day secrecy has deprived American submariners of the credit they deserve.

During the first four months of the war, as we have described in the previous volume, these ships fought doggedly under great handicaps against a confident and aggressive enemy. The Asiatic submarine bases with invaluable supplies and spare parts were lost. Intelligence of enemy ship movements was scant. Too many torpedoes proved to be duds. Prewar doctrines emphasized caution. Beleaguered garrisons demanded messenger-boy missions far from fruitful hunting grounds. Skippers were untried in combat, and the less skillful and aggressive were not yet weeded out. Although Japanese shipping sunk by American submarines up to 1 April 1942 ran up to a respectable 300,000 tons, that was only a quarter of what the war-wise Germans bagged during the same period.

---

[3] Lt. Chester W. Nimitz wrote prophetically in 1912: "The steady development of the torpedo together with the gradual improvement in the size, motive power, and speed of submarine craft of the near future will result in a most dangerous offensive weapon, and one which will have a large part in deciding fleet actions." *U. S. Naval Inst. Proceedings* Dec. 1912 p. 1198. But even Nimitz did not foresee the value of the submarine for destroying the enemy's merchant shipping.

It was rough going, but those who knew the American submariner were not surprised at the rapidity with which the silent service shook itself down. For the submarine people made up for the lack of battle traditions by a rigorous selection of volunteers who were molded into a skillful and enthusiastic corps. The promise of an early independent command attracted some of the more ambitious and intelligent young officers, and the probability of rapid promotion, excellent educational opportunities and higher pay drew the cream of enlisted men.[4] The fact that this service was both small and select made it, even more than naval aviation and the Marines, a *corps d'élite*.

Command of the submarine force was vested in a rear admiral, who exercised full administrative control, but only a limited operational control, over his boats. Submarines were assigned to squadrons and divisions on the basis of locale and type. In the early days of the war Admiral Nimitz preferred to direct submarine movements himself, but after the Battle of Midway he gradually released control of the submarines to Commander Submarine Force Pacific, with whom he still kept close liaison.

The United States was a signatory of the London Naval Treaty of 1930, in which Article 22 forbade submarines to sink merchant vessels "without having first placed passengers, crew and ship's papers in a place of safety." [5] Since that proviso made the use of submarines against armed or escorted merchant vessels impractical, and since it was assumed that Japan would arm and escort her merchant fleet in case of war, American submariners were not trained to attack merchant ships. The United States Fleet's basic doctrine was: "The primary task of the submarine is to attack enemy heavy ships. A heavy ship is defined as a battleship, a battle cruiser, or an aircraft carrier. On occasions, the primary task may, by special order, be made to include heavy cruisers,

---

[4] Before the war, officers and men actually serving in a submarine received a bonus for "extra-hazardous duty." During the war their pay, like that of aviators, was 50 per cent more than that of corresponding ranks and ratings in surface ships and on shore duty.

[5] See Vol. I of this History p. 8.

light cruisers or other types of ships." [6] Treaty and doctrine alike went by the board on the first day of the war, when the Chief of Naval Operations issued the terse order, "Execute unrestricted submarine and air warfare against Japan." The enemy, by his calculated breach of treaties and international law at Pearl Harbor, had absolved the United States from observing any rule restricting methods of naval warfare unless dictated by self-interest or the danger of retaliation. After 7 December 1941 combatant ships were still considered prime targets, but the employment of submarines to lance the arteries of enemy trade now became of major importance.

The American concept of submarines, dictated by our few and far-between bases, required that they be capable of self-sustained cruising for long periods over great distances. The building program followed these lines, so that the Navy entered the war with a preponderance of large fleet-type submarines, undersea vessels of endurance, reliability and relative comfort compared with the smaller types favored by European powers. These rugged vessels displaced in the neighborhood of 1500 tons. Variations from this mean tonnage were the smaller S-boats of 800 to 1100 tons and *Argonaut, Narwhal* and *Nautilus*, which ran up to 2700 tons' displacement. The S-boats, distinguished by numbers instead of names, and most of them old enough to vote in 1941, lacked the sea-keeping qualities of the big fleet subs. The big 2700-tonners often doubled as minelayers and troop transports.

The average fleet-type submarine was manned by a crew of 7 officers and 70 men. It had a cruising range of 10,000 miles and carried supplies for 60 days. Surface speed was 20 knots; submerged speed 9 knots. Underwater endurance at 2½ knots was 48 hours but if the boat lay on the bottom it could stay down much longer. Power on the surface was derived from a diesel-electric engine and motor combination, while storage batteries furnished juice to the electric motors when submerged.

---

[6] Comsubforce "Current Doctrine Submarines" 1939.

Armament at this period consisted of six to ten 21-inch torpedo tubes, one 3-inch 50-caliber deck gun and two .50-caliber machine guns. Some 18 spare torpedoes were stowed in the torpedo rooms fore and aft where the crewmen lived. Initially all torpedoes were propelled by turbines, operated by hot gases resulting from the combustion of a jet of alcohol and compressed air mixed with steam. Later in the war, electric torpedoes, valuable for the absence of the telltale wake, were introduced. The warheads were loaded with TNT,[7] intended to detonate whether the torpedo struck a target or passed close to the magnetic field of a metallic hull.

Unfortunately these torpedoes had grave defects in the depth-control mechanism and the exploder, which did not come to light until the war was well along. The first caused torpedoes to run ten feet deeper than set, usually so far under a ship's hull that the magnetic influence feature of the exploder was not activated. This exploder was a detonating mechanism fitted into the warhead before firing; it contained its own small "booster" explosive to jar the main charge into action. Ofttimes the tricky magnetic device functioned prematurely, endangering the boat and doing no harm to the target.[8] And the firing pin, supposed to function under physical impact, proved too fragile to stand up under a good, square, 90-degree hit; normally it would set off the charge only if the warhead hit a ship at an acute angle. Thus, the best shooting was rewarded by duds.

At the outset American submarines had no radar and relied on sighting targets by lookouts or detection by the sound-listening gear. An attack was made either by periscope observation or by tracking the target's propeller noises. This latter method never lived up to prewar expectations. During 1942 an air-search radar, the SD, and a surface-search radar, the SJ, were installed. They

---

[7] Later changed to torpex, a more powerful explosive.

[8] In addition, a so-called "anti-countermining" device, designed to prevent a sympathetic detonation from other torpedo explosions, often prevented any detonation whatsoever. It must be remembered that before the war capital ships, whose sides were protected by heavy armor plate, were expected to be the primary submarine targets; the magnetic exploder was designed for use against their unprotected bottoms.

notably increased the boats' effectiveness while adding to the congested conditions on board.

Orders to the submarines were transmitted by radio from Pearl Harbor or Australia daily, but the boats were not usually required to acknowledge. They could send in important contact reports at the skippers' discretion, and the reports had to be important because radio transmissions were generally plotted by enemy direction-finders.

In 1942 the submarine patrols in the Pacific averaged forty-seven days at sea, half of which were spent going to and from station. At the end of its patrol a boat was usually given a two-weeks' overhaul and upkeep at Pearl Harbor where elaborate rest and recreational facilities were provided for submariners. After that came a week's shakedown before the beginning of the next patrol. Southwest Pacific submarines got neither the rest nor the overhaul until after several months of hard patrolling. Individual patrols were the rule at this period; we knew about German wolf-pack tactics but had too few boats to use them so.

In the internal organization of the submarine, the captain de-decided when, what and how to attack. The execution of his orders depended on the crew, and the boat's success hinged on their intelligent precision no less than on the captain's temperament and judgment.

In a submerged daylight attack, the submarine closed the target from ahead, seeking a firing position from forward of the enemy's beam. The skipper in the conning tower acted as approach officer, giving orders for course and speed, number of torpedoes to be fired, depth settings and angular width of the spread. In order to avoid detection, he made only short and infrequent periscope observations. The periscope indicated the bearing, which was then transmitted to the target-data computer. A range-finding device in the periscope also furnished data which went into the computer to cause it to indicate enemy speed. The submarine's bow did not need to be pointed in the exact direction in which the torpedoes were to swim; a gyro-steering mechanism set itself to turn them to the proper track after firing. When the range was favorable — between 700 and 2000 yards — the captain gave the order to fire. A sailor standing by pushed a button and the first "fish" was ejected from the tube by a high-pressure air impulse. Immediately upon leaving the tube, the torpedo's engine went into action, driving a pair of counter-rotating propellers. Water rushing by the exploder mechanism turned a device which armed the torpedo after it had run 400 yards. The remaining shots were fired at five-second intervals, in order to prevent the torpedoes from interfering with each other. The process was similar to duck hunting: torpedoes "led" the target so as to hit, and angled apart to produce a shotgun effect.

The executive officer doubled as assistant approach officer and navigator; another officer operated the computer. The tiny conning tower, containing eleven men, was crowded like a subway car in the rush hour and as busy as a bargain basement. Directly below the conning tower in the control room stood the diving officer (normally the same as the engineer officer) surrounded by scores of valves, wheels, buttons, gauges and indicators. His job was to see that the boat took the required depth and kept the proper trim: down by the bow when diving, down by the stern when surfacing. Normally the submarine contained only enough sea water in its ballast tanks to give it slight negative buoyancy. Its angle was controlled by the hydroplanes, massive metal fins projecting from bow and stern hydraulically manipulated by men stationed at huge wheels in the control room. When the boat surfaced, high-pressure air forced the sea water out through ballast-tank bottoms and the planes were canted so that the submarine climbed uphill. Once on the surface, engineers in the maneuvering room shifted the source of power from storage batteries to diesel engines, opening the main induction valve to supply air. In submerging, vents opened in the tops of the ballast tanks, releasing imprisoned air and permitting sea water to come in through flood openings in the bottoms of the tanks. In these up-and-down operations, the diving officer kept a careful eye on the "Christmas tree," a vertical panel of red and green lights which told him at a glance the status of the hatches, valves and other openings.

Every inch of space below decks was utilized. In the forward and after torpedo rooms men lived among their torpedoes. If there were not enough bunks to go round, the "hot bunk" system was used; a man coming off watch climbed into a "sack" just vacated by his relief. So close did submariners live to one another, and so dependent was each on the rest, that misfits were quickly spotted and removed by the captain. And relations between officers and enlisted men were much more intimate than in surface ships. The submariner, with his cramped quarters, long patrols, nervewracking depth-charge attacks and ever-present possibility of a slow and unpleasant death by suffocation, liked the duty and frequently volunteered to make patrols rather than lie over for an earned rest which might entail his transfer to another boat. He usually claimed that his duty was the safest in the fighting Navy, but was mistaken about that; postwar records show that 16 per cent of the officers and 13 per cent of the enlisted submariners in the Pacific were lost.[9]

Although carefully selected and volunteers, submariners were not a special type but a representative group of young men. The personalities of successful captains in 1942, men like Fenno, Warder, C. C. Smith, Klakring, Burlingame and Brockman, were as divergent as the law of averages will permit. Some were quiet and scholarly, others were boisterous, hearty and cocky. All that they had in common, besides Naval Academy and submarine school background, were superior skill and aggressiveness, and a cool gambler's ability to calculate odds.

All submarine activity in the Pacific Fleet was divided into two categories: special missions and patrols. The special missions included everything done in support of the Fleet, as in the Battle of Midway, as well as operations such as minelaying, rescue and the raid on Makin. Patrols meant the normal cruises in search of enemy shipping. Unfortunately we cannot fit the story of every patrol

---

[9] Comsubpac "U. S. Submarine Losses World War II."

between these covers but must confine ourselves to the telling of a few of the more productive ones.

b. Japanese Submarines

The Japanese Navy commenced hostilities with 60 submarines, only 13 fewer than the American submarine force in the Pacific had. Results should have been commensurate with this slight disparity; yet, except during a few weeks of the Guadalcanal campaign, the Nipponese boats failed to accomplish what was expected of them either by the Emperor or by his enemies. A description of Japanese submarines and their doctrine and employment will help to explain the causes of their failure.

Japanese submarines were divided into three general classes: 47 I-class fleet submarines,[10] 13 RO-class coast defense submarines, and a small number of midgets. Displacements in the I-class ranged from 1600 to 2200 tons, the average being slightly larger than their American counterparts. Some of this type had been in commission for fifteen years; others, with the benefit of German design, were only a year or two old. Diesel engines drove them at the high speed of 24 knots on the surface, and electric motors gave 8 knots submerged. Cruising ranges at economical speeds ran from 10,000 to 17,500 miles and a few of them had a sea-keeping endurance of three months. They were supposed to have a safe-diving limit of over 300 feet but the older boats never dared venture that deep. For armament they had six to eight 21-inch torpedo tubes, mostly mounted in the bows, and carried 24 torpedoes each. On deck were either one or two guns of 5.5-inch or 4.7-inch caliber and two to four anti-aircraft machine guns. Eleven of the I-boats had an airplane hangar which housed one small float plane; four carried communication equipment for employment as squadron flagships, and five could accommodate a midget submarine apiece. The RO-class coast defense submarines varied in displacement

[10] Including 4 old I-boats, equipped for minelaying, which displaced 1142 tons and made only 14.5 knots surfaced.

from 650 to 700 tons, in age from 6 to 19 years, and the fastest could make 19 knots on the surface, 8 knots submerged. Both I and RO boats were equipped with sound-listening gear but none had radar. Midget submarines were built in 80-foot and 41-foot sizes, and carried two 18-inch torpedoes. Their endurance was limited by the time it took their storage batteries to run down.

Officers and men of Japanese submarines, always volunteers, were given a course of instruction at the Yokosuka submarine school. During the first year of the war, training was good and morale high. The complements were about the same as in equivalent American craft; the fleet boats carried 60 to 100 men, the ROs 60, and the midgets two to four.

Neither the physical characteristics of Japanese submarines nor those of their crews explain their relatively poor performance. Japanese submariners complained that their boats were very slow to submerge and, once below, clumsy. They could not dive as deep as American boats and lack of radar was a handicap. But they had two advantages which outweighed every deficiency; they could use a far-flung net of island bases to reach productive patrol areas faster than ours and stay there longer. And their simple, rugged torpedoes, equipped with a nearly sure-fire contact exploder, were very reliable.[11]

The prewar Japanese concept of submarine employment was exactly the same as the American. The boats were to operate in support of the Fleet and their primary targets were enemy warships. To this end, the newest I-boats were organized as the Sixth Fleet under Vice Admiral Mitsumi Shimizu.[12] Only the older I-boats and some of the RO-boats were portioned out to various area commanders to use in disrupting Allied supply lines.

It so happened that after Pearl Harbor there was no enemy fleet to attack, and the fast-shifting carrier task forces were few and hard to catch. Yet, instead of sending most of their boats to raid merchant shipping, the Japanese persisted in trying to find war-

[11] See Vol. III of this History p. 23.
[12] Relieved 16 March 1942 by Vice Admiral Teruhisa Komatsu.

ships. They had no scruples about unrestricted warfare, far from it; they simply failed to replace faulty strategic notions. And this is the more difficult to explain because the I-boats that reached patrol areas off California and Oregon shortly after Pearl Harbor sank several merchant vessels and alarmed the entire West Coast.

Every time the Combined Fleet moved, a submarine scouting line called the "Advance Expeditionary Force" cruised ahead. We have already seen how badly the submarines did at Midway. They did much better, sniping at carriers, during the Guadalcanal campaign; yet, even so, costly errors were made. The rear admiral in command of the scouting submarines actually rode one himself, a gallant gesture which gave him only a periscope-view of the operation. Every night the flagship would surface and the admiral would issue radio orders to his gang, but his own information was limited and the enemy could fix his position by radio direction-finding. Contrary to the general American belief, he seems to have had no radio contact with the big 4-engine flying boats which often snooped American task forces.

As the Solomons struggle grew more desperate the Japanese, like the Americans, threw nearly everything that could submerge into the disputed waters. The Germans frequently urged their Oriental allies to employ their submarine fleet against merchant shipping but they succeeded only in persuading them to dispatch a few boats on harassing missions in the Indian Ocean. The Japanese, logically enough, could not see what help that was to Dai Nippon; they withdrew these submarines and the Indian Ocean was largely left to the German U-boats, which were allowed to base at Penang, Singapore and Batavia.[13]

Much of Japan's submarine potential was wastefully diverted to special missions during 1942. The boats refueled big seaplanes on ineffective bombing missions, like the one against Oahu in March. They made long cruises to conduct nuisance bombardments, as on Midway, Johnston and Canton Islands. They carried

[13] Admiral Wenneker (German Naval Attaché to Tokyo) "German-Japanese Naval Operations World War II."

scouting aircraft great distances to make reconnaissance flights of negative value, like the one to Seattle. But the mortal blow to a successful undersea war was the Japanese Army's discovery, during the Solomons campaign, that the boats could carry supplies to isolated garrisons. Thenceforth more and more submarines were pulled off patrols to serve the Army with rice and ammunition. In January 1943 a cargo container was invented which fitted into a torpedo tube, and that started a rush to devise further means of using submarines as seagoing pack-mules. The Navy hated that sort of employment but it was overruled in Tokyo. And, as American destroyers became more adept at sonar tracking, the Japanese boats found themselves in hot water even when submerged.

Thus, while there were many faults in Japanese undersea warfare, one thing stands out like the rising sun — misconceptions engraved in the topmost minds of the military and naval hierarchy. Better submarine doctrine could not have won the war for Japan, but employment of her boats against the vulnerable supply lines would have cost the Allies dear in ships, goods and effort, and delayed the final outcome far more than did the fanatical last-ditch defense of indefensible islands.

During 1942 the Japanese Sixth Fleet was a "fleet in being." American expectation that enemy submarines would learn better imposed the costly convoy system on the United States Navy, pinned down dozens of small craft to escort duty along the West Coast and diverted valuable destroyers to escorting convoys from the West Coast and Panama across the Pacific. Later in the war, as contacts with enemy submarines fell off almost to zero, the number of escorts was cut down; and by 1944 unescorted armed merchant ships were crossing the Pacific with impunity.

2. Central Pacific Patrols

For patrol purposes the ocean west of Pearl Harbor was divided into four areas: North and Central Pacific which were covered by the boats of Rear Admiral Thomas Withers,[14] Commander Submarines Pacific Fleet; South and Southwest Pacific areas, in whose waters prowled the boats of Captain John Wilkes,[15] some based at Fremantle, others at Brisbane.

The most successful American patrol in the late spring of 1942 was made deep into enemy waters by *Trout*. This was her third patrol under Lieutenant Commander Frank W. ("Mike") Fenno. *Trout* departed Pearl Harbor 24 March and, a fortnight out, arrived off the south coast of Honshu after fueling at Midway. On 9 April, two days after arriving on station, two small freighters were sighted, chugging along toward Kobe. Fenno could not get within a mile of them but neither could he resist having a try at them because, as he later remarked, "We didn't yet know that the woods were full of ships."

Next day *Trout* followed the trail of a long smoke plume to a slow steamer. Two single-torpedo attacks failed to connect, and the freighter with an escort chased the submarine so persistently that her sailors believed they had tangled with a Q-ship. But *Trout* was as hard to catch as her finny namesake, and evaded her enemies. Next, a fat 15,000-tonner was sighted sneaking along the Honshu coast, her camouflage blending with the cliffs. Fenno got in two shots from a little more than a mile away. One of them hit, the ship's engines stopped abruptly and she fell off course with whistle shrieking, but she was not fatally stung and escaped to seaward. Fenno could not surface and give chase because he was only 3000 yards from an enemy shore battery, so he fired one more torpedo on an overtaking run, and it missed.

Trout now moved southwest to cover the approach of *Enterprise* and *Hornet*, carrying the Doolittle planes toward Tokyo,[16] so it was not until 23 April that she returned to her old hunting

---

[14] On 14 May 1942 Rear Admiral Robert H. English relieved Admiral Withers, who went to the Portsmouth Navy Yard to supervise the submarine building program. Admiral English was killed in a plane crash in Jan. 1943 and next month Rear Admiral Charles A. Lockwood Jr. became Comsubpac.

[15] Relieved 26 May 1942 by Admiral Lockwood.

[16] See Vol. III of this History pp. 389–98.

grounds. This time she literally tangled with a Japanese fishing fleet and surfaced with 50 fathom of line and a large glass float wound around the conning tower. On the afternoon of the 24th, a 10,000-ton tanker felt the bite of two *Trout* torpedoes, but they stopped her only momentarily. A small freighter foolishly came to the tanker's rescue and attracted two of Fenno's warheads, one of which sundered her amidships.[17] By this time *Trout* was hard by the beach; Fenno spun her to a reverse course, evaded a sub-chaser and hauled clear.

Four days passed before she had another chance. In a midnight attack she slapped a torpedo into a patrol vessel, which sank in two minutes. Later, as dawn was breaking, Fenno missed a cargo vessel and, two hours later, a pair of torpedoes failed against a loaded tanker. Fenno was bewildered at the failure; the target should have been a sure thing. We can now guess why — the torpedoes, set for depths of 35 and 39 feet, ran so much deeper that they had passed outside the magnetic-influence field of the ship's hulls.

On 2 May there was a repeat performance of a perfect shot failing to hit a medium-sized passenger vessel. Fenno had no time to scratch his head over the miss before a 5000-ton freighter was sighted. A second stern shot at 900-yards' range cracked the vessel's hull like an eggshell, and down she went. Two days later, con-verted gunboat *Kongosan Maru* was sent to the bottom off Honshu. The enemy retaliated with airplane depth-bombs, none of them close.

Trout now turned home, having fired 22 of her 24 torpedoes, observed 7 hits and sunk three ships. But this was better luck than most of his contemporaries had. Fenno modestly attributed this to the fact that his "fish," which were on hand in Pearl Harbor at the war's start, were more reliable than subsequent issues. Many of his misses, he believed, were caused by the rule against

---

[17] This ship will not be found in JANAC (Joint Army-Navy Assessment Committee) *Japanese Naval and Merchant Shipping Losses* because that publication omits vessels under 500 tons; but these smaller craft are covered in a later publication.

firing spreads, which had been imposed to conserve torpedoes.

Triton (Lieutenant Commander Charles C. Kirkpatrick) departed Pearl Harbor on 13 April for her third patrol along well-traveled Empire sea lanes; and a good one it was. Her first stroke of luck came when, ten days out and north of Marcus Island, she engaged with gunfire an enemy trawler after missing with two torpedoes. As this was their first gun target, the sailors made up for lack of practice with enthusiastic and rapid fire at point-blank range. It was night and black as the ocean's bottom, but 3-inch shells and .50-caliber bullets soon reduced the trawler to a tattered wreck.

On 27 April *Triton* entered the yellow waters of the East China Sea and commenced sniffing for game. Three days later, she had a chance — a convoy at which she first fired two torpedoes; both missed and she came back to fire two more, this time damaging the 5300-ton *Calcutta Maru*, whose escorts charged in for revenge; but *Triton* evaded them easily. That afternoon she did something very uncommon in those early days, she returned for another try at the crippled *Maru*. One "fish" passed harmlessly under but the second finished her off. *Triton* took some periscope pictures for proof and then hauled clear.

During the next few days the primary menace was Chinese junks, fishing all over the China Sea and showing no lights. Kirkpatrick gave these a wide berth, as old China hands had been doing for two centuries, although for different reasons. During the midwatch on 6 May, *Triton* came up astern of another convoy, missed the last ship in column, then surfaced, gave chase and sank *Taiei Maru*. Questing destroyers were easily evaded in the darkness. Kirkpatrick continued the hunt. At dawn he picked out another and larger *Maru* from the same convoy. But persistence, in submarine circles, has perils as well as rewards; the escorting destroyer went after *Triton* with a vengeance. The submarine crew were eager to experience a depth-charge attack and had their wish. They found the sensation unpleasant but their boat merely had a few bolts loosened up.

On 15 May *Triton's* gun crew had an encounter with two Japanese fishing vessels. One of them, which put up a fight, was sunk; the other hove-to and displayed a white flag. A boarding party visited the vessel and obtained a welcome load of fresh fish, valuable documents and a Japanese flag. After putting the fishermen into a boat with food and water, *Triton* destroyed her prize.

By this time Kirkpatrick had become aware that something was going on in the South Pacific. At the same time, low fuel tanks prompted him to head east for a possible interception of enemy forces. Sure enough, on 16 May, south of Shikoku, he sighted a carrier [18] and two destroyers but was unable to catch them. Next day, *Triton* deprived Yamamoto of one unit of his Advance Expeditionary Force.

Cruising submerged off Kyushu, she encountered submarine *I-164* steaming complacently on the surface. Using the Rising Sun painted on its conning tower as point of aim, Kirkpatrick shot a torpedo into the enemy. Part of the hull was tossed 100 feet into the air, and some 30 survivors were left struggling in the water when the boat went down. *Triton* had no room to spare for these castaways and continued eastward. On 21 June she fired four torpedoes at another surfaced sub but failed to hit. And on 4 July she steamed exuberantly into Pearl Harbor, where Admiral English remarked that good spirits and a successful crew went together.

Submarine *Thresher* made a late spring patrol which did not match the tonnage score of *Trout* and *Triton* but furnished plenty of thrills. On 3 April, en route from Pearl to Japan, her crew were scared but unhurt by an enemy submarine torpedo whose bubbling wake passed close aboard, emphasizing that this sort of game can be played by both sides. As was customary in underwater guerilla fighting, the two antagonists separated post haste. A day later *Thresher* aimed torpedoes at a merchantman. The "fish" appeared to be passing under but there were no explosions and no damage done to the enemy. The crew had until the 10th to grouse about that one, when their confidence was partially

[18] This was the damaged *Shokaku* limping home from Coral Sea.

restored by a single torpedo hit which split 3000-ton *Sado Maru* in two. The sinking occurred in midmorning, and Japanese escorts held *Thresher* down for the rest of the day, dropping depth charges and inflicting incidental damage. While *Thresher* was dodging the enemy explosives, she unintentionally dove far deeper than had any American submarine theretofore. Yet the boat withstood the tremendous pressure easily. This was something worth knowing; other boats used the knowledge in deep dives which left enemy depth charges growling harmlessly overhead.

Shortly after, *Thresher* was cruising on the surface when a high wave washed green water down the hatches, doing more damage than had the depth charges. She had to curtail her patrol and head back to Pearl. She had fired seven torpedoes for only one hit.

Grenadier sank the largest vessel during the spring of 1942. She had been out from Pearl for nearly a month patrolling off Japan when, on 8 May, she came on the 14,500-ton *Taiyo Maru* plodding south of Kyushu in a well protected convoy. Despite her size, the ship was poorly compartmented and two torpedoes sent her down like a lead sinker. The subsequent depth-charging did no harm and *Grenadier* was routed to the Midway action before getting any more game.

Drum, Tuna and *Pompano* were three other boats which made successful forays into the enemy's front yard prior to Midway. At midnight 1 May, *Drum* hit and destroyed seaplane carrier *Mizuho* off southern Japan. On the 13th she chased a telltale smoke plume and plopped a killing "fish" into 5600-ton *Shonan Maru;* and on the 25th repeated the performance on a smaller freighter. But, three days later, a five-torpedo spread missed a large naval transport which made a zig just as the warheads left the tubes.

Pompano started her patrol modestly by sinking a sampan. On 25 May a fire broke out in her engine room; two hours after it was extinguished she sank a small tanker. Five days later, from a range of 750 yards, which was close for those days, she sank an 8000-ton transport with two torpedoes. Some 24 depth charges in retaliation did not even touch her. On 3 June, in the Bonins, she sank a small inter-island steamer and watched a boat from Iwo Jima rescue the survivors. After blasting a trawler operating near by, she turned east to lend a hand at Midway.

The May–June patrol of *Silversides* (Lieutenant Commander Creed C. Burlingame) illustrated the difficulty of assessing damage in the early days of the war.[19] On 13 May, south of Honshu, she claimed sinking an enemy I-boat, but it escaped. On the 17th her crew were slightly embarrassed to find themselves towing a trawl buoy with a Japanese flag attached, but quickly proved they had not changed allegiance by attacking two Japanese merchantmen, one of which was sunk. Five days later, Burlingame watched his torpedoes blow the bow off a naval auxiliary and make a hit under its bridge. There followed the usual depth-charge attack, this one lasting from noon until supper time. The auxiliary was salvaged. Most of *Silversides's* patrol time was spent in hunting for the retiring Japanese Midway force.

Greenling (Lieutenant Commander Henry C. Bruton) was dispatched from Pearl Harbor on 20 April to dip down into the Mandates. West of Eniwetok she met a Japanese supply ship, fired eight torpedoes for eight misses, and started a gun action with the vessel, which proved so tough that Bruton had to break it off. On 4 May, north of Truk, the sailors were surprised that it took but one torpedo to send a 3600-ton freighter to Davy Jones's locker. For the next month the patrol was an irritating succession of ship sightings, including a carrier; never did *Greenling* get within range. But she brought home some interesting photographs and observations on the Mandates to show the top planners at Pearl, proving submarine reconnaissance of enemy-held territory to be very profitable.

So far we have recounted adventures of some of the successful boats, those that came home with facsimile Japanese flags flying on improvised halyards. Other subs had not the luck to be at the right spots at the right times to make contacts. Yet every boat

[19] Robert Trumbull *Silversides* (1945).

on patrol was a threat, and the Japanese, who had expected to be able to navigate their home waters in perfect safety, were forced to draw precious destroyers from the Fleet for escort purposes. Many of the unlucky boats brought back valuable intelligence; and some, by their very failures, saved later patrollers from wasting time in barren waters.

Cuttlefish made just such a cruise to the Marianas before Midway. An old boat with irascible engines, she could make only 14 knots. It took a long week out of Midway to reach Saipan, where the skipper reflected that his old gal had steamed over 15,000 miles since December, yet had sighted but three enemy ships. Nor were things better at Saipan. She had a brush with a small patrol boat but was unable to sink it; she sighted cruiser *Yubari* but, because of her slow speed, could not get into firing position. Again, she sighted two destroyers and was maneuvering to attack when a "sleeper," an unseen third destroyer, charged in, spoiled the attack and very nearly ruined *Cuttlefish*. Her final sighting, a tanker, she never closed near enough to shoot at. Twice she narrowly escaped aircraft bombs. On 15 June this boat was back in Pearl Harbor without a single scalp. Officers and crew had tried so hard for a score that they were dispirited; we can now see that slow speed made her useless for aggressive patrol.

The spring submarine offensive ended with preparations for the Battle of Midway, when 19 of the 26 submarines in the Central Pacific were called upon to support the Fleet, and most of the others moved off station in vain efforts to intercept the retiring enemy. In April and May, Japanese shipping losses pushed close to 250,000 tons, a high total for those days. In May alone, more enemy ships were sunk than in the previous five months of war. And not one Central Pacific submarine had been lost or badly damaged.

It was now apparent that ships in waters off the main Japanese islands were as thick as Geisha girls in Tokyo, and as easy. Comsubpac therefore divided those waters into numbered areas in order of priority, with top billing given to the entrance to

Tokyo Bay, followed closely by the passages to the Inland Sea. Midway now became a full-fledged submarine base capable of giving between-patrol refits, shortening the run to the Empire by 1100 miles. And, in order to take care of the Marshalls and Carolines without taking boats off the Empire run, it was arranged that submarines transferring to or from the Southwest Pacific Force should patrol the Mandates en route, refueling at Johnston Island when necessary.

Several boats had made the long transit between Oahu and Australia before the Battle of Midway and one of these, *Tautog* (Commander J. H. Willingham), demonstrated the profits. Two days out of Pearl on 26 April, her officer of the deck sighted a Japanese periscope as the enemy was opening range to fire. The boat's rudder was put hard over and the crew called to battle stations. One quickly-fired torpedo sent the Japanese submarine [20] down in a broil of orange-gray smoke and water. By a rare chance, a PBY on hand saw and confirmed the kill. In the Carolines on 16 May Willingham drove an enemy freighter onto the beach with a hole in its side. Next morning *I-28* was sighted on the surface, numerals and men on the bridge plainly visible. One torpedo disabled the Jap, who retaliated with two shots which Willingham dodged. The duel ended when *Tautog* registered a second hit under the enemy's conning tower. On the 24th *Tautog* snuffed out *Shoka Maru* (4467 tons). Admiral Lockwood received Willingham in Australia on 11 June with a hearty "Well Done!"

Stingray was one of the submarines to steam from Australia to Oahu as a regular patrol after Midway. Going north from Fremantle, she spent the month of June patrolling earnestly but fruitlessly off Timor, Davao Gulf and San Bernardino Strait. Finally she pointed her bow toward Guam, and after three days met a three-ship convoy from which she cut out a 1300-ton converted

---

[20] JANAC says this was *RO–30*, but Shizuo Fukui *Japanese Naval Vessels at the End of War* (a 2nd Demobilization Bureau publication 25 Apr. 1947) p. 57 proves that she was tied up throughout the war. It is certain, however, that there was a kill.

gunboat. *Stingray* escaped with minor depth-charge damage. *Thresher,* her relief, was running in the opposite direction during July. Lieutenant Commander William J. Millican took this boat right through the Marshall Islands, damaging a tanker off Maloelap early in the passage. On 9 July, at the start of the forenoon watch, *Thresher* was lying off Kwajalein in a mirrorlike sea when a big motor torpedo boat tender, *Shinsho Maru,* stood toward the lagoon entrance. She sank the tender handily and dove deep, as a patrol plane cracked the water viciously with a depth bomb. Nearly two hours later Millican and his men, serene over their easy victory, were jolted by two more airplane bombs very close aboard. Shortly after this a strange buzzing noise was heard, followed by a sinister banging and clanking on the hull as some metallic object scraped it fore and aft. While all hands were speculating what this might be, suddenly the stern rose, pitching the boat to an alarming angle. *Thresher,* like the shark she was named for, had been caught on a hook, a giant grapnel which the Japanese were towing on the end of a heavy chain! We can well imagine the consternation of the crew; the skipper even ordered secret codes destroyed. For ten heart-fluttering minutes *Thresher* writhed like a fish being played by an angler, running in fast, tight circles. Finally the grapnel was shaken loose; but the Japanese were soon back, this time with a score of well-aimed depth charges; one even bumped the conning tower. Next day the crew discovered what had given their position away. The first aircraft bomb had caused a small leak which emitted a stream of bubbles that could easily be detected breaking on the calm surface. An excellent lead for the Japanese fishermen!

Nothing more happened until *Thresher* arrived off Truk. On a dark, squally night the sound operator reported propeller noises a quarter of a mile ahead. The officer of the deck cautiously brought his rudder left. Suddenly, out of the rain and darkness, appeared a large patrol craft pounding toward *Thresher* at high speed. Millican backed emergency and ordered a dive. The Japanese skipper was so confused that, instead of continuing on his course and ramming, he turned hard right. Presently both vessels were steaming parallel, only 150 feet apart; the Americans topside watched Japanese sailors running about the deck and even heard them shout. But *Thresher* was comfortably cushioned with sea water before the enemy woke up and started shooting.

Millican's next close-up occurred off the Netherlands Indies on 4 August when he attacked a small freighter which turned out to be a scorpion with depth charges in its tail. He had a narrow escape as the "ashcans" swished and boomed all around. But *Thresher* carried her good luck into Fremantle Harbor, which she entered 15 August after a 7200-mile voyage.

Gudgeon (Lieutenant Commander W. S. Stovall), which had already sunk a Japanese I-boat,[21] made a normal passage through the Mandates. Off Truk she made a few inconclusive attacks and received some desultory depth-charging in return. On 3 August she put two good torpedoes into a 5000-ton freighter. Several days later, she claimed damage to two large transports and paid for it with an hour of heavy depth-charge attacks. Passing between Celebes and New Guinea, *Gudgeon* arrived Fremantle 2 September. The Pearl Harbor–Fremantle shuttle had proved a paying line.

By midsummer many of the boats were making their third or fourth war patrols and the effects were being felt by the crews. On *Greenling's* third patrol the skipper observed that the men most susceptible to illness and infection were those who had been longest in the business. Almost all submariners suffered from headaches, constipation and colds; in the tropics old hands developed ugly skin ulcers. Vitamin pills, sun lamps, air conditioning and fresh-frozen foods improved health conditions to some extent. Comsubpac planned to relieve one third of each crew after each patrol, but many skippers and their men were reluctant to comply. The men would volunteer to stay in a boat they knew, and one which would eventually get a Stateside overhaul; the skippers naturally liked to keep trained sailors.

[21] See Vol. III of this History p. 258.

There were many areas around Japan which no American submarine had yet penetrated, such as the coastal zone off northeast-
ern Honshu. In early August *Guardfish* (Lieutenant Commander
Thomas B. Klakring) departed Pearl on her first war patrol, bound
for these unfished waters. On the 19th, she had her first whack
at an auxiliary but the torpedoes exploded prematurely. Klakring
refrained from the usual deep dive in order to get in a shot at a
pursuing destroyer. The destroyer was so inept at tracking that no
contest resulted, but Klakring's boldness later became doctrine;
going after a heckling escort was apt to be safer than accepting a
depth-charge attack.

On 22 August *Guardfish* gun crews drew first blood against
an armed trawler, touching off its cargo of fuel oil to make a
spectacular fire. Next day the performance was repeated on a
sampan. On the 24th a 3000-ton passenger *Maru* was steaming out
of harbor when two *Guardfish* torpedoes splintered her from
hawsepipe to stack; she stood briefly on her nose and took a deep
dive. *Guardfish* shifted her locale frequently in the next few days
and had one disappointing set-to with a freighter in which defective torpedoes played a part. On 2 September she sank a 2300-ton
freighter. But her real pay-off came on the 4th. In the late afternoon she hit two ships in a convoy within a minute. One went
down stern first, the other bow first, while excited submariners
took turns squinting through the periscope.[22] Less than an hour
later, she fired a long single shot at a freighter entering Kuji Bay.
This remarkable shot from a range of nearly four miles took
seven-and-a-half minutes to reach the end of its journey, where
it blew out the vessel's midship section and left it wallowing in
the mud. And yet the day was not done. Before another hour
passed, *Guardfish* sank a fourth ship, almost in the same spot.[23]
At all times she sailed almost within scraping distance of a rock-
bound shore.

[22] *Guardfish* boys were great observers; it is about her that the story is told
that she hove-to off a Japanese racecourse to watch a horse race!

[23] The fourth is unconfirmed in JANAC, but the *Guardfish* boys saw it sink;
anyway, the other three totaled 6268 tons.

The next five days *Guardfish* spent evading angry patrol craft. On 15 September she entered Midway lagoon with a broom at the masthead, having fired all but one of her 24 torpedoes for eleven hits and eight sinkings. Klakring modestly attributed his success to the fact that Admiral English had given him permission to try for contact hits rather than under-the-keel magnetic explosions.

In August and September *Haddock*, another new submarine, was the first to carry on patrol the modern SJ radar, which in submarines corresponded to the SG in surface craft. Unfortunately, her patrol area to the westward of Okinawa contained little shipping at the time; she had but seven enemy contacts and sank two. Eventually the SJ radar was to make night attacks and wolf-pack tactics highly profitable.

As early as October 1942, *Finback* (Lieutenant Commander Jesse L. Hull) found good hunting in the Formosa Channel. On the 14th she saw 7000-ton transport *Teison Maru* steaming in convoy, signal flags flying merrily, and with one torpedo sent crew and passengers scrambling into lifeboats, and the ship to the bottom. A week later she chased a convoy at night, attacking on the surface. There was the too familiar sight of torpedoes "running under the target and failing to explode," but Hull kept right on doling out warheads until he got two ships, totalling 15,000 tons. And on her way back to Midway *Finback* polished off a sampan with gunfire.

Trigger (Lieutenant Commander Roy S. Benson) was on her second war patrol not far from Tokyo Bay, one dull gray morning in October, when through the murky haze a thin finger of smoke took form. Benson moved in for a look-see which convinced him that the target was a freighter too small to warrant the expenditure of a torpedo, so manned his deck gun and automatic weapons. No sooner had *Trigger* opened fire than the enemy replied in kind, and shells whistled all around the exposed gun crew. A sub is no match for that sort of thing, so Benson sent his gun crews below and maneuvered to fire a torpedo. But the enemy had an answer for that, too, and came charging in like a wounded whale.

By adroit twisting *Trigger* avoided the deadly prow, passing the *Maru* at a close 50 feet while machine-gun bullets rained down. *Trigger* kicked the Jap in the groin with a stern tube shot and then submerged. A few minutes later she surfaced, and this time an enemy torpedo whizzed down the port side. The duel went on until after daylight, with torpedoes and depth charges. Benson finally lost touch and we have never learned whether this "little freighter" was a Q-ship or a converted gunboat; anyway, she escaped.

At dusk, 17 October, *Trigger*, after sending 5800-ton *Holland Maru* to the bottom and missing another close shot, was lying on the surface enjoying the night air when a Japanese destroyer charged in to ram, guns firing and depth charges ready. *Trigger* discreetly submerged and danced a grim ballet with the depth charges. Each time the enemy approached the sub would sheer off, but the "ashcans" fell jarringly near. Finally, *Trigger* turned bow to the Jap and let fly three torpedoes, a "down-the-throat" shot. At least one of these made a premature explosion and none hit. The Jap then tried a torpedo on *Trigger* but the sub came back with another at him. Reinforcements now churned the water on all sides, so *Trigger* went deep. This gave the destroyer the initiative, and charge after charge went off close aboard the sub, while her crew bailed water from wet to dry bilges. Just when the enemy really had the submarine cold, he did what so many of his fellows were prone to do; he gave up. *Trigger* lay low with run-down batteries until after midnight, then surfaced and high-tailed away. She returned to Pearl Harbor with empty torpedo tubes.

The sea lanes from Japan south to Truk and thence on to the South Pacific were the logistic link between the homeland and the front. Here the Central Pacific boats might strike telling blows at shipping and, at the same time, indirectly support fleet operations. So additional boats were assigned as marauders in the Carolines over and above the Australia–Pearl Harbor transfer patrols. It was a tough assignment because ships here had more and better air and surface escorts than elsewhere and the glassy seas of low latitudes made concealment difficult. *Greenling*, on the Truk–Japan route when the Marines landed at Guadalcanal, made five attacks. She nailed the 12,700-ton *Brazil Maru* with 400 soldiers and 200 other passengers on board (as a survivor taken prisoner stated) and also a 4500-ton passenger vessel, by surface attacks during darkness. *Flying Fish* in late August had the chance of a lifetime when a battleship showed up in her periscope sights, but she failed to hit and the subsequent depth-charge attack sent men reeling, broke crockery, knocked down insulation and damaged machinery. She escaped only by going deep to where a layer of sound-distorting cold water gave protection long enough for her to escape and retire to Pearl.

The landings on Guadalcanal helped the Japanese merchant marine through the latter half of 1942, because Admiral Nimitz reluctantly transferred a dozen boats to the Bismarck–Solomons area, leaving only about eleven to patrol Empire waters; and of these five were usually in transit. Boats operating off Japan or China had more targets than they could handle.

Greenling, on a businesslike patrol in October, sank 20,000 tons of *Marus* and claimed damage to an auxiliary carrier. *Kingfish* made five attacks, two kills. *Drum* saw plenty of targets but poor torpedo performance (only 4 hits out of 23 shots) cut her bag down to one small freighter. *Nautilus*, after transporting Marines to Makin, swam into the waters off Hokkaido and, despite bad weather, made nine attacks and sank three ships. Her skipper was willing to fight anything, anywhere; on occasion he brought *Nautilus* to the surface where her 6-inch guns could follow up the torpedoes.

Whale in October was the first American submarine to plant mines in Empire waters. These, shaped like long cylinders, were placed in torpedo tubes for discharge. Her example was followed by *Sunfish*, *Drum* and *Trigger*. Rarely is the success of mining determined until after war's end; but *Trigger* in December was startled and pleased to see an enemy merchantman blow up in a mine field a few minutes after it had been laid. Nobody on the American side knew until late in 1945 the tremendous execution these mines had wrought. *Whale* received postwar credit for five enemy ships sunk in her mine field; *Sunfish* and *Trigger* got two each in theirs. All told, 16 enemy ships fell victim to offensive mines laid by American submarines before February 1943.

In December *Halibut* used her new SJ radar to good advantage, making numerous contacts and attacking mostly at night. She destroyed three small ships and somewhat revived confidence in American torpedoes by getting 9 hits out of 19 shots. *Kingfish* had the satisfaction of sinking a 4400-ton *Maru* on Pearl Harbor day and a larger merchantman, in a radar-controlled attack, three days after Christmas.

The first and only planned lifeguard mission of 1942 was carried out by *Triton, Pike* and *Finback* in December. These boats took station along the route to Wake Island during a bombing mission by Army B–24s. Their duties were to guide the bombers in by radio and rescue any that might be forced to ditch. It was perhaps too bad that nobody gave them an opportunity for a dramatic rescue, which might have brought maturity a year earlier to the project of submarine lifeguards.[24]

The changing pattern of submarine tactics was illustrated by *Tarpon*. Cruising near Tokyo Bay on the night of 1 February 1943, she picked up a radar contact, ran it down on the surface and sank an 11,000-ton *Maru* without using her periscope. In darkness on the 8th she picked up a radar contact, chased it on the surface, and using radar ranges and periscope sighting put four hits into the 17,000-ton *Tatsuta Maru*. That pride of the Japanese merchant marine went to the bottom. The enemy never found an answer to these tactics, which made the American submarine one of the most formidable weapons of the war.

While *Tarpon* was making her score, a submarine division commander at Pearl was writing a significant endorsement on a patrol report submitted by *Whale:* —

[24] The Japanese employed submarines as lifeguards at war's outset.

"Thirty-seven-and-one-half per cent of the torpedoes fired were defective. . . . The case against the torpedo is well founded. . . . Every effort is being made to improve torpedo exploder performance and it is hoped that the fruits of this effort will not be delayed much longer." [25]

3. *North Pacific*

Aleutian waters were bad enough for large ships which could stand the buffeting of the wild williwaws and the pounding of heavy northern seas; for submarines these waters were the world's worst. Unfortunately, it was the uncomfortable little S-boats that found themselves out on Uncle Sam's Arctic limb. A fair bag of big game would have been some compensation for nasty cruising, but during the whole of 1942 only six enemy ships took the plunge as victims of North Pacific submarines.

The experience of *S-34* (Lieutenant Commander Thomas L. Wogan) was representative of early Aleutian patrols. She, in company with *S-35*, sailed from Dutch Harbor 12 April, bound for the Kurile Islands. The two boats were barely in open water when bad weather separated them. On the second day of the voyage a wave washed over the bridge of *S-34* and tossed the quartermaster so savagely that his nose was half torn off and his body badly bruised. The engines were cranky and the weather foul, but a great-circle track was made through the Bering Sea to reach enemy waters. On 22 April a Japanese merchantman was attacked from close range but he dodged the "fish." The captain took his boat around Kamchatka through the Kuriles into the Sea of Okhotsk, where drifting ice stopped her. Two torpedoes from 900 yards missed an enemy freighter.

That was Wogan's last contact with the enemy except for an occasional plane. On 27 April, *S-34* ran into another ice field. Her patrol now became a tussle with drifting ice and unpredictable cur-

---

[25] Comsubdiv 102 endorsement on *Whale* Report of 2nd War Patrol.

rents, the barometer escalating as much as 0.15 inch an hour and the weather changing as fast. No stars were visible and landfalls in the foggy Kuriles were chancy. Sound gear indications were often drowned by rumblings from under-water volcanoes. Heavy seas dumped so much green water on the bridge that the conning tower hatch had to be closed even when surfaced. Below decks, everyone sniffled with colds. The only break for them came on May Day when the boat anchored for a few hours in Chichagof Harbor, Attu; during an entire watch the men basked in fresh air and sunshine. Next day, while *S-34* was at anchor in Kiska, the wind blew up a whole gale which plagued the submariners until the 10th when they wearily returned to Dutch Harbor. So rugged a routine could be endured neither by men nor machinery, so it was decided to rotate the S-boats between the North Pacific and a relatively soft job in San Diego, acting as "tame submarine" for destroyers practising anti-submarine tactics.

The navigational hazards of operating an S-boat in the Aleutians claimed a victim in June, after the Japanese had occupied Attu and Kiska. *S-27*, commanded by Lieutenant H. L. Jukes, reconnoitered Amchitka Island for Admiral Theobald on 19 June. Daylight lasts for 18 hours at this time of year, so that when *S-27* surfaced at 2200 she hove-to five miles off shore to recharge batteries. Fog closed in and the submarine, without fathometer or radar, was swept by unpredictable currents onto a reef off Amchitka. The boat took a heavy list, the motor room flooded, and chlorine fumed out of a wet battery. Jukes sent out a distress call which was heard, but nobody picked up his broadcast position. As the ship was untenable, all hands went ashore in a rubber boat, carrying food, guns and ammunition. Fortunately on Amchitka they found an abandoned church and other buildings where they lived fairly comfortably until rescued a week later by Catalinas from Dutch Harbor.

When the Japanese invaded Kiska and Attu, the S-boats were reinforced by seven fleet submarines to assist in patrolling cold northern waters. *Growler* (Lieutenant Commander Howard W.

Gilmore) departed Pearl Harbor 20 June, called at Midway and headed north for station off Kiska. She spent three days watching and dodging enemy aircraft before finding worth-while targets. In the late Arctic twilight of 5 July Gilmore sighted destroyers *Arare, Kasumi* and *Shiranuhi* off Kiska Harbor entrance. *Growler* crept silently up on them and methodically put a torpedo into each, then launched an extra one at *Arare*, who retaliated with torpedoes of her own which narrowly missed, and *Growler* made a quick getaway, pursued by patrol craft. She had sunk *Arare* and damaged the other two destroyers at a cost of four torpedoes and a jammed periscope.

On 7 July a Japanese destroyer with a good sound operator gave *Growler* a bad hour, damaging her propellers and sound gear with depth charges. But she escaped on the surface after dark, made Dutch Harbor safely and was shifted back to Pearl and Central Pacific operations. Her crew, with radar, fathometer, efficient sound gear and air conditioning, had enjoyed a luxury cruise compared with the S-boat submariners.

Triton also did good work in the Aleutians. Lieutenant Commander Kirkpatrick took her north from Pearl on 25 June and arrived on station off Agattu Island near Attu on 4 July. The skipper spent most of the holiday trying for a navigational fix; but in midafternoon he forgot navigation when destroyer *Nenohi* appeared through the mist, steaming at a cautious 9 knots. Kirkpatrick carefully fired two torpedoes and dove to await results. In less than a minute a resounding explosion prompted a peek through the periscope. The delighted submariners watched *Nenohi* roll over, a hundred men still clinging to her cold and slimy bottom. Twenty minutes later she sank, leaving her crew to fight for places in a single lifeboat. To add to *Triton's* joy, the fog lifted enough for Kirkpatrick to correct an eight-mile error in his dead reckoning. He hung about until 12 July when periscope trouble developed, and then proceeded to Dutch Harbor for repairs. For three days the crew had such liberty as an Aleutians base afforded, then shoved off for Kiska. Admiral Theobald's cruisers conducted a bombardment of that island on 8 August and *Triton* hoped to catch enemy ships trying to escape, but none did. During that month *Triton* was mostly at sea, but targets were not plentiful and she damaged only one. She also carried Army reconnaissance troops from Dutch Harbor to Adak. Early in September 1942 the submarine was gratefully returned to Hawaiian sunshine.

Another Kiska watch-stander was *Grunion* (Lieutenant Commander Mannert L. Abele), a new fleet submarine which had arrived at Pearl Harbor in late June and had taken off for Aleutian patrol on the 30th. Between 15 and 28 July she made five attacks on Japanese subchasers, sank two and badly damaged a third. On 30 July she reported heavy anti-submarine activity at the entrance to Kiska and was ordered to report at Dutch Harbor; but *Grunion* never acknowledged and was never seen again. How and where she was lost still remains a mystery.

Other fleet-type submarines in the North Pacific made no killings during the summer of 1942, and the meager results of these patrols prompted Admiral Nimitz to pull most of the big boats out of Theobald's bailiwick and send them to more profitable hunting grounds.

During an October patrol by *Halibut,* an effort was made to employ aircraft in finding targets for her, but this was a new experience for both and communications were not good enough. One plane gave *Halibut* an enemy ship position in latitude-longitude coördinates, which would have been fine except that the boat had been running so long in a dense fog that she had no idea where she was herself. On 11 October *Halibut* was close enough to an enemy ship, apparently a freighter, to see a PBY making near-misses. The submarine skipper decided to join in as the "freighter," unescorted, was steaming in slow circles. During his surface approach the Japanese crew started to swing out lifeboats, apparently in preparation for abandoning ship. *Halibut* fired four torpedoes but all missed, at least one passing under the target. The submarine then received a nasty surprise in the shape of a torpedo from the "freighter" and several close shots from a concealed deck gun. Her target was a Q-ship, and *Halibut* was lucky to get out with a whole hull.

All summer and fall the plucky little S-boats continued their Arctic vigil, but *S-31* (Lieutenant Commander Robert F. Sellars) was the only one to sink anything, a 3000-ton *Maru* on 26 October. The S-boat was patrolling the main route from the Kuriles to the Aleutians when she came upon the target anchored in the open roadstead off Paramushiro, and punctured its hull with two well-aimed torpedoes. A minute later *S-31* grounded, and for the next half hour scraped and bounced along the bottom of the bay, finally clearing the foul ground. Commander Sellars later observed, "There is no sensation quite like that obtained when twisting and turning, trying to stay at periscope depth, searching for a path through the reefs to deep water." But he added, "There is nothing like hearing torpedoes explode and a good sinking to keep the crew happy." *S-31* cruised over 4000 miles for this one kill and, like her sisters, was mauled by monstrous seas; one man had cracked ribs and two others were injured by waves over the bridge.

Winter brought more grief for the S-boats and the experience of *S-35* was particularly chilly. Lieutenant Henry S. Monroe took this boat on a pre-Christmas patrol off Amchitka. An Arctic blow made up on 21 December, and the submarine crawled desperately up and down the steep slopes of pale green frigid waves which frequently inundated the tiny bridge. On the second dogwatch a wave slammed Monroe into a hatch, spraining an arm and a leg. He limped painfully below and turned in, only to be routed out by the dread shout of "Fire!" from the control room where salt water had short-circuited electric cables. Crackling white electric arcs and wicked blue flames lit up the control room; when one fire was quenched another broke out. Noxious fumes forced the men to secure engines and drove them topside. The sailors worked desperately, as they were in imminent danger of grounding on Amchitka, but finally they put out the fires and restarted the engines. Next morning fire broke out again; and, since there was no flame-extinguishing chemical left, all hands were driven to the exposed bridge where they huddled miserably, praying that the fire would suffocate for want of air. All day the struggle continued, engineers alternating between smoky interior and icy topsides. Eventually Monroe and his men won the fight and completed a slow passage to Adak. *S–35* sailors were convinced that theirs was the toughest patrol of the war to date, and many another submariner would agree.

4. *South and Southwest Pacific*

On 1 April 1942 there was not much left of the old Asiatic Fleet but six old destroyers and Captain John Wilkes's submarines,[26] then based at Fremantle, Australia. Even they were slowed down by shortages and by frequent demands for defensive and evacuation missions. Wilkes's force was now split; the S-boats were sent to base under General MacArthur at Brisbane, in order to patrol the Australian Mandates, while the fleet boats continued to overhaul at Fremantle [27] or Albany and to patrol the Indies and the Philippines. At the same time Wilkes was relieved of some of the area for which he was responsible by the assignment of Formosa, the East China Sea north of the Philippines and the Western Pacific as far as Palau, to Central Pacific submarines. The South Pacific, east of long. 159°, the meridian of Russell Island, became an "orphan zone" where control of American submarines was vested in Nimitz or Halsey, but the boats to do the work were based at Brisbane.

At the beginning of April, Wilkes had under his command 21 fleet boats and five S-boats. Three replacement fleet boats and six S-boats were on their way out. The latter group (Subdiv 53, Lieutenant Commander E. E. Yeomans) took 45 days to reach Brisbane from Panama, arrived in mid-April and started patrolling only six days later. About the same time the five S-boats from Fremantle

[26] See Vol. III of this History p. 375.
[27] The port of Fremantle is at the mouth of a river 12 miles below Perth. Submariners referred to the base by either name.

arrived in Brisbane and all eleven were organized as the Eastern Australia Submarine Group (TF 42) under the command of Rear Admiral Francis W. Rockwell, who was relieved 12 August by Captain Ralph W. Christie in tender *Griffin*.[28] Fremantle remained the headquarters and Captain Wilkes the commander of the fleet boats (TF 51).

Patrols from Fremantle during April and May 1942 were neither spectacular nor profitable. Boats would make quick runs northward to pass through the narrow tide-swept Lombok Strait in darkness. Thence they would steer north or northeast to their patrol stations. As a rule, few sightings were made and more often than not the boats would be ordered to evacuate Europeans or stranded American aviators from an enemy-occupied island. *Sturgeon* sank a small freighter en route to her station and on 3 April blew up a Japanese frigate. Her patrol was broken off in late April when she was sent in to Tjilatjap to pick up stranded British fliers, but an officer, Lieutenant Chester W. Nimitz Jr., who went ashore in this Japanese-held port, could not find them and she returned to Fremantle 7 May after having been at sea 170 out of the previous 200 days.

Spearfish had better luck off western Luzon, sinking one 4000-ton freighter and a week later one of 7000 tons. Then she was pulled off patrol to evacuate Army and Navy nurses from Corregidor. *Seawolf* on April Fool's Day, south of Java, mangled light cruiser *Naka* with hits in two firerooms. *Naka* barely managed to make port and was out of the war a full year. *Searaven* performed a satisfactory rescue mission in mid-April, evacuating 33 Australians from Timor under trying conditions. Ensign George C. Cook USNR swam in through the surf and, after failing to find the Aussies, tried again three nights later and brought these debilitated men through the surf; their gratitude was touching. *Porpoise* rescued five Army aviators from an island near Halmahera and received in return a case of Scotch whisky with General MacArthur's thanks.

Lieutenant Commander Eugene B. McKinney took *Salmon* up

[28] See Coral Sea Task Organization in chap. 1 above, for boats and skippers.

the Lombok–Makassar–Sulu route and on the morning of 25 May sighted smoke on the horizon, closed and sank the 11,000-ton repair ship *Asahi*. The Japanese never seemed to realize the menace of a smoking stack. A few days later McKinney followed another such sign to the kill of 4000-ton *Ganges Maru*.

On 14 April *Skipjack* (Lieutenant Commander James W. Coe) sailed via Timor and the Celebes and Sulu Seas to Camranh Bay, Indochina. On 6 May she made a pre-dawn spurt to get ahead of a 2500-ton freighter and sank her before sunrise. Later the same day, she missed a French passenger ship with two prematures, but on the 8th two of her torpedoes crumpled a 4800-ton *Maru* and damaged a companion freighter. The escorting destroyer worked over *Skipjack* with 39 depth charges but did no damage. A few days later, "Red" Coe saw the wake of one of his torpedoes pass directly under a fat transport; "a bitter dose," as he reported. "I now have little confidence in these torpedoes." On 16 May the same thing happened; even the sinking next day of 5500-ton *Tazan Maru*, while her white-clad crew scrambled into life-boats, failed to allay the skipper's wrath. On tying up in Fremantle he wrote, "To make round trips of 8500 miles into enemy waters to gain attack positions undetected within 800 yards of enemy ships only to find that torpedoes run deep and over half the time will fail to function, seems to me an undesirable manner of gaining information which might be determined any morning within a few miles of a torpedo station in the presence of comparatively few hazards."

Coe's pungent remark was not the first intimation of disgust with torpedoes in the Southwest Pacific. As far back as December 1941, Lieutenant Commander T. D. Jacobs, C.O. of *Sargo*, had experimented with shallow depth settings and had inactivated the magnetic influence device, hoping to account for the failure of 13 torpedoes to explode. Jacobs later requested test firing to check depth control. Complaints to the Bureau of Ordnance brought an equivocal reply, in February 1942, that the torpedoes ran four feet deeper than the setting only during the first half-mile of their run.

Submarine crews were losing confidence in their captains and the captains were losing confidence in their torpedoes and themselves. On 20–21 June Captain Fife, of the Southwest Pacific Command, took matters into his own hands and caused torpedoes to be fired, under his personal supervision, against a special fisherman's net target. Exercise heads were specially weighted to simulate a standard warhead, the results proving that torpedoes ran about ten feet deeper than set. In July the test was repeated with the same damnably conclusive results. Admiral King now directed the Bureau of Ordnance to recheck its data. Finally, on 1 August 1942, eight months after the war's start, word was passed to the Fleet that torpedoes were actually running ten feet too deep! [29]

There still remained the premature explosions and contact firing-pin failures to be dealt with, and no remedy was found during the period which we are now discussing. So we must bear in mind that in all attacks described in this volume the American submariner was a gladiator without his cestus. Torpedoes were both unreliable and in short stock. Many were abandoned in the Philippines. Stateside production and overseas distribution were barely able to keep pace with expenditure. This had two bad effects; patrols made with less than full torpedo allowance were cut short by running out of "fish" and frequently a target escaped because the submarine could afford to fire only one or two torpedoes where a full spread should have been used.

Swordfish, in May and June 1942, swept through the South China Sea, sank two ships and damaged one. When ordered over to the Malay Peninsula, she located the spot where lay the bones of H.M.S. *Prince of Wales* and *Repulse* [30] and ascertained that the Japanese had marked it with a buoy. Returning to Fremantle on 4 July, the skipper complained that his men had not been separated from the ship in eight months and made a modest request that

[29] Technicians in tender *Holland* in Apr. 1942 discovered that the anti-counter-mining device was erratic and in June the Bureau of Ordnance authorized inactivation of the device at discretion.

[30] See Vol. III of this History pp. 188–90.

36-hour liberties be granted to a portion of his crew. Not long after this, an elaborate recreation and relief system was established in Australia as at Pearl Harbor. There were seaside and inland resort hotels where pallid submariners could tan themselves on the beach or go on kangaroo hunts; and, as one of their number remarked, "We enjoyed going ashore there because there were women, plenty of them, and they spoke English."

On 26 May 1942, when Rear Admiral Lockwood[31] relieved Captain Wilkes as Commander Southwest Pacific submarines, Japanese pressure in the Solomons and New Guinea brought a gradual shifting of fleet boats from western to eastern Australia. Throughout the summer and fall, Lockwood sent occasional patrols into the South China Sea, Philippine waters and the Flores Sea. There were a few successes, such as the blasting of a big aircraft ferry. Coasting on the surface during a violent electrical storm on 11 September, *Saury* put three torpedoes into this vessel, sending planes, men and fragments of ship sky-high.

Lieutenant Commander Frederick B. Warder took *Seawolf* into Philippine waters on her seventh war patrol, and he was out for blood.[32] On his fifth patrol he had been plagued by enemy escorts and had sunk only one ship, a converted gunboat. On his sixth patrol, although firing 17 torpedoes at a variety of targets, he had sunk only two medium *Marus*. This seventh patrol he was determined to get the enemy if it meant going right into the harbor after him. And that is just what he did. On 2 November at the entrance to Davao Gulf he fired three stern shots at *Gifu Maru*

[31] Charles A. Lockwood Jr., Virginia born (1890) and Missouri raised, Naval Academy '12, began his underwater career two years later, commanded a submarine at the age of 24 and a division in 1917. After several more submarine commands he served on the Yangtze Patrol and had destroyer duty for a year. From 1926 on, he was with submarines except for two years on the Naval mission to Brazil and two years as first lieutenant of *California* and "exec" of *Concord;* and two years instructing at the Naval Academy. Comsubdiv 13, 1935–37; submarine desk under C.N.O. and chief of staff to Comsubs. U. S. Fleet to Jan. 1941, when he acted chief of staff to Admiral Ghormley in London. Comsubs SW Pacific with rank of rear admiral, May 1942, Comsubpac Feb. 1943.

[32] Gerold Frank and J. D. Horan *U.S.S. Seawolf, Submarine Raider* (1945) contains good photos and anecdotes.

(2933 tons), took a photo of her sinking, counted 41 survivors in the water and cut in his position less than five miles from a light-house. The next day he charged into Davao Harbor, watched men loading hemp on board the 7189-ton *Sagami Maru*, lined her up in his periscope sights and put a fish through the starboard side of her engine room. The crew fought back with deck guns but Warder calmly put a second shot into her starboard side aft. This took all the fight out of the Japanese, who manned boats and rowed for the dock 800 yards away. A third torpedo adroitly placed in the bow sent this big ship to the bottom, and *Seawolf* hauled clear, furiously pursued by patrol craft and planes. Warder did not abandon Davao Gulf, and on the 8th polished off con-verted gunboat *Keiko Maru* in three deliberate hitting attacks which the victim's disciplined and alerted crew were unable to fight off.

Exploits such as these were too few to break Japan's "rice line" between the Indies and the Empire. The most valuable accom-plishments of the Australia-based boats were in the enemy-infested waters of the Bismarcks, the Solomons and New Guinea.

During the spring and early summer of 1942, the brunt of submarine war in that area was borne in discomfort and danger by the venerable S-boats. In theory this was an excellent employ-ment for craft of limited endurance, but practice soon uncovered their defects. On the surface the S-boat could do but 11 knots, nowhere near enough to make approaches on warships. If a target obligingly came within range of a waiting S-boat, primitive methods of torpedo control prevented accurate shooting. After getting off her "fish," the S-boat could go under water neither as deep nor as far nor as fast as the fleet boats, and her riveted hull frequently leaked a revealing trail of oil. Machinery and men were soon worn out by cruising in tropical waters with no air conditioning. Never-theless these boats made a wonderful record.

Lieutenant Commander Oliver G. Kirk took *S-42* up to the Bismarck Archipelago and on 11 May fired four torpedoes at minelayer *Okinoshima*, flagship of the Japanese Tulagi Occupation group.[33] He saw three hits, "like long thin horizontal phosphorescent bands," start fatal fires amidships. The ensuing counterattack brought everyone to the point of heat exhaustion; one man threw a fit, others collapsed in their tracks when the strain was over. *S–47* (Lieutenant Commander James W. Davis) in the same waters had trouble from start to finish. She could not move fast enough to get in a shot at a cruiser, whose escort's depth charges shook her like a kitten in a dog's mouth. She missed a freighter, which turned and nearly rammed her. Machinery breakdowns were frequent and difficult to repair. Living conditions were intolerable; mildew whiskers grew on food and clothing, rust attacked metal, heat rash broke out on irritated skins. Men slept on the slimy steel decks rather than in their sweat-soaked bunks. In the hope that the crew might have more rest during the submerged hours of daylight, meals were up-ended, with breakfast at nightfall, dinner at midnight and supper at dawn. *S–44*, equipped with air conditioning, found life more bearable and sank converted salvage ship *Shoei Maru* on 12 May off Cape St. George.

Navigating an S-boat was accomplished more by smell and feel than through science. There was no radar, no fathometer and only inferior sound gear. Submergence all day in unpredictable currents threw off dead reckoning and without bubble sextants star fixes could not be obtained at night; even their horizon sextants were almost worn out, so that twilight fixes were uncertain. On the night of 13–14 August, *S–39* (Lieutenant F. E. Brown) grounded on a submerged reef off Rossel Island in the Louisiades, listed 35 degrees to port and commenced pounding to pieces on the rocks. Backing with the engines, blowing ballast and fuel, discharging torpedoes and jettisoning ammunition had little effect. As the day wore on, the list increased to 60 degrees and there was danger that the boat would roll completely over. Fortunately the Australian corvette *Katoomba* appeared and rescued all hands, leaving *S–39* to be destroyed by Allied bombers.

In spite of all their difficulties, the Brisbane-based S-boats helped

[33] See chapters i and ii of this Volume.

to reduce the Emperor's merchant marine, and during the Guadalcanal campaign they won some outstanding duels. On 8 August
S–38 (Lieutenant Commander H. G. Munson) disposed of transport *Meiyo Maru*, loaded with reinforcements for Guadalcanal;
two days later *S–44* (Lieutenant Commander J. R. Moore) sank
heavy cruiser *Kako*, retiring after the Savo Island battle. In October 1942 the S-boats were sent Stateside and underwater patrols
in these waters were turned over to fleet boats from the Aleutians,
under the direct control of Admiral Halsey, Commander South
Pacific Force. As the boats for tactical reasons had to be based at
Brisbane, Captain Leon J. Huffman, a submariner, was assigned to
Halsey's staff as liaison officer. Frequently, during the darker days
of the campaign, Huffman's tally of underwater victories was the
only good news the Admiral got.

Let us try to see this campaign through the eyes of the submarine skipper, for whom each patrol was an operation in itself.
Sculpin (Lieutenant Commander Lucius H. Chappell) of the
old Asiatic Fleet was one of the first fleet subs to take station off
New Britain. Early in the morning of 28 September she possibly
damaged a tanker but then found out that she was up against
the Japanese varsity. For hours, two well coördinated destroyers
tossed depth charges down on her, tearing a small hole in the
pressure hull which had the crew sweating and bailing but did
not force them to break off their patrol. On 7 October Chappell
saw a destroyer and a transport in his periscope, and was tempted
to retaliate on the destroyer, but "prudence prevailed over personal
animosity" and his torpedoes sank the 4700-ton transport. After
the usual depth-charge shivaree, *Sculpin* swam clear. On the night
of 10 October Chappell and his watch topside were able to applaud
an air raid on Kavieng, then moved down to Rabaul where they
witnessed the same thing on the 13th. Next day *Sculpin* started
some fireworks of her own, making a surface chase to sink a 3000-
ton passenger-cargo *Maru*. On the 18th the sub was routed into
New Georgia Strait, where she tussled with a ship which had
"started life as a tramp" but now had guns and depth charges to

defend herself. *Sculpin* missed this one with her last torpedo and then went "back to the barn" at Brisbane.

In October our old friend *Gudgeon*, 13 days out of Brisbane, sighted a rusty five-ship convoy south of New Ireland, pounding painfully along. Lying in wait on the convoy's starboard bow, she fired torpedoes at the two leading ships, which were in line abreast, then dove and headed underneath the others so as to blend her propeller noises with theirs. Even so the two escorts located and attacked her with 51 depth charges. One of the targets, a 6800-tonner, sank and the other was probably damaged.

Sturgeon, on a seven-week patrol along the seaway between Rabaul and the Shortlands, made contact with 36 targets, many of them big and juicy but moving at terrifically high speed. Warships on this "Tokyo Express" run were hard to catch, and *Sturgeon* managed to sink only the 8000-ton aircraft ferry *Katsuragi Maru*.

Silversides parted from her tender in Brisbane with the executive officer tootling on his trombone and the crew softly humming the favorite Australian melody, "Waltzing Matilda." This was her fourth war patrol and she was a good boat and a lucky one.[34] On 23 December off Bougainville a fireman named Platter came down with a terrible bellyache which the "doctor," Pharmacist's Mate T. A. Moore, diagnosed as appendicitis. Lieutenant Commander Burlingame consented to let Moore operate when it became apparent that the man would die if something were not done in a hurry. A chief radioman was called to lend a hand and two husky seamen held the patient on the wardroom table. The boat submerged to twenty fathoms and the operation began. There were difficulties in finding the appendix, keeping the man drugged, and preventing the operating crew from passing out from the ether; but after five hours' work Platter was sewed up shipshape and stowed in his bunk. *Silversides* surfaced just in time to avoid a collision with an enemy destroyer. Her batteries were nearly

[34] Her commissioning day in Mare Island had been rainy and foreboding until just before the ceremony, when the clouds rolled back and opened up a blue and sunny sky, a happy omen which the crew never forgot.

depleted, but she submerged again and Burlingame played tag with the destroyer while a Japanese plane came over and dropped a salvo of bombs close by his exposed periscope, knocking it off and locking the bow planes so that the boat started up-end. Everyone on board lost footing and the patient was thrown from his bunk. An ensign ran forward to ask the chief torpedoman what he was doing about the bow planes; the chief replied that he was doing all he could – he was praying. Prayers were effective and *Silversides* eventually squared away on an even keel and evaded pursuit. In recompense for this rugged bout, *Silversides* sank a 10,000-ton tanker on 18 January 1943 and two days later sank three freighters, totalling 18,000 tons, with six torpedoes. And the patient recovered and returned to duty.[85]

Nautilus, the submarine hero of Midway, had an experience on New Year's Day 1943 in keeping with the Jules Verne tradition. She hove-to off a Bougainville beach and took on board a refugee group consisting of 14 Catholic nuns, 3 children and 12 other persons, whom skipper Brockman greeted with "Happy New Year!" – as indeed it was for them. *Nautilus* entertained these guests until they could be transferred to a patrol craft in friendly waters.

Albacore (Lieutenant Commander Richard C. Lake) made a significant kill without realizing it. After dark 18 December she was cruising off Madang Harbor, New Guinea, when the skipper unleashed two torpedoes at what he thought was a cargo ship. Countermeasures kept him down, but in the morning he saw large quantities of debris marked with Japanese characters. He returned to base claiming a freighter; actually he had sunk a victor of the Wake and Savo Island battles, light cruiser *Tenryu*.

Not all the boats were lucky. *Growler* (Lieutenant Commander Howard W. Gilmore) put out from Brisbane for the Bismarcks

---

[85] *Grayback* had a similar experience with a bad appendix on Christmas Eve 1942. Pharmacist's Mate Robe, described as the ship's best lookout, best machine-gunner and best helmsman, was assisted by a Yale man who had "once considered studying medicine." *Grayback*, too, had action after the operation, destroying several landing barges that night.

in January 1943 and on the 16th made a brilliant attack on a well escorted 6000-ton freighter, sending her down with two torpedoes. After several other scrapes with enemy ships, *Growler* on the night of 7 February was suddenly attacked, on the surface, by a Japanese destroyer at very close range. Before Gilmore could turn her, he inadvertently rammed the enemy at 17 knots. The boat shuddered and heeled 50 degrees while enemy machine gunners poured a shattering fusillade onto the exposed superstructure. Gilmore, badly wounded, ordered the bridge cleared and shouted, "Take her down!" *Growler* submerged with the skipper and two others still on deck. She was saved by this unselfish action, which cost brave Gilmore his life.

Argonaut, the big 2700-tonner which in August transported Marine raiders to Makin Island, was sent on a routine patrol in January, 1943. On the 10th, in full view of an American Army bomber, she attacked an enemy convoy and damaged one destroyer. The other destroyers attacked with depth charges, damaging *Argonaut* so that her bow came up like a giant buoy. The Japs then circled and pumped shells into the hull until they had destroyed it. Lieutenant Commander John R. Pierce and his entire crew of 103 perished.

It is surprising that more submarines were not lost in the Solomons–New Guinea campaigns. Enemy transports seldom traveled unescorted, the escorts were usually well trained, and the oily calm prevalent in those low latitudes made a periscope easy to detect. There were plenty of enemy airfields on which to base anti-submarine aircraft, and Japanese submarines offered another threat. Finally, American fliers regarded all submarines in these waters as hostile and frequently bombed American boats. Such hazards kept our submarines from running up high scores; in the six months of the Guadalcanal campaign their total bag was 23 ships and 85,361 tons.

In October and November 1942, minelaying by submarines began in the Southwest, as in the Central Pacific. *Thresher, Gar, Tautog* and *Grenadier* made successful plants far into enemy waters, even in the Gulf of Siam. In postwar tabulation *Tautog's* mines received credit for blasting three ships, and *Grenadier's* for two.

During the Solomons–New Guinea campaign there had been little or no contact with the Philippine guerilla forces, but in January 1943 *Gudgeon* landed six men and a ton of supplies on Negros. Thenceforth submarine runs were made about every five weeks, doing much to hearten and support the Filipino patriots.

5. Sub Summary for 1942

Compared with their later successes, the performance of American submarines in the first year of the war was disappointing. Certain factors that kept that performance down have appeared in the stories of war patrols, but the reasons for these defects are not so apparent.

Particularly does the question "Why did the Navy enter the war with faulty torpedoes?" cry for an answer. Japanese torpedoes were wickedly effective and certainly the Japanese were not superior to Americans in technical know-how. Why, then, this difference? The answer is not simple.

In prewar days, torpedo development, manufacture and testing were lodged in one place, the Naval Torpedo Station, a large establishment on Goat Island in the harbor of Newport, Rhode Island.[36] But the Navy's Bureau of Ordnance directly supervised the Torpedo Station and so cannot escape responsibility. There was no direct link between the Station and the Fleet, and only tenuous liaison was maintained by line officers, skilled in torpedo engineering, who rotated between sea billets and the Torpedo Station. These few officers were almost the only ones in the Navy whose technical knowledge of torpedoes exceeded what was required for normal overhaul and practice firings. The submariners'

[36] The Torpedo Station received some assistance from the research staff of the General Electric Company and from the Massachusetts Institute of Technology.

weapon was designed, built and tested under the direction of specialists; the ultimate consumer was allowed no say in the matter.

The situation would not have been so bad except for the policy of top secrecy maintained by the Bureau of Ordnance. For instance, when the magnetic-influence exploder was designed and tested, knowledge of its mechanism, even of its existence, was bottled up and sealed in the minds of a few men for 16 years. It was finally issued to the Fleet in 1941 with an injunction that captains and torpedo officers keep it ultra-secret. Later, torpedomen were reluctantly given some details so that at least they would know how to handle the device. Service experience with the exploder was practically nil when war started; men on the firing line were largely ignorant of its functioning.

Prewar economy was another factor that made for poor performance. A torpedo is an expensive weapon, costing between $8,000 and $10,000 in 1941, and the Navy was governed by a budget before the fighting started. Only a handful of men in service had ever seen a live warhead fired. In practice a special exercise head was fitted which caused the torpedo to float at the end of its run, in order to facilitate recovery. When a firing drill was conducted, officers and men were interested only in making the costly torpedo run *under* the target, and having it surface for recovery afterwards. If the torpedo ran under the target's keel it was presumed to be a "hit"; the magnetic-influence exploder was never given a chance to explode, and nobody questioned but that it would function. And nobody found out that the torpedoes were running much deeper than they were set. The Torpedo Station tested them against a fish net mounted on the Newport range between Coasters Harbor and Gould Islands, where the water was too shoal for deep running. Depth-recording mechanisms, installed within the body of the torpedo, indicated promptly when its depth changed, but were unreliable in measuring the depth. Besides it was assumed that, with the influence exploder, it would make no difference if the depth were a few feet off one way or the other. As for the contact firing mechanism, hundreds of practice shots were fired with the torpedo swinging from a pendulum against a plate representing a ship's side, and torpedo drops were made against a concrete ramp; but these tests were evidently inadequate as the most important defect was never disclosed.

There is some consolation in learning that the Germans, with all their previous torpedo experience, had much the same sort of trouble with magnetic-influence exploders in this war; but the Germans solved their problem much more quickly than did the Americans. And it is humiliating to think that poor "have-not" Japan liberally expended live torpedoes and hulls in realistic tests, which "rich" America felt she could not afford.

It is only fair to say that the torpedo took more than its share of blame; that misses caused by errors of judgment were sometimes improperly ascribed to torpedo faults. Blunders were made by submariners in approaching targets, in firing spreads and in control, owing to lack of combat experience. Torpedo maintenance was occasionally neglected, and duds due to careless upkeep were blamed on the mechanism. But the torpedoes were defective, and nothing is more disastrous to military morale than faulty weapons. It is a matter of pride that the submariners of the Pacific Fleet never gave up trying and were eventually rewarded when the defects of their torpedoes were corrected.

The torpedo shortage of 1942, which reduced spreads and shortened patrols, was caused partly by the loss of 233 torpedoes at Cavite and partly by American politics. As early as 1930 the Bureau of Ordnance had foreseen a torpedo shortage in the event of war and endeavored to reopen a World War I torpedo station at Alexandria, Virginia. Civilian employees of the Newport plant saw in this a threat to their jobs, and as the Torpedo Station was regarded by certain politicians as a part of their patronage, they successfully prevented the reëstablishment of the Alexandria Torpedo Station until July 1941.[37]

---

[37] *Submarine Operational History* and conversation with numerous persons "in the know." The Newport Torpedo Station made an excellent torpedo, apart from the features mentioned, but the work was slow and during the war the infiltration

The year was one of exploration rather than exploitation. Submarines probed everywhere to feel out the principal Japanese shipping lanes, and much of this search was unproductive. For instance, submarines patrolled fruitlessly off certain passages into the Palaus for months until, in October 1942, a captured chart revealed that the Japanese were routing traffic into and out of that group of islands by a secret passage many miles away from the patrol route.

Excessive caution was another deterrent to success. This was partly the fault of a convention in prewar target practice which imposed severe penalties on a submarine that was sighted before firing. Early in the war, American submarines stayed submerged all day, often waited for targets to appear instead of seeking them out, fired from extreme ranges, dove deep at the slightest sign of countermeasures. Night attacks on the surface, penetration of enemy harbors, counterattack on escorts — all normal procedures in years to come — were daring innovations in this exploratory year.

In addition to tactical improvements, future submariners were to have the advantage of technological advances such as radar. And, as more boats were completed and more bases were wrested from the enemy, the number of patrols vastly increased.

On the bright side there were many happy discoveries in 1942. Shipbuilders had done even better than they knew. Submarine hulls withstood pressures and pummelings far beyond anticipated limits. Before the war, the Portsmouth Navy Yard tested hull strength by actually depth-charging submarines — even with crews inside — and from these tests made important improvements. The engines were rugged and reliable; the boats were long-winded and far-ranging. Even prosaic details such as the Kleinschmidt water distiller added immeasurably to comfort and human endurance in

---

of labor politicians made conditions worse. The Torpedo Station was by no means the only instance of the effect of political pressure on the Navy, but it was one of the worst, in more ways than one. The whole subject awaits a thorough investigation.

American submarines. On the other side, Japanese anti-submarine technique was poor initially and improved little during the war. From 7 December 1941 to 8 February 1943, only five American submarines were lost in action, and one of these was lying alongside a dock.[38]

By February 1943 the best hunting grounds were known, some of the torpedo defects had been corrected, and there were plenty of aggressive skippers who could be depended on to make the most of opportunities.

[38] See Vol. III of this History pp. 172, 304; *Argonaut* above, and *Grunion,* which may have been an operational loss.

CHAPTER XI

The Makin Raid[1]

16–18 August 1942

East Longitude dates, Zone minus 12 time.

THE MOST ambitious of the many special missions assigned to the submarines occurred as an offstage act of the Guadalcanal–Tulagi landings — a scheme to distract Japanese attention during the early days of the Solomons campaign. It involved transporting a raiding force over some 2000 miles of ocean to Makin, one of the Gilbert Islands. Selected to do the job were the big 2700-ton *Nautilus* and *Argonaut;*[2] the passengers were 222 Marines of the 2nd Raider Battalion commanded by Lieutenant Colonel Evans F. Carlson USMC.

Early in the war the Japanese moved into the Gilbert Islands and announced to reluctant natives that henceforth Hirohito was their boss, but they did little to implement the pronouncement. On Makin Atoll, for instance, the entire garrison consisted of 43 fighting men. Admiral Nimitz was well aware of the enemy's weakness in the Gilberts and believed that a small force of Marines could stir up a rumpus out of all proportion to their numbers. He was right; but the rumpus was not to our ultimate advantage.

Events were happening so fast in the Pacific that there was little

[1] Action Reports of units involved; Cincpac "Battle Experience from Pearl Harbor to Midway" (Secret Information Bulletin No. 1); O.N.I. Combat Narrative *Miscellaneous Actions in the South Pacific;* Capt. Walter Karig USNR and Cdr. Eric Purdon USNR "*The Makin Island Raid*" U. S. *Naval Inst. Proceedings* Oct. 1946; Japanese "Records of Various Base Forces," WDC Translation No. 161,013.
[2] *Nautilus* was commanded by Cdr. William H. Brockman; *Argonaut* by Lt. Cdr. John R. Pierce.

time to plan and still less to train the expedition. On 8 August the two submarines poked their black noses out of Pearl Harbor, separated, and settled down for a long and uncomfortable voyage. There was no place to sit and no place to stand, so the Marines and off-watch sailors kept to their bunks except when eating. The air was hot and fetid with the odor of unwashed bodies. Meals were a continuous performance for the cooks and stewards since it took tnree hours to feed all hands. The only breaks were the morning and evening exercise periods, but even these were trying since the appearance of an enemy ship, sub or plane meant a pell-mell scramble for the hatches before submerging. That sort of thing went on for over a week, yet the sailors and raiders managed to retain their good spirits.

Nautilus, carrying Commander John M. Haines, the task force commander, arrived off Makin Atoll before dawn 16 August and spent the day sizing up the island through her periscope. That night the two boats joined company and final orders were given.

During the midwatch the submarines inched cautiously toward the beach, a ticklish navigational problem with inaccurate charts and current tables. Rubber boats were brought topside, inflated, rigged with outboard motors and stowed with the raiders' gear. The next problem was getting the boats into the water and the men into the boats. The first was easy, but the second required that some of the *Nautilus* Marines ride in *Argonaut* boats. *Nautilus* wallowed noisily in the swell like a playful hippopotamus, water sloshing and wheezing through the limber holes in the superstructure. From the beach came a steady roar of surf lashing against the reef. With all this noise, Colonel Carlson was unable to make his orders heard and was very nearly left behind. Not knowing whether his men were in the proper boats, he decided to make the landing in one spot instead of two as planned, but one boat didn't get the word.

Makin is a typical Pacific atoll, a necklace of palm-shaded coral islets around a quiet lagoon. On the seaward side of Butaritari, the largest island, is a fringing coral reef. Carlson elected to land over the reef opposite the principal settlement, which lay on the lagoon only 1500 feet across Butaritari.

The rubber boats skimmed through the surf and made their landings undetected, 15 of them hitting the correct spot at 0500 August 17, three others landing somewhat to the north; the one which hadn't got the word beached a full mile to the south. Carlson paused long enough to hide boats in the underbrush, post a guard and establish radio communication with the submarines.

So far so good. Now prospects for surprise, as rosy as the dawn light which was streaking the eastern sky, were suddenly shattered by a rifle shot. A Marine had accidentally discharged his piece. So, abandoning all pretense of secrecy, Carlson ordered one company of raiders to dash across the narrow island and seize the coastal road on the lagoon side.

The rifle shot was not a complete surprise to Sergeant Major Kanemitsu and his men. Several days previously, the Japanese high command, uneasily aware that the Americans were on the move and not knowing whither, had ordered a general alert. Makin was a soft billet for the Japanese, situated as it was in the pleasant flow of the trade winds and far from the shooting war, but Kanemitsu had taken the alert seriously. Each day his little garrison held maneuvers. Machine-gun nests were built and tree-climbing snipers were ready to station themselves in the tops of coconut palms. Hence, although the warning came before reveille, the Japanese were quick to organize defenses.

Not quick enough, however. Lieutenant Merwin C. Plumley and his company reached the lagoon shore, took over a building without opposition, then commenced a southward advance. It was 0630 before the Japanese, arriving afoot, on bicycles and in trucks, made their first effort to stop the Marines. For the rest of the day the Japanese were to fight with last-ditch bravery.

Eager natives joined the Marines early and told Carlson that the bulk of the enemy lay two miles to the southward congregated around a radio station at the head of a wharf. Carlson asked for and received bombardment support from *Nautilus* but *Argonaut* did not receive the message. The submarine bombarded the land positions to the best of its ability although handicapped by poor observation and lack of bombardment-type shells. While the shooting went on, the Marines reported a small transport and a patrol boat in the lagoon standing down from the northward. *Nautilus* gunners could not see these targets but scattered 23 salvos from the two 6-inch guns in their direction. The results were surprising; both craft sank and 60 Japanese went down with the transport.

At 0905 Kanemitsu admitted the hopelessness of his situation with a final radio message, "All men are dying serenely in battle." That was hardly the phrase for it. From the tops of the coconut trees they sniped at every raider that moved, especially those who appeared to be wearing telephones or operating radios. From their machine-gun emplacements they fired until all the gunners were killed. Carlson found it necessary to employ his second company when the southward advance slowed down.

At 1039 an enemy reconnaissance plane appeared and the two submarines went under. This was forerunner of several aërial attacks, the first at 1130 when two planes dropped bombs harmlessly, and the second at 1255 when twelve planes of motley description flew into the fight. Ten of these bombed and strafed the island without success while two others, big "Mavis" flying boats, landed troops in the lagoon. Marine automatic-weapon fire hit and burned one plane on the water and caused the other to crash in taking off. Even so, about 35 troops made the shore in Japanese territory. By midafternoon, snipers concealed in the palm groves became so difficult to locate that Carlson pulled his men north into more open terrain, hoping that the enemy would give chase and be easier targets. As the Japs fell for this ruse, another bombing raid came over and dumped bombs right on them.

Meanwhile Lieutenant Oscar F. Peatross USMC and eleven men from the boat which had landed far to the south found themselves to the enemy's rear. They immediately went on a destructive rampage, destroyed the radio station, killed Japs, searched houses and burned equipment. That evening Peatross and seven men breasted the surf and reached their submarine.

At 1700 Carlson began a deliberate withdrawal to the embarkation point and at 1900 launched his boats. But the surf which had been so easy on the way in was a different story on the way out. Outboard motors declined to work, and no matter how hard the men paddled few could clear the breakers. Boats capsized, men lost their weapons and most of their clothing, and finally were cast up on the beach exhausted. Only seven boats and fewer than 100 men made it back to the submarines that night.

This was low tide for Marine spirits. Here were 120 of them on a hostile shore deep in enemy waters without sufficient arms and hampered by wounded, four of them stretcher cases. The only light in the sky was a cheering signal blinker from the submarines, to the effect that they would stay indefinitely to make the rescue.

During the night there was but one brief skirmish with a Japanese patrol and in the morning a new effort was made to get off. Carlson sent Major James Roosevelt USMCR, his executive officer, out through the surf with four boats. In the meantime a volunteer five-man Marine crew headed into the shore from *Nautilus*, hoping to get a line through the surf and pull the remaining boats out to sea. One swam ashore but a plane strafed the boat, which disappeared and was never seen again. There were still 70 men left on Makin but Japanese aircraft became so active that it was decided to postpone further embarkation efforts until nightfall.

Apparently these raiders thought they had been abandoned on Makin. In a popular Japanese history that came out during the war, there is published in facsimile a note signed by a Marine captain offering to surrender his unit of "approximately 60" men.[3] Fortunately, when they were looking around for someone to receive the note, these Marines made the surprising discovery that

[3] *Dai Toa Senshi* (Story of the Greater East Asia War) 1944 II p. 470. Copy in Library of Congress. The name of the signer is obliterated. Either one of the 9 Marines subsequently taken prisoner retained this note and the Japanese obtained it from him; or it was picked up elsewhere. It certainly was never delivered.

there were no Japanese left! Most of them were dead; a few had fled to remote islets of the atoll. The situation was indeed well in hand. During the remainder of the 18th the raiders wandered about, picking up important documents in Kanemitsu's headquarters and destroying weapons and equipment. Eighty-three dead Japs were counted and only three live ones, who soon joined the majority. After dark, four rubber boats were carried across the island to the quiet waters of the lagoon, lashed to a native outrigger canoe, and before midnight had reached the submarines. Flames from burning Japanese aviation gasoline made a beacon as the two undersea boats departed for Pearl Harbor, convinced that all living Marines were on board. But nine of them were left behind.

At the time it looked as if this foray were a great success, at a cost of 30 Marines killed and missing. It caused the enemy to divert forces, secured interesting intelligence, and taught valuable lessons about raiding islands and about submarine troop transport. Nevertheless, this raid prompted Tokyo to order the fortification of the Gilbert Islands on a scale which later cost the Americans dear. Within a month of Carlson's departure, a detachment of Japanese Special Naval Landing Force landed on Tarawa. More troops followed, so that by November 1943, when the Marines stormed ashore, over 2500 well entrenched Japs were on hand to meet them – a striking contrast to Kanemitsu's 43-man garrison at Makin.

The story of nine missing Marines provides a sad sequel. Left behind in the rush, they were captured a few days later and shipped to Kwajalein for transportation to Tokyo. At Kwajalein the prisoners received good care at the hands of curious Japanese, who frequently gave them candy and cigarettes and joshed with them about the sights they would see in Tokyo. For six weeks the raiders lived there in barracks, never doubting the good faith of their captors. But early in October Vice Admiral Koso Abe, commanding Marshall Island bases, became impatient over the delay in moving them out, and after a brief conference with an officer from Truk headquarters summarily ordered the men executed. The onerous task fell on the shoulders of Captain Yoshio Obara, Kwajalein garrison commander. Obara, who had two brothers in America and nephews in the United States Army, protested vehemently against the inhuman and illegal order, but Abe remained adamant. The Captain was unable to find a single volunteer executioner and at last detailed four officers, who reluctantly obeyed. Dubious homage was accorded the doomed men when Captain Obara selected a date for the execution which coincided with Japan's annual memorial to departed heroes, the Yasukuni Shrine festival. On 16 October the nine Marines were led to a large grave and ceremoniously beheaded in the presence of the sadistic Abe.

After the burial, Obara's men placed flowers on the grave and considered the incident closed. But a Marshallese native had witnessed the execution from a hiding place in the bushes and, after the war, testified against the principals. Admiral Abe was tried for atrocity and hanged at Guam; Captain Obara received a ten-year prison sentence.[4]

[4] Commander Marianas "Records of Proceedings of a Military Commission," 1946.

PART III

The First American Offensive

10 July–8 August 1942

CHAPTER XII

Strategic Decisions[1]

March–July 1942

THE GUADALCANAL operation was the first in the Pacific War — excepting the operations of submarines — in which the United States took the strategic offensive. Earlier carrier strikes and sharp backlashings on the enemy like those on Balikpapan and Badung Strait were offensive only in a tactical sense. Moreover, they were hit-and-run affairs; this was a hit-and-stay proposition. Since it was initiated by the United States, the discussion among top-level planners which led to the strategic decision to occupy the Solomons goes back almost to the very start of the Pacific War, and the objectives of that decision were not fully attained until 1944.

Although the decision to "beat Hitler first" to which the American Chiefs of Staff had agreed even before America entered the war[2] imposed a strategic defensive in the Pacific, that decision never implied mere passivity. It did not preclude raids, attrition tactics by submarines or the exploitation of favorable opportunities for limited offensives. Admiral King, eager from the first to seize such opportunities, germinated the Guadalcanal operation in a memorandum to General Marshall dated 18 February 1942.

That was only four days after the fall of Singapore. General

---

[1] Data for this chapter are derived from Cominch and C.N.O. files and records. Captain Tracy B. Kittredge USNR kindly checked accuracy. Also, Cincpac files and papers by courtesy of Admiral Nimitz; Admiral Ghormley's Narrative of his Command, written in 1944, and conversations with him.

[2] See Vol. I pp. 46–8; Vol. III pp. 51–2; this decision was confirmed at the "Arcadia" conference between Roosevelt and Churchill at Washington in early Jan. 1942.

Wainwright was still battling on Bataan, Darwin was being bombed, and the Japanese octopus was closing in on Java.

King requested the Chief of Naval Operations (Admiral Stark) and his opposite number on the Joint Chiefs of Staff (General Marshall) to approve the establishment of an American base in Efate Island of the New Hebrides, 300 miles northeast of Nouméa and 600 miles southeast of Guadalcanal. Marshall, with his usual perspicacity, replied that such a step had far-reaching implications; air power commitments in other theaters would seem to preclude expansion in the Southwest Pacific for some time to come; but, if the Admiral wanted it, "the entire situation must be reconsidered." King developed his thoughts further on 2 March. The occupation of Efate would provide a bastion to the United States–Australia lifeline; but, more important, would be the first of a series of strong points, near enough for mutual air support, "from which a step-by-step general advance could be made through the New Hebrides, Solomons and Bismarcks." In other words, he anticipated the entire course of the war in the South Pacific to the middle of 1944.

Three days later the Admiral expressed the same concept in a memorandum to the President. By that time, 5 March, the situation in the Southwest had further deteriorated. The surrender of Java was a matter of hours and General MacArthur had been ordered to retire to Australia. Nobody seemed able to stop the Japanese, and in Washington there was even serious talk of abandoning Australia and New Zealand to the enemy. But, as King told the President, "We cannot in honor let Australia and New Zealand down. They are our brothers, and we must not allow them to be overrun by Japan." And the President agreed.

As Admiral King saw it, the approaches from Japan to Australia should be actively and continuously probed in order to hamper the enemy's southeasterly advance and prevent his consolidation of conquered areas. The Allies already possessed strong points in Samoa, Suva and Nouméa, and the Navy was about to set up a base at Tongatabu. The time was ripe to occupy and fortify Efate in the New Hebrides and Funafuti in the Ellices. When reasonably secure in these new bases the Navy could cover the West Coast–Australia sea route more effectively, and also "drive northwesterly from the New Hebrides into the Solomons and Bismarcks."

Accordingly, on 14 March 1942, the Joint Chiefs of Staff reconsidered the entire situation. The U-boat offensive against Atlantic shipping was then most alarming; American ground and air forces were being accumulated in the United Kingdom for an offensive the nature of which was still under intense discussion; the British were under heavy pressure in the near East; and the Russians, locked with the German Army along an extensive front, were loudly demanding the establishment of a second front in Europe.[3] But, on the other side of the world, Japan had gained territory which would enable her to attain economic self-sufficiency in all strategic materials if given time to organize them. If not pressed by us on her southward and eastward flanks, Japan as her next move might drive through Burma into India and strike hands with the eastward-advancing Germans; or she might invade Australia or New Zealand; or turn on Russia and invade Siberia. Her success in any one of these three possible operations would make ultimate Allied victory exceedingly difficult to attain.

Wherever the Joint Chiefs turned, the situation seemed urgent. In their opinion the United Nations "would constantly be on the verge of ultimate defeat during 1942." Faced by this dilemma, the Joint Chiefs recommended a limited deployment of American forces into the Southwest Pacific, with the object of securing the antipodes and putting such pressure on Japan as to prevent any further westward or southward offensive on her part.[4] They estimated that 416,000 United States troops would be required in

---

[3] In Admiral Stark's conversation with the President on 25 Apr. he remarked "If we win in the Atlantic we will win everywhere; if we lose in the Atlantic . . ." F.D.R. finished the phrase, "We will lose everywhere." "No," said Stark, "I'd put it 'we might not win anywhere.'" "That's right!" said F.D.R.

[4] Their planning committee even made the tentative suggestion to revaluate the basic strategic concept of the war if the British refused to launch a European offensive in 1942, "in order to consider the possibility of concentrating U. S. offensive effort in the Pacific Area." This tentative feeler became more emphatic in June, when it looked as if the British were stalling. See Vol. II p. 14.

overseas positions in the Pacific to secure Australia and New Zealand; 225,000 were already there or en route. As for naval forces available then or during 1942, this table tells the story: —

DEPLOYMENT OF UNITED STATES SHIPS, 1942

	Available 15 March		Expected Additions, 1942	Recommended Deployment	
	Atlantic	*Pacific*	*1942*	*Atlantic*	*Pacific*
Battleships [5]	2	7	3	2	10
Large Carriers	2	5	—	1	6
Escort Carriers	1	—	10	7	4
Heavy Cruisers	4	13	—	4	13
Light Cruisers	8	12	6	13	13
Destroyers	78	92	44	106	108
Submarines	50	61	13	28	96

The Joint Chiefs concluded their session of 14 March by recommending the following general course of action for the fighting forces of the United States during 1942: —

1. Secure the territory and coastal waters of the Americas.

2. With British and Canadian assistance, secure the transatlantic sea and air routes.

3. Secure the British antipodes and the islands and sea lanes between them and our West Coast and Panama.

4. Contain Japanese forces where they now are, and attempt to reduce them with attrition tactics by submarines and carriers.

5. Give limited air assistance to the defense of the India-Burma-China area.

6. Exert the maximum Anglo-American effort in offensive operations against Germany.

It looked as though King's Efate-Solomons offensive were indefinitely postponed, unless it could be worked in under 3 or 4. But Admiral King knew of more than one way to skin a cat or start a base.

About 500 men of the Americal Division, the United States Army garrison of New Caledonia, were sent up to Efate about 25 March; Marine Fighter Squadron 212, diverted from Tonga-

[5] Exclusive of the old *Texas, New York* and *Arkansas* in the Atlantic.

tabu, arrived about the same time, and the 4th Marine Defense Battalion also. Work was started on the airfield at Vila Harbor, and before the Guadalcanal operation began there was a serviceable strip for land-based planes there.[6]

On 17 March (East Longitude date) General MacArthur arrived in Australia. The Anzac Command was now obsolete; Abda had ceased to exist. After about two weeks' negotiations, conducted mostly in London among representatives of the American, British, Australian, New Zealand and Netherlands-in-exile governments, a new division of Pacific Ocean areas and assignment of commands was decided upon, about 1 April 1942. This delimitation endured with little change for two years, and, in its main division between the Nimitz and MacArthur commands, until the end of the war.

As outlined in the directives to Nimitz and MacArthur on 4 April, the areas and commands were as follows: —

1. *Southwest Pacific Area,* General Douglas MacArthur, Supreme Commander Allied Forces. The northern and eastern boundary between this and the Pacific Ocean Areas started at the China coast on lat. 20° N, ran east to long. 135° E, south on that meridian through the Philippine Sea to the Equator, along the Line eastward to long. 165° E (between Nauru and Ocean Islands), south on long. 165° E to lat. 10° S, southwesterly to lat. 17° S, long. 160° E, and south on that meridian to the Pole. Thus, General MacArthur's area included the Philippines, Australia and all waters between them; the whole of New Guinea and all the Bismarck and Solomon Islands.[7]

[6] Efate in the New Hebrides, an irregularly shaped island about 25 by 14 miles, has two good harbors, Vila and Havannah, with enough level ground at each for the construction of airfields. Vila, a town with about 1000 white population, is the capital of the New Hebrides, an Anglo-French condominium (locally known as the "pandemonium") that had been functioning since 1906. There was a seaplane base there before the war which the Navy improved, and it established another at Havannah. Development at Efate was planned in order to provide a reserve air and naval base as an alternate to or overflow from Nouméa, with secure anchorage and limited supply base for a large task force, and air facilities for the operation of two carrier-based and two land-based air groups, and a hospital.

[7] Since Admiral King has been accused of attempting to hamper and restrict General MacArthur's command, it is worth recording that the addition of the

2. *Southeast Pacific Area.* Everything east of a line drawn from the Mexico-Guatemala boundary to lat. 11° N, long. 110° W (near Clipperton Island) and thence south to the Pole. Rear Admiral John F. Shafroth continued to command in this area, with a small Southeast Pacific Force consisting of three old light cruisers and a few destroyers.

3. *Pacific Ocean Area,* Admiral Chester W. Nimitz, Commander in Chief, included everything between these two. It, in turn, was divided more or less laterally into

a. *North Pacific Area.* North of lat. 42° N, to include the Aleutians and Alaska. No commander was appointed or force assigned until just before the Battle of Midway.

b. *Central Pacific Area.* From lat. 42° N to the Equator, including the Hawaiian, Gilbert, Marshall, Caroline and Marianas Islands. No subordinate commander was appointed under Admiral Nimitz.

c. *South Pacific Area.* From the Equator to the Pole, including the Ellice, Phoenix, Marquesas, Tuamotu, Samoa, Fiji and New Hebrides island groups and New Caledonia and New Zealand.[8]

Vice Admiral Ghormley,[9] whose long and varied naval experience qualified him for this important command, arrived in Wash-

---

Bismarcks and Solomons to it was his idea, as he felt it was essential to engage the attention of Australia to the defense of the approaches to their country, and shake them out of their isolationist attitude. He objected however to including New Zealand, New Caledonia, the New Hebrides and the Fijis in it, as the New Zealand and Australian governments wished, on the sound strategic ground that Australia and New Zealand were distinct strategic entities. Australia was doubly menaced by enemy troops in the Bismarcks and New Guinea, so defense was a land-air task, for which the best naval support was a fleet free to maneuver without restrictions imposed by the local situation. New Zealand on the other hand could not be threatened as long as the Allied navies controlled the sea approaches; its defense was primarily a naval task for which Nouméa, Fiji, Tongatabu, etc. were key points in support of the line of communications.

[8] West of the Southwest Pacific Area was the China-Burma-India Area, for which the United States had no strategic responsibility, and in which very limited American ground and air forces were committed.

[9] Robert L. Ghormley, b. Portland, Ore., 1883, Naval Academy '06 (12th in class), aide to C. in C. Pacific Fleet, Rear Admiral Southerland; 1st Lieut. *Nevada*

ington from London on 17 April, to be informed that he was to command the South Pacific Force and Area. Next day he saw Admiral King who said, as he remembered: —

"You have a large and important area and a most difficult task. I do not have the tools to give you to carry out that task as it should be done. You will establish your headquarters in Auckland with an advanced base at Tongatabu. In time, possibly this fall, we hope to start an offensive from the South Pacific."

Ghormley spent two weeks at Washington collecting a staff of some forty officers, of which the senior members were Rear Admiral Daniel J. Callaghan and Brigadier General DeWitt Peck USMC. He also collected Admiralty charts of 1897 and German charts of 1908, the only ones available for the Solomons; and these were based on surveys going back to the eighteenth century. The United States Navy never did get accurate charts of the Solomons until after it had seized them and sent in survey vessels.

When Ghormley was in Washington he found that the planning sections of the War and Navy Departments had been working for three months on the establishment of bases, equipment and garrisons in the South Pacific Area. It had been slow work in view of the magnitude of the task, the enormous distances involved, the primitive conditions in most of the islands, inadequate shipping and civilian war production just beginning to function. Samoa was well garrisoned by Marines; the naval fueling station for the Panama–Pacific route was ready at Bora Bora; an advanced naval base was in the course of being set up at Tongatabu; and, in order to facilitate the ferrying of planes to Australia, a serviceable chain of island airfields, with naval fueling and minor repair stations, had been established to break the air journey from Oahu.

----

and aide to Vice Admiral A. W. Grant in World War I, C.O. destroyer *Sands* 1920, aide to Asst. Secretaries T. Roosevelt Jr. and Robinson 1923–25, "exec." of *Oklahoma* 1925, General Board 1927, asst. chief of staff to C. in C. of Fleet, Admiral Schofield, 1931, in charge of tactical section fleet training division C.N.O. 1932–35, C.O. *Nevada* 1935–36, on staff of C. in C. Admiral Hepburn 1936. Head of war plans division, office of C.N.O. 1938–39, Asst. Chief of Naval Operations 1939–40, special naval observer London 1940–42. See Vol. V. Ret. 1946; died 1958.

These included Johnston, Palmyra and Canton Islands, Suva and Nandi in the Fijis, Nouméa and Efate, and Christmas Island.

As only common — very common — labor by natives could be had in these islands, it was fortunate that the Navy had set up "tailored" units of men and machines to construct different classes of naval and air bases — an "Acorn" for an advanced land and seaplane base, a "Cub" for a medium-sized fuel and supply base and a "Lion" for a full-sized naval operating base. Ghormley asked for one Cub and one Lion to be alerted on the West Coast for shipment to New Zealand as soon as shipping was available, and a Naval Construction Battalion (Seabees) for handling cargoes at Auckland. But they could not yet be had. One Cub and the 7th Seabees were the first to arrive, in early August. Admiral King was so disturbed by the delay in base construction that he appointed a special inspection board, headed by Rear Admiral Richard E. Byrd the Antarctic explorer and including representatives of all Navy Department bureaus concerned with logistics, to inspect the sites and make recommendations. Their tour of inspection was made in May and June and their report dated 15 August — one week after the Guadalcanal campaign had started — laid out a plan of development that in the main was followed.[10]

Admiral Ghormley left Washington with his staff on 1 May, and spent about a week conferring with Admiral Nimitz and staff at Pearl. At his request Rear Admiral John S. McCain, who later won fame as a carrier task force commander, was appointed Commander Aircraft South Pacific Area. McCain set up headquarters on board U.S.S. *Tangier* in Nouméa Harbor shortly after, and exercised operational control of all Allied planes, with a few exceptions, in the South Pacific.[11]

In the meantime the Battle of the Coral Sea had been fought. The Japanese lunge at Port Moresby had been thrown back, but their seaplane base at Tulagi in the southern Solomons, facing

[10] See note at end of chapter.
[11] Before the Guadalcanal campaign opened McCain shifted his flag to *Curtiss* and moved to Efate; later to Espíritu Santo.

Guadalcanal, had survived its bombing by Admiral Fletcher's carrier planes on 3 May. Tulagi was a new threat to the line of communications which it was Ghormley's prime duty to defend. If King's long-deferred plans to move into the Solomons were to be carried out, it was high time a start should be made.

Ghormley arrived at Nouméa 17 May, to find a tense political situation. New Caledonia and all the French Islands in the Pacific except Wallis had declared for General de Gaulle, who had sent out one of the two French admirals who had broken with Vichy, Contre-Amiral d'Argenlieu, as his high commissioner. D'Argenlieu had just ousted a popular governor for alleged disaffection from the Allied cause, a counterrevolution was imminent, many of the local French were pro-Axis and others wavered in their allegiance with the fortunes of war; ship and troop movements were constantly reported to the Japanese. Even the Free French authorities were suspicious and un-coöperative. D'Argenlieu had a couple of French corvettes under his command, and wished to use them to oust the Vichyites from Wallis (Uea), the French island of the Samoan group. Permission was gladly accorded by Admiral Ghormley, and the operation was executed by *Chevreuil* on 26 May; next day the island was occupied by Marine and Seabee detachments sent up from Samoa in U.S.S. *Harris* and *Zeilin.*

The military situation at Nouméa, however, was satisfactory. Major General A. M. Patch was there in command of the "Americal" (America-Caledonia) Infantry Division United States Army, which had started arriving from Australia in March; and Brigadier General Chamberlin, an old cavalry officer who became a tower of strength to Ghormley, commanded the small garrison at Efate. Sixteen Catalinas were based on tender *Tangier* in Nouméa harbor, four Flying Fortresses and 34 Army fighter planes were on the Gaiacs field at the center of the island, and the advanced base at Efate was already operating under difficulties imposed by malaria, terrain and lack of bare necessities.

This was not enough. The two Generals and the Admiral promptly decided that, in order to counter the new Japanese base at Tulagi, another advanced air and naval base must be set up at Segond Channel, Espiritu Santo. Washington replied that no airfield should be constructed there until adequate defense forces were available, but that Ghormley could start a seaplane base at any time. General Chamberlain, who (said Ghormley) would have taken troops up in fishing boats if necessary to get started, released the original Efate garrison, which went up to Espiritu Santo to start Base "Button" on 28 May. Soldiers, Seabees and Marines started a road from the harbor to what appeared to be a good airfield site, and then started to construct the field; but the terrain proved to be unsuitable, the first coral surface sank into the bog, and the first runway was barely ready for use on D-day, 7 August. Within a few months Espiritu Santo had become the principal advanced base for the support of Operation "Watchtower," the occupation of Guadalcanal and Tulagi.

On 28 May Admiral Nimitz proposed to General MacArthur that the 1st Marine Raider Battalion, then at Tutuila, pull off a raid on Tulagi. MacArthur rejected the plan on the ground that we had insufficient strength to hold Tulagi if captured, and Ghormley agreed.[12] Many in the Navy, however, believed that we missed a golden opportunity to slip into Tulagi and Guadalcanal when the enemy's back was turned, for at that time almost the entire Japanese Navy was converging on the Aleutians and Midway.

By the end of May, Vice Admiral Ghormley had broken his three-starred flag in U.S.S. *Rigel* in Auckland Harbor, resisting the pressing invitation of the New Zealand government to establish his headquarters ashore at the capital, Wellington. They, not he, were responsible for the land defense of the sub-continent, so his place was in the outport, although at that time he had no fighting ships under his command, not even old Anzac Task Force 44. On 19 June, the date when the South Pacific Force and Area were formally activated, the New Zealand light cruisers *Achilles* and

---

[12] The danger was that the Japanese 25th Air Flotilla at Rabaul would bomb the hell out of any Marines in Tulagi before we had any air base nearer to it than Townsville, Australia, about 1000 miles distant.

Leander, two destroyers at Samoa, and all the other auxiliaries in the area, were placed under Ghormley's command.

The logistics problem did not become acute until the plan of operation came out. Captain M. C. Bowman, with the best sort of coöperation from the Dominion authorities, managed to set up a system whereby a large part of the fresh provisions consumed by the South Pacific Force as it marched up the Solomons was furnished by the farms of New Zealand.[13] In Nouméa facilities for handling military cargoes were even less than at Auckland, and supply ships sometimes swung around the hook for weeks before they could get unloaded. The absolute necessity of sending up cargo-handling equipment, stevedore personnel, cranes, tugs and the like ahead of the fighting forces was a lesson we learned the hard way in Operation "Watchtower."[14]

On the Glorious Fourth of June the Battle of Midway dispelled Japanese dreams of further conquest. Operation plans for the occupation of New Caledonia, Fiji and Samoa had been issued on 18 May; now they were shelved and on 11 July were formally canceled. The center of enemy effort shifted to Rabaul, where the garrison originally intended for Port Moresby was waiting. Formerly the Bismarcks, Papua, the Solomons and the Coral Sea had been the responsibility of Admiral Inouye's Fourth Fleet based at Truk, but on 10 June a new Eighth Fleet was created to take care of that area. Vice Admiral Gunichi Mikawa, the first commander

---

[13] All the excess production of dairy products and mutton in New Zealand had been promised to Great Britain, who released them to U. S. forces on being supplied with corresponding calories from the U. S. It got so that soldiers and sailors of the South Pacific Force would baa and bleat when they saw a supply ship come in from New Zealand.

[14] Admiral Ghormley observed in a memo. to Cincpac of 1 Oct. 1942 that the original base plans of Feb.–Mar. 1942 called for Auckland to be the major and Tongatabu the minor Sopac bases, Nouméa being reserved for the Army. Consequently New Zealand, Tongatabu, Samoa, Bora Bora, Fiji and Efate had priority in base development, to the neglect of Nouméa. He had urged before leaving the U. S. that reservoirs of base materials and personnel (Cubs, Acorns, etc.) be established in New Zealand ready to be sent where the strategic situation demanded, but this was not done. The area was still dependent on shipments from the U. S. to fill urgent needs. Hence Nouméa and Espiritu Santo were suddenly overwhelmed with material for the Guadalcanal campaign, and bad unloading bottlenecks developed.

in chief, arrived with his staff at Rabaul in heavy cruiser *Chokai* on 29 June. His initial combat force of five heavy and three light cruisers and a number of destroyers was soon augmented, and the program of airfield construction and air-power concentration was intensified. By the end of June, Rear Admiral Yamada's 25th Air Flotilla at Rabaul comprised 24 land-based bombers and 30 fighter planes, together with ten seaplanes and ten float-plane fighters at Tulagi.[15] Besides two large airstrips at Rabaul (eventually expanded to five or six) the Japanese were building others on New Ireland, at Gasmata on the south coast of New Britain, at Lae and Salamaua in New Guinea and on Buka, the little island at the north end of Bougainville. They were determined to make the Bismarck-Solomons area a bastion against American advance through Dampier Strait, as the Central Pacific route was already blocked by the Marshalls and Carolines.

Two more advanced airfields were needed to complete this bastion; one in the lower Solomons and another at Port Moresby. For the first, the terrain at Tulagi and Florida Island was unsuitable, but across the sound on Guadalcanal was a fine level plain. It was the start of airfield construction there, before the end of June, that sparked off the whole Guadalcanal operation. And, as the attempt to take Port Moresby by sea had been frustrated by the Coral Sea battle, the Japanese high command now decided to reach the Gulf of Papua overland, by ferrying troops to Buna across the Bismarck Sea, which the Eighth Fleet controlled, and marching them across the Owen Stanley Range. That operation was set to start on 25 July. The Japanese had no plan as yet for an offensive from Guadalcanal south. That would doubtless have come in good time; but for the present the rôle of Guadalcanal was to assist the Tulagi-based seaplanes in preventing Allied interference with the Buna-Port Moresby thrust.

Now turning our attention to Pearl Harbor and the Central Pacific, we see that the Pacific Fleet after the Battle of Midway enjoyed a brief period of upkeep, rest and training; that is, all

---

[15] Lt. Cdr. Salomon's notes taken at Tokyo p. 25.

except Admiral Theobald's North Pacific Force which had to watch the Aleutians, and the depleted carrier air groups. They were sent to San Diego and other training centers to act as nuclei for the new pilots and planes being prepared to take the place of those whose sacrifice had made the Midway victory possible. Admiral Nimitz on 15 June observed that new aircraft deliveries and flight school graduates had done little more to date than balance operational and battle losses. A replacement pool must be built up at the Hawaiian Islands; plane, pilot and carrier production must be expedited; training methods must be improved.

Rear Admiral Spruance now became chief of staff to Admiral Nimitz. Carrier *Wasp*, having completed her Malta ferry duties,[16] the new battleship *North Carolina*, heavy cruiser *Quincy*, light cruiser *San Juan*, and seven destroyers passed through the Panama Canal on 10 June. This was the first substantial reinforcement to the Pacific Fleet in 1942. Cincpac therefore reorganized his carrier striking forces as follows on 15 June: —

TASK FORCE	11	16	17	18
C.O.	R. Adm. Fitch	R. Adm. Fletcher	R. Adm. Mitscher[17]	R. Adm. Noyes
CVs	*Saratoga*	*Enterprise*	*Hornet*	*Wasp*
CAs	*Minneapolis*	*Louisville*	*Northampton*	*Quincy*
CAs	*New Orleans*	*Portland*	*Salt Lake City*	*Vincennes*
CAs	*Astoria*	*Chester*	*Pensacola*	*San Francisco*
CLs		*Atlanta*	*San Diego*	*San Juan*
DDs	Desron 1 [18]	Desron 6	Desron 2	Desdivs 15, 23

Fletcher's and Mitscher's forces were placed on 48-hour notice at Pearl for rest, reorganization and training. "Sara" was then on a plane-ferrying mission to Midway, and Task Force 18 would be formed at San Diego shortly.

The busiest American naval officers, other than those engaged

---

[16] See Vol. I pp. 151, 194–97.

[17] Pending Admiral Halsey's return to duty.

[18] These and the other destroyer screens did not follow strict organizational order.

in training, were the higher command. What would happen next? What should be our next move?

One basic condition that limited possibilities in the Pacific was Atlantic priority. Although our African adventure, Operation "Torch" of November 1942, was not formally adopted by the Combined Chiefs of Staff until 25 July, it had been on the cards since June, and the preparations for it absorbed a major part of new naval construction, as well as all combat-ready divisions of the United States Army. The anti-submarine war in the Atlantic was also in a very acute stage. Admiral Nimitz and the Pacific Fleet planners, therefore, had no hope of getting additional ships, planes and men for a strategical offensive during the ensuing twelve months. They must do with what they already had, together with the forces that had been promised to the Pacific Fleet on 14 March.

Yet the question remained, What should we do with what we had? The sanguine General MacArthur had a proposition ready, immediately after Midway. Give him one division trained in amphibious warfare, a naval task force including two carriers and a few score big bombing planes, and he would jump off next month to recapture Rabaul. That sounded fine; even in retrospect the General's strategy appeals to one as bold and incisive, sparing the long agony of conquering the Solomons island by island. But the Joint Chiefs (greatly to the relief of the Navy) turned down this proposal for several reasons. No transports were yet available for troop lift. Rabaul, at the end of an "air pipeline" from Japan, could be readily and steadily reinforced by the enemy, yet was beyond fighter-plane range from the air bases then in Allied possession. There is no doubt that the decision against moving into Rabaul was wise. In June 1942 the balance of naval power in the Pacific was too delicate to warrant an attempt to seize and hold a position so exposed to Japanese counterattack. Rabaul had to be left in enemy possession, a formidable barrier to MacArthur's advance, until Allied forces became much stronger; and, by the time they were strong enough, it seemed better strategy to beat down, encircle and neutralize rather than to assault Rabaul.

Actually what we would do depended as much on what the Asiatic enemy did as on what we had. Despite his defeat at Midway he still had the interior lines and the strength to stage a new offensive at any one of several points, provided not many carriers were needed. That proviso limited his probable offensive moves to the Aleutians and the Solomons. One guess as to his intentions was a declaration of war on Russia. If that assumption were correct, every effort should be made to strengthen the Aleutians and to wrest Kiska and Attu from the Japanese. But the last thing the Japanese wanted was to wage war on two fronts. They allowed Russian-flag merchant vessels (mostly Liberty ships given to Russia under lend-lease) to carry munitions from the United States to Vladivostok; and, in their military convention with Germany, insisted that any German raiders or submarines that might penetrate the Pacific must respect the Russian flag! The American high command concluded that there would be no Russo-Japanese war for a long time and that the Aleutians could be crossed off as the scene of an enemy offensive. But there was no possibility of the Pacific Fleet's undertaking an advance into the Gilberts and Marshalls until very heavily reinforced, which could not be until 1943.

Thus, the one promising target left was Tulagi. That, too, had the advantage of leading somewhere — toward Rabaul, for the capture of which the forces under MacArthur's command might ultimately be employed.

Admiral King, who had never given up his concept of a gradual advance up the line of the Solomons, returned to it in a memorandum to General Marshall on 25 June. He predicted that the enemy would not stay still in the South Pacific, or permit us to do so. It was urgent that we take the initiative. Using the 1st Marine Division, then en route to New Zealand, an offensive could be mounted in the South Pacific about 1 August. Admiral Nimitz in fact had already suggested this: an amphibious operation to retake Tulagi, covered by the two carrier task forces he had in readiness at Pearl.[19]

General Marshall thought well of the idea, but suggested that it be entrusted to MacArthur rather than to Nimitz. King replied (26 June) that in his opinion any such operation "must be conducted under the direction of Cincpac and cannot be conducted in any other way." One can readily understand why: the only amphibiously trained troops available were Marines; the only troop lift available was Navy transports; the only covering and supporting force (other than Ghormley's tiny force) was the Pacific Fleet. And the only assistance that MacArthur could render would be land-based air cover from distant Australian fields. King believed that, after the amphibious phase was completed, MacArthur with Pacific Fleet support should take charge of troop movement into the southern Solomons and of consolidating the area. Marshall agreed, and King then flew to San Francisco to consult with Nimitz, bringing with him the Joint Chiefs of Staff directive which, with some modifications, governed Allied movements in the South Pacific for the next eighteen months.

Nimitz's plane crash-landed at Alameda 30 June, but fortunately the Admiral was only slightly injured. Cominch and Cincpac quickly agreed on the broad lines of the operation.

The gist of the 2 July directive is interesting to record, as circumstances forced a change in many important particulars.

Joint Chiefs of Staff Directive of 2 July 1942 (IN SUMMARY)

I. *Ultimate Objective:* Seizure and occupation of the New Britain–New Ireland–New Guinea area.

II. *Tasks:* —

1. Operation "Watchtower." Seize and occupy the Santa Cruz Islands, Tulagi and adjacent positions. Cincpac to be in charge. Target date 1 August.

2. Seize and occupy the rest of the Solomon Islands, Lae, Salamaua, and Papua. MacArthur to be in overall command.

[19] Nimitz also predicted a second Japanese attempt to take Port Moresby, but thought it would be made by sea like the first.

3. Seize and occupy Rabaul and adjacent positions in New Guinea and New Ireland. MacArthur's again.

III. *Other important clauses:* —

1. Direct command of tactical operations will remain with naval task force commander throughout all three tasks.

2. The Joint Chiefs may order the withdrawal of naval attached units after the completion of any one task, in the event that in their judgment conditions require their employment elsewhere.

3. The boundary from 1 August between the Southwest Pacific (MacArthur) and the Pacific (Nimitz) Areas will be shifted westward to long. 159° E, which runs a few miles west of Guadalcanal.

Anticipating a bit, let us note briefly how much of this directive was or was not carried out, and why.

Task 1. The target date for beginning "Watchtower" was very nearly met, but the Santa Cruz Islands were never occupied in strength because they proved to be forbiddingly malarial and rugged. Guadalcanal, which became the main objective of Task 1, was not secured until early February 1943.

Task 2 was, in the main, completed between July and November 1943, but its execution had to be divided between the South Pacific and the MacArthur forces, and it was found desirable to by-pass several large Solomon Islands.

Task 3 never was carried out as planned. It proved to be more profitable and less costly to pound down, neutralize and encircle Rabaul, a task that was completed in February 1944 when the Admiralties were secured. The Army and the Navy swept over the Philippines and up to the shores of Japan with Rabaul still in Japanese possession, and more than 100,000 enemy troops were isolated in that area.

On 5 July Admiral Nimitz received a bit of news that sparked off the whole operation. An American reconnaissance plane observed that the Japanese were starting to build an airfield — the future Henderson Field — on Guadalcanal. This news had very different effects on the Ghormley–MacArthur team and on the King–Nimitz team.

Admiral Ghormley flew to Melbourne to confer with General MacArthur, General Sutherland, his chief of staff, and Vice Admiral Arthur S. Carpender, about to be appointed Commander Naval Forces Southwest Pacific under General MacArthur.[20] They liked neither the proposed operation nor the target date of 1 August. MacArthur voiced his and Ghormley's views in protesting to King and Nimitz on 8/9 July against a premature and possibly disastrous beginning. In view of the recently developed enemy airfields, and the shortage of Allied planes, airfields, transports and troops, they warmly urged that Operation "Watchtower" be deferred until adequate means were available for a quick seizure and rapid follow-up.

To Marshall, when he received this discouraging opinion, King observed, "Three weeks ago MacArthur stated that, if he could be furnished amphibious forces and two carriers, he could push right through to Rabaul. . . . He now feels that he not only cannot undertake this extended operation but not even the Tulagi operation." Nevertheless, King felt it necessary to stop the enemy's southward advance without delay. An airfield in his possession in Guadalcanal "will hamper seriously if not prevent our establishment in Santa Cruz," would put him "in a position to harass Espiritu Santo." To MacArthur he wrote the same day (10 July) that he could not sanction any delay. Even if additional demands for Operation "Torch" or elsewhere should postpone the follow-up into the Solomons, the Tulagi operation must go on.[21]

He was right. The Tulagi–Guadalcanal operation was indeed a perilous undertaking at that time; the armed forces involved liked to refer to it as "Operation 'Shoestring.' " But the risk had to be taken. This new Japanese spearhead had to be cut off then and there, lest it sever the lifeline between the United States and "down

---

[20] This force was the nucleus of the future Seventh Fleet. Vice Admiral Herbert F. Leary, General Marshall and General DeWitt Peck USMC also took part in the discussion.

[21] King to MacArthur 10 July; King to Marshall 10 July. C.N.O. files.

under." In accepting the grave responsibility for ordering the seizure of these islands, Admiral King made one of the great decisions of the war.[22]

[22] State of South Pacific Area Bases, May–June 1942, from "Inspection Report by South Pacific Advanced Base Inspection Board, Rear Admiral R. E. Byrd, senior member," 15 Aug. 1942: —

Bora Bora. Naval fueling base (capacity 120,000 bbls, to be more than doubled). Army garrison (3412 officers and men). Eight OS2U-3s stationed in harbor, 81 naval officers and men, plus one Seabee battalion.

Palmyra. One 5400-ft. airstrip and small N.A.S. with 14 Marine Corps F2A-3s and a Marine Defense Battalion. Total personnel, 1413.

Samoa. (1) Pago Pago and Tutuila. N.A.S., airfield with 5280-ft. runway, 18 F4F-3s, 17 SBCs, a number of seaplanes with tender *Swan,* a Marine Defense Battalion and a Raider Battalion. Total personnel, 7995. (2) Apia on Upolu Island and Savaii (the New Zealand mandate), a Marine Defense Battalion, a Naval Air Detachment and a Seabee unit; N.A.S., seaplane base with 11 planes, airfield just begun. Total personnel, 5074. (3) Wallis, the French island. Marine Defense Detachment, 3 seaplanes in lagoon, plans for a 7000-ft. airstrip. Total personnel, 2602.

Tongatabu. Fuel base, alternate staging point for aircraft on South Pacific air ferry route and air support point for Fiji and Samoa, started 9 May with arrival of 10-ship convoy bringing 147th Infantry and attached units, 24 P-40s, Seabee battalion and 8 OS2U-3s to operate from Nukualofa Harbor. Warm coöperation from Queen Salote and the Tongans. Airfield with 3 runways already built by British. Hospital ship *Solace* stationed in Nukualofa Harbor. 7800 Army and 862 naval personnel.

Fiji (1) at Suva, the colonial capital, large seaplane base and a smaller one two miles away. A U. S. infantry division arrived 11 June to relieve the New Zealand garrison of about 13,000 troops, and brought staff and materials for a large Army hospital. (2) at Nandi, on NW side Viti Levu, 26 R.N.Z.A.F. sea and land planes, 17 P-39s, 6 PBYs en route. Two 7000-ft. runways and satellite field (Narewa) with two 5000-ft. runways; a third seaplane base at Lautoka Bay. About 223 U.S.N. personnel and 545 of R.N.Z.A.F.

New Caledonia. In and around Nouméa, American Division and attached units, 22,216 officers and men. Seaplane base about to be activated on Ile Nou; about 152 naval personnel. Sixteen PBYs and 5 OS2U-3s based on U.S.S. *Tangier,* about to be relieved by *Curtiss.* Tontouta airfield, 33 miles from Nouméa, two airstrips to be closed for resurfacing by U. S. Army Engineers for about two months 1 July. Plaine des Gaiacs at center of south coast, one 7000-ft. strip and one 5000-ft. constructing, also 8 emergency and satellite fields, 4 B-17s, and 34 P-39s and -40s at these fields. Unloading conditions at Nouméa very unsatisfactory.

Efate. Seaplane base and 4000-ft. airstrip at Vila, with 8 OS2Us and 18 F4F-3s of VMF-212, 4th Marine Defense Battalion and half of 3rd Seabees. 4609 Army and 1209 Navy and Marine personnel, much weakened by malaria.

Espiritu Santo. Two OS2U-3s operating from Segond Channel; 500 troops building airfield.

CHAPTER XIII

Plans and Preparations[1]

June–July 1942

East Longitude dates in the South Pacific; West Longitude dates at Hawaii.

1. *Operation "Shoestring"*

O N 10 July Admiral Ghormley received Admiral Nimitz's operation order for the seizure of Tulagi, Guadalcanal and Ndeni (Santa Cruz), including a list of available ground and air forces and ships. A day or two later he observed that enough ships and men had been given him to do the job, provided General MacArthur could interdict interference by enemy planes based at Rabaul and near-by fields. "I desire to emphasize," he said, "that the basic problem of the operation is the protection of ships against land-based aircraft attack during the approach, the landing and the unloading." General MacArthur remarked that his air force would need heavy and quick reinforcement to accomplish that. It certainly did.

The movements of forces had already begun. Nimitz informed McCain on 11 July that he was building up the number of Flying Fortresses in the South Pacific Area to 35, and that a thousand men of Army Air Force ground crews and 1500 tons of freight were being sent to him in the *President Tyler*. Ghormley and Nimitz were already thinking ahead to Task 2. Assault troops cannot be used for garrisons; where were these garrisons to come

---

[1] See note 1 to previous chapter for sources.

from? King warned him that no new troops were available; neither the Hawaiian Army command nor MacArthur could spare any; Ghormley would have to roll up garrisons from Samoa and the other South Pacific bases.[2] Nimitz, with prophetic insight, pointed out that once we had occupied Guadalcanal our forces on land and in air would be in close contact with the enemy, who would be in a position to move up amphibious forces under cover of land-based aircraft to recover his lost positions. It must be assumed that the Japanese would exert every effort to do that, and the process was bound to be costly for both sides. Unless provision were made for a steady flow of replacements from the United States, "not only will we be unable to proceed with Tasks 2 and 3 but we may be unable to hold what we have taken." [3] But, alas for Operation "Watchtower," no such provision would or could be made. Operation "Torch" was getting all the gravy; even the 3rd Infantry Division, amphibiously trained by the Marines at San Diego, had sailed away in several large transports en route to Africa via Norfolk.

The movement of the 1st Marine Division to New Zealand had long been planned, but not with a view to their immediate employment in combat. One of its regiments, the 7th, had been sent to Samoa as early as March 1942. Of the other two regiments, about one half were embarked in two large passenger transports (*Wakefield* and *Ericsson*), and stores and equipment in nine cargo ships — "commercial-" rather than "combat"-loaded,[4] because as recently as May it had been assumed that the Marines would have at least six months to train at New Zealand. This echelon, with Major General Vandegrift the division commander, arrived at Wellington 14 June. The General did not know what he was in for until the 26th. By that time most of the transports had been unloaded and were on their way back to the Atlantic to participate in Oper-

[2] King to Ghormley, 14 July.
[3] Nimitz to King 17 July.
[4] *Del Brazil, Electra, Lipscomb Lykes, Alcyone, Libra, George F. Elliot, Barnett, Mizar* and *Alchiba* were the AKs. For the distinction between the two types of loading see Vol. II of this History p. 27.

ation "Torch." Captain Reifsnider then brought up a division of
Pacific Fleet transports. All supplies had to be reloaded during
the cold and rainy southern winter, and with inadequate ware-
house space so that thousands of tons of supplies in cardboard
containers were spoiled. Fortunately there was a good, high camp
area about 35 miles from Wellington where the Marines kept in
fine physical condition and trained in the near-by forest.

This first echelon reëmbarked and reloaded its equipment and
supplies in transports *American Legion, Fuller, Bellatrix* and
Neville, beginning 2 July, in order to leave port facilities available for the second echelon when it arrived. A working team of
300 Marines to each vessel did practically all the reloading, since
New Zealand labor was found to be lazy, expensive and inefficient.
The second echelon reached Wellington on 11 July and sailed
on the 22nd; the third, in six transports, combat-loaded at San
Diego, sailed thence 1 July escorted by the *Wasp* carrier group;
stopped off two days at Tongatabu to wait for the carrier, which
had had an engineering accident,[5] and sailed on the 20th for the
grand rendezvous south of Fiji.

If there is one factor more important than surprise for the
success of an amphibious operation, it is Intelligence.[6] Exact information is wanted, both hydrographic and topographic, so that the
ships may know where to anchor and the troops where to land
and where to go when they get ashore. Admiral Ghormley's turn-
of-the-century charts of the Solomons were distressingly vague.
He did not need a prompting from Nimitz on 4 July to fly an
"Intelligence team" to Australia to obtain more information from
evacuated planters, skippers of coastal craft and the like. MacArthur's command and the Australian Navy helped; but the amount
of new information thus obtained was disappointing both in quan-
tity and quality. Data imparted orally by former residents of the

---

[5] On 13 July the starboard high-pressure turbine stripped its impulse blading;
Wasp slowed to 7½ knots in order to lock the starboard shaft, and proceeded on
the port engine. The ship's own force removed and replaced the blading, and all
repairs were completed by 20 July. *Wasp* War Diary.
[6] See also Vol. II pp. 25–6.

Solomon Islands proved to be of slight use in many cases and misleading in others. For instance, Mount Austen, one of the principal landmarks near the future Henderson Field, was assigned as a D-day objective on the basis of an old resident's information. Actually it was located nine miles WSW of the landing beach across thick jungle. Our informants were both honest and intelligent, but they had never looked at Guadalcanal through military binoculars. Let the reader try to describe a beach area that he has long been familiar with as a summer visitor, and he will be surprised to find how little he knows that would be of any use to an amphibious force commander.

In the planning of an amphibious operation, there is no substitute for an intensive study of the area by military people in time of peace (which nobody had even thought of doing here) or aërial reconnaissance just before the operation. For Guadalcanal, the most useful sources of information were aërial photographs and an observation flight undertaken on 17 July by two Marine Corps officers, Colonel Twining and Major McKean, in one of General Brett's Army Air Force B–17s. They checked up on the installations Tulagi-side, but, before they were ready to inspect enemy activities on Guadalcanal, the float-fighter planes from Tulagi got after them and the Flying Fort had to vamoose. She made Port Moresby all right, with fuel tanks almost dry.

A third product of Intelligence, important for any military or naval operation, is knowledge of the movements of enemy forces. At about the time of Midway the Japanese generally tightened up on their security and appeared to be on their guard to such an extent that, in July and August, Naval Intelligence was largely deprived of its best sources and had to rely almost wholly on the observations of reconnaissance planes.

A certain number of local pilots and former residents volunteered to accompany the task force, in order to identify landmarks and pilot the ships through unfamiliar waters. These men, mostly Australians, gave excellent service.

On 16 July it seemed impossible to meet D-day, only two weeks off. Admiral Ghormley therefore postponed it six days, to 7 August. This important and salutary decision was made after consultation with Rear Admiral Richmond K. Turner, newly designated commander of the amphibious force, who called at Auckland 15 July en route to Wellington. Rear Admiral Turner, whom we have already encountered at several points in this history, had been the chief naval planner on the boards that had developed the vital strategic decisions in Washington. At the time Admiral King became Chief of Naval Operations in March, Turner was eager for a sea command; but King, who knew his ability, had kept him in Washington as an assistant chief of staff in order to save him for the Solomons show, which might be described as a sea command plus. Turner, detached from Washington 11 June, only revealed on the 30th, at San Francisco, that he was to command the amphibious forces. From that moment he began to plan for Operation "Watchtower." King and Nimitz approved the rough project that he then drafted, and at Pearl Harbor, between July 4 and 7, he had opportunity for further consultation with Admirals Nimitz, Fletcher, Kinkaid and Fitch. Turner took command of the Amphibious Force of the South Pacific at Wellington 18 July. Promptly he and his small staff began intensive planning for the landings, working day and night. This admiral, like President Roosevelt, had an equal capacity for broad views and for minute details; and, although his was the first amphibious operation of the war, he carefully planned it down to the employment of every landing craft and the exact times and amounts of naval gunfire support. For, as Turner often remarked, he "hated above all things to see soldiers swimming."

Readers who are allergic to catalogues of ships may now skip to the next chapter if they will bear in mind the command setup and the essential components of the force.

Admiral Ghormley as Comsopac was the overall strategic commander charged with the general direction of the campaign; but the O.T.C., the officer in tactical command, was Admiral Fletcher. Turner, commander of the amphibious spearhead and the embarked

Marines, was in the command echelon below Fletcher, but actually he had complete autonomy from the moment of sailing. The command setup was such that General Vandegrift's landing force remained subordinate to Turner, even long after it had been engaged in battle. Admiral Fletcher limited his command in practice to the three carrier groups, whose function was to provide air cover for the landings.

Admiral Crutchley RN, in command of the small Australian and United States cruiser and destroyer force formerly known as Task Force 44, was second in command to Turner and actually in command of the ships that furnished gunfire support and anti-aircraft protection to the amphibious operation.

There were two mutually independent components of land-based air power: Rear Admiral McCain's planes (Army, Navy and Marine Corps), operating from bases in New Caledonia, Fiji, Efate and (presently) Espiritu Santo; and General MacArthur's, operating from Port Moresby and the same Queensland fields that were in use during the Coral Sea battle. Each was responsible for air search over a definite area of ocean, the dividing line being longitude 158° E, which cuts through the Solomons between Choiseul and Santa Isabel.[7] General MacArthur's air plan, which he communicated to Admiral Ghormley 20 July, provided for air reconnaissance over Port Moresby, the Bismarcks and the whole line of the Solomons to Guadalcanal up to 2 August; and thereafter, daily searches up to the dividing line, with a view to interdicting Japanese flights southward from Rabaul as well as reporting enemy ships. This plan had to be considerably modified because on 21 July the enemy landed several thousand troops at Buna and Gona on the north coast of Papua, commenced his march over the Owen Stanley Range to take Port Moresby from the rear, and on the 30th shot down five out of seven Army bombers from Port Moresby that had attacked his new position. MacArthur now had a defensive campaign on his hands; and for some time, as we shall

[7] This was one degree west of the area boundary between South and Southwest Pacific.

see, it was doubtful whether his troops could keep the Japanese up in the mountains and out of Port Moresby.

McCain's air-search plan may best be described when it comes into play, as seen in a chart in the next volume. His headquarters were in tender *Curtiss* at Segond Channel, Espiritu Santo. Although the airstrip there was ready for fighter planes 28 July, it could not yet accommodate Flying Fortresses, whose nearest bases in Efate and New Caledonia were too remote to permit them to bomb Guadalcanal unless spare gas tanks were fitted.

Two groups of submarines were sent on the prowl: one from the Pacific Fleet, to watch the Japanese advanced naval base at Truk; six S-boats of Captain Christie's command, based at Brisbane, to watch Rabaul.

2. *Task Organization* [8]

SOUTH PACIFIC FORCE, PACIFIC FLEET
Vice Admiral Robert L. Ghormley in *Argonne*

Rear Admiral Daniel J. Callaghan, Chief of Staff

TF 61 EXPEDITIONARY FORCE
Vice Admiral Frank Jack Fletcher

TG 61.1 AIR SUPPORT FORCE, Rear Admiral Leigh Noyes
Unit directly under Admiral Fletcher (old TF 11)

	SARATOGA	Captain DeWitt C. Ramsey

Air Group: 1 SBD-3 (Dauntless), Commander Harry D. Felt

VF-5	34 F4F-4 (Wildcat) [9]	Lt. Cdr. Leroy C. Simpler
VB-3	18 SBD-3	Lt. Cdr. Dewitt W. Shumway
VS-3	18 SBD-3	Lt. Cdr. Louis J. Kirn
VT-8	16 TBF-1 (Avenger)	Lt. Harold H. Larsen

Heavy Cruiser	MINNEAPOLIS	Capt. Frank J. Lowry
Heavy Cruiser	NEW ORLEANS	Capt. Walter S. DeLany

[8] The task organization in the O.N.I. Combat Narrative *The Landings in the Solomons* has been consulted but rigorously checked and corrected.
[9] The first of the Wildcat series to have folding wings.

Destroyer Screen, Captain Samuel B. Brewer (Comdesron 1)

PHELPS	Lt. Cdr. Edward L. Beck
FARRAGUT	Lt. Cdr. Henry D. Rosendal
WORDEN	Lt. Cdr. William G. Pogue
MACDONOUGH	Lt. Cdr. Erle V. Dennett
DALE	Lt. Cdr. Anthony L. Rorschach

Unit under Rear Admiral Thomas C. Kinkaid (old TF 16)

ENTERPRISE   Capt. Arthur C. Davis

Air Group: 1 TBF-1 Lt. Cdr. Maxwell F. Leslie

VF-6	36 F4F-4	Lt. Louis H. Bauer
VB-6	18 SBD-3	Lt. Ray Davis
VS-5	18 SBD-3	Lt. Turner F. Caldwell, Jr.
VT-3	14 TBF-1	Lt. Cdr. Charles M. Jett

Battleship   NORTH CAROLINA   Capt. George H. Fort

Cruisers, Rear Admiral M. S. Tisdale

Heavy Cruiser	PORTLAND	Capt. Laurance T. DuBose
AA Light Cruiser	* ATLANTA	Capt. Samuel P. Jenkins

Destroyer Screen, Captain Edward P. Sauer (Comdesron 6)

BALCH	Lt. Cdr. Harold H. Tiemroth
MAURY	Lt. Cdr. Gelzer L. Sims
GWIN	Cdr. John M. Higgins
* BENHAM	Lt. Cdr. Joseph M. Worthington
GRAYSON	Lt. Cdr. Frederick J. Bell

Unit under Rear Admiral Noyes

* WASP   Capt. Forrest P. Sherman

Air Group: 1 TBF-1, Lt. Cdr. Wallace M. Beakley

VF-71	29 F4F-4	Lt. Cdr. Courtney Shands
VS-71	15 SBD-3	* Lt. Cdr. John Eldridge Jr.
VS-72	15 SBD-3	Lt. Cdr. Ernest M. Snowden
VT-7	9 TBF-1	Lt. Henry A. Romberg

Heavy Cruiser	SAN FRANCISCO	Capt. Charles H. McMorris
Heavy Cruiser	SALT LAKE CITY	Capt. Ernest G. Small

Destroyer Screen, Captain Robert G. Tobin (Comdesron 12)

LANG	Lt. Cdr. John L. Wilfong
STERETT	Cdr. Jesse G. Coward
AARON WARD	Lt. Cdr. Orville F. Gregor
STACK	Lt. Cdr. Alvord J. Greenacre
* LAFFEY	* Lt. Cdr. William E. Hank
FARENHOLT	Lt. Cdr. Eugene T. Seaward

* Lost during Guadalcanal operations before 10 Feb. 1943.

Fueling Group

PLATTE	Capt. Ralph H. Henkle
CIMARRON	Cdr. Russell M. Ihrig
KASKASKIA	Cdr. Walter L. Taylor
SABINE	Capt. Houston L. Maples
KANAWHA	Cdr. Kendall S. Reed

TF 62 SOUTH PACIFIC AMPHIBIOUS FORCE

Rear Admiral Richmond K. Turner in *McCawley*

TG 62.2 ESCORT, Rear Admiral V. A. C. Crutchley RN [10]

CA	H.M.A.S.	AUSTRALIA	Capt. H. B. Farncomb RAN
CA	H.M.A.S.	* CANBERRA	* Capt. F. E. Getting RAN
CL	H.M.A.S.	HOBART	Capt. H. A. Showers RAN
CA		* CHICAGO	Capt. Howard D. Bode

Desron 4, Capt. Cornelius W. Flynn

SELFRIDGE	Lt. Cdr. Carroll D. Reynolds
PATTERSON	Cdr. Frank R. Walker
RALPH TALBOT	Lt. Cdr. Joseph W. Callahan
MUGFORD	Lt. Cdr. Edward W. Young
* JARVIS	* Lt. Cdr. William W. Graham Jr.

Desdiv 7, Cdr. Leonard B. Austin

* BLUE	Cdr. Harold N. Williams
HELM	Lt. Cdr. Chester E. Carroll
HENLEY	Cdr. Robert H. Smith [11]
BAGLEY	Lt. Cdr. George A. Sinclair

TG 62.1 CONVOY,[12] Captain Lawrence F. Reifsnider in *Hunter Liggett*

Major General Alexander A. Vandegrift USMC, Commander Ground Forces
Brigadier General William H. Rupertus USMC, Assistant Div. Commander

Embarking 1st and 5th Regiments 1st Marine Division, 2nd Marine Regiment
2nd Division, 1st Raider Battalion, 3rd Defense Battalion and attached Marine
Corps units; 959 officers, 18,146 enlisted men.

TRANSPORT GROUP X-RAY (for Guadalcanal), Capt. Reifsnider

Transdiv A, Capt. Paul S. Theiss

5th Marine Regiment (less 2nd Battalion) and attached units, Col. LeRoy P.
Hunt USMC.

FULLER	Capt. Theiss
AMERICAN LEGION	Capt. Thomas D. Warner
BELLATRIX	Cdr. William F. Dietrich

* Lost during Guadalcanal operations before 10 Feb. 1943.

[10] Also second in command of TF 62.
[11] Relieved by Lt. Cdr. E. K. Van Swearingen 14 Aug. and became Comdesdiv 7 in *Blue.*
[12] Here arranged as organized for the landings.

Transdiv B, Capt. Charlie P. McFeaters

Divisional headquarters and 1st Marine Regiment, Col. C. B. Cates USMC.

MCCAWLEY	Capt. McFeaters
BARNETT	Capt. Henry E. Thornhill
* GEORGE F. ELLIOTT	Capt. Watson O. Bailey
LIBRA	Cdr. William B. Fletcher Jr.

Transdiv C, Capt. Reifsnider

Embarking part of Support Group, HQ and Service Battery, Special Weapons Battalion, 5th Battalion 11th Marine Regiment and attached units, part of 3rd Defense Battalion.

HUNTER LIGGETT	Cdr. Louis W. Perkins USCG
ALCHIBA	Cdr. James S. Freeman
FOMALHAUT	Cdr. Henry C. Flanagan
BETELGEUSE	Cdr. Harry D. Power

Transdiv D, Capt. Ingolf N. Kiland

Embarking 2nd Marine Regiment (less 1st Battalion) and attached units, Col. John M. Arthur USMC.

CRESCENT CITY	Capt. Kiland
PRESIDENT HAYES [13]	Cdr. Francis W. Benson
PRESIDENT ADAMS [13]	Cdr. Frank H. Dean
ALHENA	Cdr. Charles B. Hunt

TRANSPORT GROUP YOKE (for Tulagi), Capt. George B. Ashe

Transdiv E, Capt. Ashe

Embarking 2nd Battalion 5th Regiment, 1st Battalion 2nd Regiment, Battery E 11th Regiment, half 3rd Defense Battalion, 1st Parachute Battalion, Company E 1st Raider Battalion and other units; Brigadier General Rupertus commanding.

NEVILLE	Capt. Carlos A. Bailey
ZEILIN	Capt. Pat Buchanan
HEYWOOD	Capt. Herbert B. Knowles
PRESIDENT JACKSON	Cdr. Charles W. Weitzel

Transdiv 12, Cdr. Hugh W. Hadley

1st Raider Battalion (less Company E), Lt. Col. Merritt A. Edson USMC, embarked in Destroyer Transports:

* COLHOUN	Lt. George B. Madden
* LITTLE	* Lt. Cdr. Gus B. Lofberg Jr.
MCKEAN	Lt. Cdr. John D. Sweeney
* GREGORY	* Lt. Cdr. Harry F. Bauer

* Lost during Guadalcanal operations before 10 Feb. 1943.

[13] These ships moved across the Sound on the night of 7–8 Aug. and landed their contingents Tulagi-side.

FIRE SUPPORT GROUPS

TG 62.3 Fire Support Group L, Capt. Frederick L. Riefkohl

Heavy Cruiser	* VINCENNES	Capt. Riefkohl
Heavy Cruiser	* QUINCY	* Capt. Samuel N. Moore
Heavy Cruiser	* ASTORIA	Capt. William G. Greenman

Destroyers

HULL	Lt. Cdr. Richard F. Stout
DEWEY	Lt. Cdr. Charles F. Chillingworth Jr.
ELLET	Lt. Cdr. Francis H. Gardner
WILSON	Lt. Cdr. Walter H. Price

TG 62.4 Fire Support Group M, * Rear Admiral Norman Scott

AA Light Cruiser	SAN JUAN	Capt. James E. Maher
Destroyer	* MONSSEN	Cdr. Roland N. Smoot
Destroyer	BUCHANAN	Cdr. Ralph E. Wilson

TG 62.5 MINESWEEPER GROUP, Cdr. William H. Hartt Jr.

HOPKINS	Lt. Cdr. Benjamin Coe
TREVER	Lt. Cdr. Dwight M. Agnew
ZANE	Lt. Cdr. Peyton L. Wirtz
SOUTHARD	Lt. Cdr. Joe B. Cochran
HOVEY	Lt. Cdr. Wilton S. Heald

TG 62.6 Screening Group, Rear Admiral Crutchley RN
Same as TG 62.2, less Desdiv 7

TF 63 LAND-BASED AIR, SOUTH PACIFIC FORCE [14]

Rear Admiral John S. McCain

At Efate: 16 B-17 (Colonel L. G. Saunders USA), 18 Marine Corps Wildcats, 6 Scout-Observation planes (Maj. H. W. Bauer USMC).

In New Caledonia: 21 PBY-5, 1 PBY-5A (Patrons 11 and 23 from Patwings 1 and 2, based on tender *Curtiss*) Army Bomron 69, Colonel Clyde Rich USA, 9 B-17, 10 B-26 equipped with torpedoes, 38 P-39, 16 F4F-3, 6 R.N.Z.A.F. Hudsons, 3 Scout-Observation planes, 17 SBD of Marine Corps.

In Fiji: 6 PBY, 3 R.N.Z.A.F. Singapores, 12 R.N.Z.A.F. Hudsons, 12 Marine Corps Wildcats, 12 B-26 equipped with torpedoes, 8 B-17, 9 R.N.Z.A.F. Vincents.

In Tongatabu: 6 Scout-Observation planes, 24 Marine Corps Wildcats.

In Samoa: 17 SBD, 18 Marine Corps Wildcats, 10 Scout-Observation planes.

SOUTHWEST PACIFIC AREA

General Douglas MacArthur USA

ALLIED AIR FORCES, SOUTHWEST PACIFIC

Lt. General George C. Kenney USA [15]
Northeast Area Command, Air Commodore F. W. F. Lucas RAAF
Air Command No. 2, Brig. Gen. Martin F. Scanlon USA

* Lost during Guadalcanal operations before 10 Feb. 1943.

[14] This list from Admiral Ghormley's records. The "hundreds of planes" mentioned in the O.N.I. Combat Narrative is an exaggeration.

[15] Relieved Lieutenant General Brett 4 Aug. 1942.

Available for Guadalcanal Operation

19th Bombing Group, an average of 20 B–17s operational.

435th Reconnaissance Squadron component at Port Moresby

4 B–17, 27 B–26, 12 B–25, a few R.A.F. Hudsons and PBYs.

22nd Bombing Group and 3rd Bombing Group, based in Australia and staging through Port Moresby, took care of Lae and Salamaua.

Two fighter squadrons of the 35th Group, with about 35 P–40s at Port Moresby.

Two R.A.F. Squadrons, with about 30 P–40s in the area.

SUBMARINE FORCE SOUTHWEST PACIFIC
Rear Admiral Charles A. Lockwood Jr.

TF 42, Captain Ralph W. Christie, based at Brisbane[16]

S–38	Lt. Cdr. H. G. Munson
S–39	Lt. F. E. Brown
S–41	Lt. I. S. Hartman
S–43	Lt. Cdr. E. R. Hannon
S–44	Lt. Cdr. J. R. Moore
S–46	Lt. Cdr. R. C. Lynch Jr.

As the question has often been asked whether the Pacific Fleet contributed all it could to the South Pacific Force at this critical juncture, an effort has been made to find out how the rest of that fleet was employed.

Vice Admiral William S. Pye[17] was still in command of old Task Force 1, the seven prewar battleships and a destroyer screen. They sailed from San Francisco 1 August for Pearl Harbor and remained in the Islands throughout September, engaged in training exercises when not in harbor. As these battleships would have been valueless in the Solomons operation,[18] it was proper to use them to cover and protect Hawaii; but they tied up eight to ten destroyers and three flag officers who might have been better

---

[16] These boats were on patrol at the time in this area. *S–38* sank *Meiyo Maru* bringing reinforcements to Guadalcanal 8 Aug. and *S–44* sank heavy cruiser *Kako* 10 Aug. See above, Chapter X, Sec. 4. In addition, Pacific Fleet submarines *Greenling* and *Drum* patrolled off Truk.

[17] Relieved by Vice Admiral H. F. Leary at Pearl 20 Sept. 1942.

[18] General MacArthur wanted them under his command, although there was nothing they could have done in Australia or New Guinea waters; the Bismarck Sea was so imperfectly charted and so dominated by aircraft from Rabaul that not even destroyers could be risked on the north coast of Papua.

employed around Guadalcanal. Hawaii, moreover, had protection in the shape of Rear Admiral Murray's Carrier Task Force (17), built around *Hornet* and including heavy cruisers *Northampton* and *Pensacola,* and *San Diego.* This force was on 24-hour notice at Pearl, from which it sortied on 9 August to make a sweep and engage in flight and gunnery training. It was certainly not excessive for defending an important flank of America's Pacific defenses against an enemy still capable of making a thrust in that direction.[19] The Japanese Navy still had fleet carriers *Shokaku* and *Zuikaku* and a number of small ones. Admiral Nimitz had to guard against their raiding Midway, Johnston or Canton Islands while Ghormley's forces were busy at Guadalcanal.

Eight old four-stacker destroyers, battered veterans of the Java Sea, were left at San Francisco for conversion; four destroyers (*Shaw, Barker, Dunlap* and *Fanning*) operated out of Pearl on convoy and other duties. Rear Admiral Theobald's North Pacific Force (TF 8), two heavy and three light cruisers, five destroyers and two tankers, remained intact. It would have been useful at Guadalcanal, but the possibility that the Japanese might try an invasion by the Aleutians–Alaska route could not be ignored.

Everything else in the Pacific except one light cruiser, on a special mission, was tied up in convoy duty.[20]

The British Admiralty was invited to make a diversion on the far western flank, hoping it might convince the Japanese that weight was about to be thrown in that direction. So the Far Eastern Fleet of the Royal Navy put on a little show in the Bay of

---

[19] At the time there was much criticism in the South Pacific because Cominch sent to TF 62 *Quincy* and *Vincennes* instead of "blooded" cruisers of the Pacific Fleet. But it must be admitted that *Astoria* and *Chicago,* which fitted that description, were no better handled at Savo Island than were the two cruisers from the Atlantic Fleet.

[20] *Manley* and *Stringham* en route Nouméa via Bora Bora; *Long Island, Aylwin* and *W. W. Burroughs* at Pearl about to proceed to Suva; *Gamble, Breese* and *Tracy* en route Espiritu Santo; *Montgomery, Ramsay, Dorsey, Boggs* en route Palmyra, where *Schley, Ward, Allen* and *Chew* already were; *Helena* en route Nouméa; *Raleigh, Wasmuth, Perry, Conyngham* in San Francisco–Pearl escort group; *Preston* and *Clark* en route Wellington. All these were engaged in convoy duty on 2 August. Cincpac War Diary.

Bengal. Three convoys covered by Admiral Somerville's battle-ships and carriers steamed out of Vizagapatam, Madras and Trincomalee before dawn on 1 August, apparently headed for the Andaman Islands off Burma. They continued in that direction for sixteen hours, reversed course and returned to port. It is not known what effect this demonstration had on the Japanese.

CHAPTER XIV

The Landings[1]

7–8 August 1942

East Longitude dates, Zone minus 11 time. The
Japanese constantly employed Tokyo time, Zone
minus 9; Allied task forces were not consistent.

1. Rendezvous, Rehearsal and Approach

THE LANDINGS were only three weeks away when Admiral Ghormley issued his operation plan and made final assignments of ships and troops within his command.

Admiral Turner was responsible for the detailed operation plan for the landings. Nineteen large transports and cargo ships were to carry the major load of the landing force, supplemented by four of the tiny converted destroyer transports. Cruisers *Quincy, Vincennes, Astoria* and *San Juan* and six destroyers must blast the enemy away from the landing beaches. If enemy mines lay in the narrow approaches, five converted destroyer minesweepers would cut the unseen hazards adrift. Rear Admiral Crutchley RN was to command a group composed of H.M.A.S. *Australia, Canberra* and *Hobart*, U.S.S. *Chicago* and nine United States destroyers; his task was to protect the other groups from air, submarine and sea attack. His own fighter director augmented by two carrier teams con-

[1] This account follows closely that of the excellent O.N.I. Combat Narrative *The Landings in the Solomons* (1943); additional details from General Vandegrift "Division Commander's Final Report on Guadalcanal Operations Phase II" 24 May 1943; Maj. John L. Zimmerman USMCR, Marine Corps historical monograph *The Guadalcanal Campaign* (to be printed; I saw only the 1st preliminary draft, Sept. 1948); Action Reports of individual ships; statements by participants; personal examination of the terrain in Apr. 1943.

trolled Fletcher's carrier planes when they arrived over Savo Sound. The landing force was split into a Guadalcanal Group under the overall commander Major General Vandegrift and a Tulagi Group under Brigadier General Rupertus.[2]

Rear Admiral McCain's land- and tender-based aircraft had to reconnoiter the Solomons for several days before the landings. This essential function could be performed only if sufficient planes and bases were available in the outward fringes of Allied territory. So the month of July was a busy one for the birdmen and their servicing components; airfields were hacked out of jungles in the New Hebrides, New Caledonia and the Fijis;[3] planes bearing the insignia of Army, Navy, Marine Corps and New Zealand air forces were ferried to the jumping-off points. By 25 July the seven air task groups were ready to go. The Army's 69th Bombardment Squadron sent scouts winging 400 miles north of New Caledonia. Long-stepping B–17s flying from Efate kept the southern Solomons under observation. Aircraft tender *Curtiss* (Commander Maurice E. Browder) of Pearl Harbor fame prepared to shift berth from Nouméa to Espiritu Santo, her flock of patrol seaplanes to base in both places and Efate as well. Tenders *McFarland* and *Mackinac* stood by to provide Catalina bases in Ndeni, Santa Cruz Islands, and Maramasike Estuary, Malaita. Marine Corps fighter and scout planes took over the local defense of the vulnerable New Hebrides bases. General Kenney dispatched his Southwest Pacific planes on far-ranging searches west of 158° East Longitude.

Ghormley's small planning staff deserves no small credit for a successful rendezvous, right on time, of a number of task forces which started out from places as wide apart as Wellington, San Diego, Nouméa and Sydney. He gave all subordinate flag commands an opportunity to confer by designating a rendezvous 400 miles southeast of the Fiji Islands. Forenoon watch 26 July found

---

[2] Admiral R. K. Turner's War Diary for 18–30 July, Comsopac Op Plan No. 1 of 16 July, Task Force 62 Op Plan A3–42 of 30 July 1942.
[3] Koumac in northern New Caledonia was ready in time.

Admirals Turner, Kinkaid, Noyes, McCain and Callaghan and General Vandegrift boarding Admiral Fletcher's flagship *Saratoga* for this mid-ocean forum.[4]

Admiral Ghormley, the top commander, was already flying up to Nouméa to his flagship, the hybrid vessel-of-all-work *Argonne*, and had no opportunity to view this South Pacific Force, so recently swollen from Anzac remnants and assorted oddments to fleet dimensions. But every man in the force enjoyed the sight of a sea sprinkled with fighting ships to the horizon's rim — the great flattops lunging into the wind to launch and recover planes, the cruisers briskly maneuvering to keep step, the destroyers in their never-ending quest for sound contacts, the transports stolidly zigzagging, their topsides green with Marine "zoot suits" (the herringbone twill coverall of that era), the bright signal hoists constantly being run up, answered and lowered, and the drone of Wildcats and SBDs overhead. Fletcher's expeditionary force was small in comparison with later ones which set out to take the Marianas and the Philippines; but it was mighty impressive to sailors of the Pacific Fleet in 1942. Particularly did they welcome recent arrivals from the Atlantic Fleet (three of them, alas, destined to sink in these waters) — carrier *Wasp* fresh from her plane-ferry duties in the Mediterranean, heavy cruisers *Quincy* and *Vincennes* and, most of all, *North Carolina*, first new American battlewagon to roll over the Pacific surges, bringing a 16-inch main battery to blast the Japs, her topsides bristling like a porcupine with the new allowance of anti-aircraft guns, double or treble what her elder sisters had had at Pearl Harbor. A brave sight altogether; but, after all, a scratch team. None of them, except two of the carrier groups, had ever operated together before. Admiral Crutchley did not even have an opportunity to meet the captains of the American cruisers suddenly placed under his command.

---

[4] The only information available to the writer about this conference, other than a few recollections of the participants, is a record of the conclusions drawn up by Admiral Ghormley's representative, Admiral Callaghan.

The operation had been planned so hurriedly that there were a thousand details to be worked out at this mid-ocean conference, and worked out they were, in about forty-eight hours. Fletcher already had his own plan for air support of the landing, but arrangements had to be made for the B-17s based at Efate and New Caledonia to help out. He told Turner that he had been ordered not to hold his carrier force within supporting distance of Guadalcanal for more than two days and Turner protested in no uncertain terms that he would need air protection while the AKs — cargo ships — were being unloaded; but his protest was unavailing. "Everyone deplored lack of time to plan carefully and thoroughly," reported Admiral Ghormley's representative, "but saw no way out except to whip plans into shape as rapidly as possible."

Turner's Amphibious Force rehearsed the landings at Koro Island in the Fijis between 28 and 31 July. These exercises were useful in teaching Marines, carrier planes, naval gunners, transport and landing craft crews to coöperate in a large-scale, ship-to-shore boat movement, but were a failure as far as landing was concerned because a coral reef prevented all but a few boats from going ashore.

Rehearsal completed, the Amphibious Force and its escorts formed up according to Admiral Turner's approach plan, steered westward to about lat. 16°36′ S, long. 159°06′ E, and then due north for Cape Esperance, Guadalcanal. At 2000 August 6 the van, led by Admiral Crutchley's flagship *Australia*, had reached a position 60 miles southward of the nearest shores of Guadalcanal.[5] So far as anyone knew — and so far as we now know — even the existence of this force was unknown to the enemy. It had been assembled so quickly and secretly, and had been so favored by a weather front which thwarted enemy plane search, that surprise was complete. Early in the morning the Japanese radio station at Tulagi reported: "A large force of ships of unknown number and

[5] Lat. 10°23′ S, long. 158°59′ E. *Chicago* War Diary.

types is entering the Sound. What can these ships be?" They would soon find out.[6]

Now it was D-day, with H-hour coming up. This was the first amphibious operation undertaken by United States forces in World War II; the first, indeed, since 1898. It cannot be said, in that favorite phrase of military writers, that "the atmosphere in the force was one of sober confidence." Even the Marines, who had studied and practiced amphibious warfare for many months, felt a little queasy when they reflected that this time they were not going to meet dummy opposition but the famous jungle fighters who had run us out of the Philippines and the British out of Singapore and the Dutch out of Java. As for the naval officers, some had taken part in exercises at Culebra or San Clemente, but most of them knew nothing of amphibious warfare except theory, and the more of that they knew the less confidence they felt in this operation. For the whole history of war from Syracuse to Gallipoli proves how difficult amphibious warfare is at all times and how disastrous it may be to a force unfamiliar with its practice; how easily such a force may be thrown into confusion by stout opposition, want of exact timing, foul weather or even ordinary bungling. The time would come when both fleet and ground forces were at home with this work, schooled by experience and fortified by success; when Admiral Turner's "V 'Phib" with the alligator shoulder patch would become a proud and confident force, making web-footed operations so formidable that the enemy would flinch from defending his own beaches. But that time seemed far, far away on 7 August 1942.

Furthermore, there is something sinister and depressing about that sound between Guadalcanal and Florida Islands, from which the serrated cone of Savo Island thrusts up like the crest of a giant dinosaur emerging from the ocean depths. It is now hard to dissociate this feeling from events and from the remembrance of those

---

[6] Japanese Crudiv 6 Battle Report 7–10 Aug. 1942 (WDC No. 160,997). The first dispatch from Tulagi notifying Rabaul of the approach of surface forces was dated 0635 and received 0725, our time (WDC No. 161,730).

who there met death in its most horrible forms. Yet there is that which eludes analysis; one never felt so, for instance, about the blood-soaked ashes of Iwo Jima. Men who rounded Cape Esperance in the darkness before dawn of 7 August insist that even then they felt an oppression of the spirit — "It gave you creeps." Even the land smell failed to cheer sailors who had been long at sea; a rank, heavy stench of mud, slime and jungle arose from the faecaloid island of Guadalcanal.

A brief lift was given by a fine message from Admiral Turner that was read over the loud-speaker of every ship before the landings began: —

On August seventh this force will recapture Tulagi and Guadalcanal Islands which are now in the hands of the enemy.

In this first forward step toward clearing the Japanese out of conquered territory we have strong support from the Pacific Fleet and from the air, surface and submarine forces in the South Pacific and Australia.

It is significant of victory that we see here shoulder to shoulder the United States Navy, Marines and Army and the Australian and New Zealand Air, Naval and Army services.

I have confidence that all elements of this armada will in skill and courage show themselves fit comrades of those brave men who already have dealt the enemy mighty blows for our great cause.

God bless you all!

R. K. TURNER

2. *Landings at Guadalcanal*

Transport Group "Yoke" destined for Tulagi separated from Group "X-ray" destined for Guadalcanal about 0300 August 7, when the cruising disposition was about ten miles northwest of the big island; the one steered north of Savo Island, the other between it and Cape Esperance, to parallel the north coast of Guadalcanal. It was a silent night and a silent dawn; no sign of life could be seen afloat or ashore as the ships' bows hissed through the calm

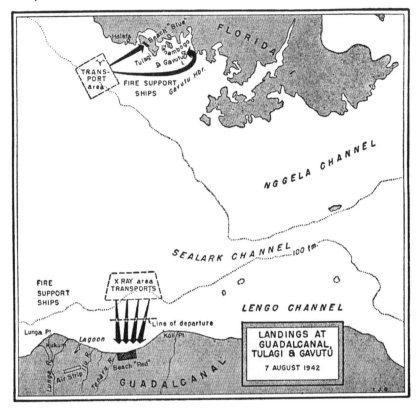

LANDINGS AT
GUADALCANAL,
TULAGI & GAVUTU
7 AUGUST 1942

waters of that sound where so many of them would find their graves. We shall follow the fortunes of the X-ray group first. This was much the larger of the two, in view of the expectation that the enemy on Guadalcanal was some 5000 men strong. As far as can now be ascertained, there were actually no more than 2230 Japanese then on the island, and 1700 of these belonged to naval construction units.[7]

At 0613 cruiser *Quincy* broke silence to begin her scheduled bombardment of the coast west of Lunga Point, where there was supposed to be a coastal battery. A few minutes later an auxiliary schooner was sighted, carrying gasoline from Tulagi to Guadal-

---

[7] "Translation of Answers to Questionnaires on Guadalcanal Operation" ATIS No. 22,729; Marine Corps *Guadalcanal Campaign* p. 35 of preliminary draft.

canal; a carrier's Wildcat promptly sank it. The other fire support ships began seeking out gun emplacements and storehouses along shore, and presently 44 planes from *Saratoga* and *Enterprise*, arriving on schedule, began doing their part in the shore bombardment. At 0647 the 15 transports coasted to their assigned positions in the debarkation area off the beach designated "Red," a thousand yards of black sand just east of the Tenaru River,[8] and at 0650 Captain Reifsnider made signal from *Hunter Liggett*, "Land the Landing Force!" The sun was just rising to a fair morning with partial overcast; temperature was 80° Fahrenheit, and it only rose two or three degrees during the day.

As this was the first full-scale American amphibious operation of the war, it followed very closely the prewar doctrine worked out by the Navy and Marine Corps at Culebra,[9] and it differed from the landings in North Africa, which came three months later, only in being made in full daylight.[10] At Guadalcanal the operation proceeded fairly smoothly because of lack of opposition; the Japanese, mostly labor troops and concentrated at Kukum several miles to the westward, appear to have been dazed by this great panoply of force. The landing craft employed were the old, blunt-nosed 36-foot Higgins boats for the Marines and the 36-foot ramped LCPR, together with a few 45- and 56-foot LCMs capable of carrying a small tank or 15 tons of cargo. Preceded by a short but superfluous shore bombardment, the first wave gathered at the line of departure,[11] 4000 yards from the inner line of transports and 5000 yards from the beach, and at 0913 the first troops were

---

[8] In all the early reports and charts the Ilu and Tenaru Rivers are confused. The one that bordered Beach "Red" is the Tenaru; the one about 2 miles to the westward, where the battle of 21 August took place, is the Ilu. Beach "Red" was selected as lying about halfway between 2 points where the enemy was supposed to be in force; but there were none at the eastern point.

[9] See Vol. I of this History, Introduction pp. li-liii.

[10] See Vol. II of this History pp. 59-65. The North African landings began in darkness because the Army so wished it; but the Navy ran the war in the Pacific and conducted all major landings in daylight to prevent confusion.

[11] For explanation of this and other terms and description of equipment used in amphibious landings, see Vol. II pp. 29, 266-71. Each transport group also carried a few experimental amphtracs (LVTs).

ashore. The Marines landed two battalions abreast. In view of the lack of resistance and the minesweepers' report "negative" after a preliminary sweep, the transports moved in nearer to the beach at 1100. All day the ship-to-shore movement continued, interrupted only by the noon air attacks; by nightfall about 11,000 Marines were ashore. The only untoward feature of this landing was the failure to provide an adequate working party, understandable since an immediate fight had been anticipated. By late afternoon, supplies were stacked high on Beach "Red," laden landing craft circled offshore for hours waiting for a clear spot to ground; and, although the work continued well into the night under artificial light, it had to be called off because of beach congestion. This slow-up turned out to be very serious for the Marines because no transports were completely discharged when forced to retire on 9 August.

While a part of the first combat team to land occupied and organized the immediate beachhead, the second marched west along the water's edge and a third pushed southwesterly through dense jungle into the interior, hoping to capture the rugged, nine-mile-distant Mount Austen, which had been located much nearer on the maps. Both prongs of the advance continued early on 8 August without encountering any Japanese except a few stragglers who were taken prisoner. As these reported that the enemy had retreated to Kukum near Lunga Point, where his major installations were, General Vandegrift made a quick change of plan, abandoned the hopelessly remote Mount Austen objective, and sent Colonel Hunt's team along the coast road to seize Kukum and the Lunga River mouths. Crossing the Lunga at noon, Hunt's men encountered their first opposition — light rifle and machine-gun fire which was quickly silenced — and entered the main Japanese encampment at 1500. In the meantime Colonel Cates's team overran a small enemy patrol and by 1600 had occupied the 3600-foot Japanese airstrip, soon to be renamed Henderson Field. According to the Japanese it was ready to handle 60 planes,[12] but none were yet there.

---

[12] Intelligence summary in Crudiv 6 Battle Report (WDC No. 160,997).

The Marines were now in possession of an airfield, machine shops, two large radio stations, two large electric light plants, an air-compressor plant for torpedoes, and great stores of rice, soybean sauce, canned vegetables and beer which came in very useful during the lean days ahead. The rest of 8 August was spent in relieving the supply congestion at Beach "Red" and shifting the landing place to a beach some two miles nearer to Kukum, just west of the Tenaru River. So far so good; but it never remains good long on Guadalcanal.

3. *Landings Tulagi-side* [13]

The landings Tulagi-side were a different story. Planned as the lesser of the two, Group "Yoke" had only four large transports and four destroyer-transports (APDs) as against 15 big ones in Group "X-ray," and carried only three battalions of Marines — but the enemy opposite proved to be in sufficient strength to fight back viciously. The terrain, too, was complicated.

Tulagi, a narrow island only 4000 yards long, lies in a bight of Florida Island, 18 miles across the sound from the landing beach on Guadalcanal. The southern third of the island had been developed as the capital of the Solomon Islands Protectorate, with the usual Residency on a hill, cricket field, golf links, courthouse, jail, wharves and cluster of Chinese shops and native dwellings. These had been taken over by the Japanese in May, almost intact. The harbor is on the northeast side of the island. Across the harbor mouth, some 3500 yards east of the southern point of Tulagi, lies the small, high island of Gavutu connected by a causeway with the even smaller Tanambogo Island to the north. The two resemble a weight-lifter's bar bell and are only 1200 yards long from north to south. On Gavutu the Lever firm had built its offices, stores, machine shop and wharves, before the war; and

---

[13] Same general sources as in footnote 1; the Action Report of *Heywood*, Capt. H. B. Knowles, is most valuable for Gavutu.

there in May the enemy established his seaplane base. Both Tulagi and Gavutu-Tanambogo had to be taken. The Japanese expected an attack, although not now; they had about 500 troops well dug in on the larger island (we buried 427) and 1000 on the two smaller ones (we buried 980).[14] Brigadier General Rupertus commanded all the Marines Tulagi-side.

This terrain required a complex landing plan, which Admiral Turner's staff and General Vandegrift's had worked out to the last detail; and it worked surprisingly well. The Tulagi landing was effected on Beach "Blue" on the northern, unsettled part of that island, since it could be expected that the enemy would be prepared to defend the better beaches farther south. Gavutu was so reef-ringed that the only possible landing beach lay inside the harbor, by a long and complicated approach. As the boat lanes both to Beach "Blue" and to Gavutu passed close under the Florida Island shore, two small Marine units landed early at Halevo and Haleta to prevent firing on the boats. The Japs had not thought of that, and these Marines had no trouble.

For landing on Beach "Blue," Tulagi, the inner line of four destroyer-transports carried most of Lieutenant Colonel Edson's 1st Raider Battalion. No finer officer than Merritt A. Edson ever wore the Anchor and Globe; no tougher Marines existed than the 1st Raiders. As they were waiting to enter their landing craft, Edson read them a remark made by "Tokyo Rose" the previous day: "Where are the United States Marines hiding? . . . No one has seen them yet!"

The first wave of raiders waded ashore on Beach "Blue" at H-hour, 0800 August 7, and nobody was there to meet them; but the boat movement had been observed, for at 0715 Radio Tulagi sent off a dispatch: "Enemy has commenced landing."[15] They promptly plunged into the jungle, crossed the island ridge to Sesape — soon to be our motor torpedo boat base — and worked cautiously

---

[14] About 600 of the 1500 were labor troops. When the writer visited Tanambogo in April 1943, the hill was being razed by bulldozers, which uncovered the remains of many more Japs who had been smothered in caves and dugouts.

[15] Records of Air Flotilla 25 at Rabaul (WDC No. 161,730).

south along the eastern shore. The second wave, which landed a few minutes later, advanced along the island crest and along the western shore, with a battalion landing team of the 5th Marine Regiment close behind. "Enemy strength is overwhelming," radioed Tulagi to Rabaul at 0800, its last message before a salvo from cruiser *San Juan* smothered the radio station. Before noon the Marines on both flanks found the going very rough. The scheduled naval bombardment, as usual at this stage of the war, was too brief to be of much assistance to the ground troops. *San Juan*, *Monssen* and *Buchanan* had fired about 1500 rounds of 5-inch shell into Hill 208,[16] but had succeeded only in driving the defenders underground. Dive-bombers from the carriers, directed by Lieutenant Commander Beakley in a TBF, pounded positions on the eastern shore. There were plenty of Japs topside, too; it was here that the Marines first encountered enemy snipers tied up in the fronds of coconut palms. "If they had been good shots, few of us would have survived," said Major Chambers of the raiders. More naval fire support was requested, but for some reason the word did not get through, and the Marines had to take the hill with rifle fire and hand grenades.

By nightfall only Hill 281 on the southeast end of Tulagi was in enemy hands. During the midwatch the enemy made four or five separate counterattacks, one penetrating even to battalion headquarters in the Residency, but the Japs made no effort to consolidate and were thrown back. Infiltration, sniping, shouting and whistling went on all night. "The Japs practically slept with us," said Major Chambers. But the Marines held. Soon after daylight on 8 August two battalions of the 2nd Marine Regiment, one of them originally earmarked for Guadalcanal, were landed on Beach "Blue" with orders to help sweep Tulagi clean. They found Edson's Raiders already doing that. In the morning, with the capture of Hill 281, Tulagi was practically secured. "Each Jap fought until he was killed," reported General Vandegrift, "each

---

[16] The numbers of these hills usually, as here, designated their height in feet above tidewater.

machine-gun crew to the last man, who almost invariably killed himself rather than surrender." Only three prisoners were taken, but about 40 escaped by swimming to Florida Island.

Tiny Gavutu and Tanambogo were tougher than Tulagi. Early in the morning of 7 August, planes from Admiral Fletcher's carriers bombed and strafed the Japanese seaplane base, destroying its entire complement of aircraft — 19 float planes and two 4-engined flying boats. After that, the two small islands received all the attention that fire support ships and air bombers could spare from Tulagi, but no great damage was done to the caves and dugouts where 1000 Japs were waiting to sell their lives dear. That was the situation at noon when the 1st Parachute Battalion of the Marine Corps (Major R. H. Williams) moved in to take these islands by assault.

The paratroops were boated from transport *Heywood* in the Yoke area, which meant a rough trip of seven to nine miles off a lee shore with wind and sea making up; the men were two hours afloat, cramped, drenched, and many seasick. Owing to the reefs around Gavutu, they almost had to circle the island before reaching the only possible landing place, the seaplane ramp. Although *San Juan* and two destroyers delivered a brisk bombardment just before the landing, and one destroyer followed the boats in, shooting, the three boat waves met scattered rifle fire before landing and a severe machine-gun fusillade rattled out of the hills as they debarked a few minutes after noon. These hills were lined with earth-and-coconut-log dugouts, which the Japanese always built very cleverly. Before two hours had elapsed, one Marine in ten had become a casualty and the majority were pinned down to the beach. But on the left flank the paratroops overran Hill 148 on Gavutu and at 1800 raised the American flag on its summit.

Tanambogo, still full of live and angry Japs, remained to be dealt with. During the afternoon it was pounded both by naval guns and air bombs until the trees were completely stripped of leaves and most of the trunks were down too; but the defenders could still deliver such a murderous fire on the causeway leading from Gavutu that there was no question of taking it that way. As all other Marines were well occupied, General Rupertus had the bright idea of reëmbarking the unit that had gone ashore at Haleta in the early morning, and sending half of it to take Tanambogo from the rear, and the other half to reinforce Gavutu. The first three boats reached the smaller island at dusk, hoping to land under cover of darkness. Unfortunately the preliminary bombardment by the destroyers exploded a gasoline tank that lit up the scene brilliantly. The Japs opened fire and killed or wounded every occupant of one boat and decimated the other two. These Marines were forced to retire and join the other three boatloads at Gavutu. Thus, at midnight 7 August, Tanambogo, like Tulagi, was still in enemy hands.

In view of the easy situation on Guadalcanal, transports *Adams* and *Hayes*, carrying the 2nd and 3rd Battalions of the 2nd Marine Regiment, were sent Tulagi-side and Lieutenant Colonel Hunt's 3rd Battalion was given the job of cleaning up Tanambogo. It landed on Gavutu in seven waves shortly before noon 8 August; but the problem of getting men across that fireswept causeway remained. Fortunately, the Colonel had two tank lighters from *Adams* at his disposal. Well on in the afternoon, each LCM carried one tank and a number of ground troops from Gavutu around the reefs to the inside of Tanambogo, covered by vigorous and effective bombardment at point-blank range from destroyer *Buchanan*.[17] One tank landed safely but got ahead of its supporting troops, the Japs rushed out of their dugouts, stalled the tank track with an iron bar and killed all but one of the crew with hand grenades. But the other tank, aided by perhaps 60 infantry, worked around the little island, blasting out the dugouts until the Marines on Gavutu could cross the causeway in safety, as they promptly did. By 2200 August 8 the two ends of the bar bell were in American hands.

[17] *Buchanan* and *Monssen* had stood by Gavutu and Tanambogo since the afternoon of the 7th. With the aid of Lt. G. H. Howe RANR, who knew those waters, as pilot, they circled the islands and threaded the reefs again and again, giving most valuable fire support to the troops. Rear Admiral Scott's Action Report.

The taking of Tulagi, Gavutu and Tanambogo had cost the lives of 108 Marines, with 140 wounded;[18] but the force of about 1500 Japanese was wiped out, except for isolated snipers in holes and caves, who made trouble for a week or more.

4. *Air Counterattacks, 7–8 August* [19]

Admiral Ghormley well said that a basic problem of the operation would be to protect ships from land-based air attack during the landing and the unloading. True, General Kenney's Flying Fortresses and medium bombers did their best; 13 Flying Forts raided the Rabaul fields 7 August and destroyed a number of planes, but they were too few to prevent enemy counterattacks. So the main responsibility for protecting the amphibious force fell on the planes from Admiral Fletcher's carriers, and on the ships' anti-aircraft guns.

Rear Admiral Yamada, Commander 25th Air Flotilla, had some 48 long-range bombers ready on 7 August as well as 12 to 15 big flying boats based on tender *Akitsushima* in Simpson Harbor. A staging field for land-based planes was already in use at Buka Passage between Buka and Bougainville. It did not take Admiral Yamada long to react to the report of our landing at Tulagi. At 0900 August 7 his orders went forth to the 5th and 6th Air Attack Forces under his command, and at 1045 an Australian coastwatcher in Bougainville sighted many twin-engined bombers flying south-easterly, and passed the word to Admiral Turner at Guadalcanal. At 1315, the radar in *Chicago* picked up this flight 43 miles away; five minutes later, about 27 of them covered by fighter planes were

18 I believe these figures, which are from Zimmerman's monograph, include bluejackets in the landing force. Paratroops claimed a (total) loss of 50 to 60 per cent. Cruiser *San Juan* when delivering fire support had 5 killed, 13 wounded in a turret explosion.

19 O.N.I. Combat Narrative *Landing in the Solomons* pp. 47–50, 59–62 for the defense; Daily War Report of 25th Air Flotilla at Rabaul (WDC No. 161,730, National Archives No. 12,264, trans. by Lt. Pineau) for the enemy. This document reveals that the Japanese bombers were also looking for our carriers but failed to locate them.

seen coming in high over Savo Island. The attack was a high-level one that did no damage. At about 1500, two unheralded groups, of 16 dive-bombers, singled out the X-ray group off Guadalcanal and scored a hit on destroyer *Mugford* that killed 22 men but did slight damage.

Both counterattacks would undoubtedly have been more effective but for the work of the combat air patrol furnished by carriers *Enterprise* and *Saratoga*, then operating with *Wasp* southwest of Guadalcanal. These were directed by the fighter-director team in *Chicago*. The first group of six Wildcats from *Enterprise* was given the reciprocal bearing of the approaching enemy, and so went wild. The second, third and fifth groups, each of eight Wildcats, claimed one or two kills; the fourth, of six Wildcats, tangled with a bomber-fighter formation and lost three planes with their pilots; two more made forced landings but the pilots were recovered. *Saratoga* planes, too, were in the combat air patrol; two groups of eight Wildcats each attacked an enemy formation over Savo Island, had no time to gain altitude, and together lost five of their number to "Zekes"; a third group of eight *Saratoga* F4Fs intercepted eleven Japanese dive-bombers, whose approach had not previously been detected, and claimed to have shot down all but one. *Wasp* had charge of combat air patrol over Admiral Noyes's carrier formation on the 7th, but six of her SBDs that were on a bombing mission against Tulagi contributed to the general mêlée. They were attacked by six "Zekes" and lost one of their number; the pilot was recovered.

Considering that almost all the carrier-plane pilots were naval aviators of the latest crop, with a little leaven from the victors of Midway; that this was the first American amphibious operation to be covered by carrier-based air, and that the enemy was energetic and relentless, these American pilots did exceedingly well. They certainly saved the transports from damage, and paid for it by the loss of eleven F4Fs and one SBD. As usual, their claims of planes shot down were excessive, owing to duplication; but Admiral Yamada admitted the loss of 14 out of 43 bombers and two out of

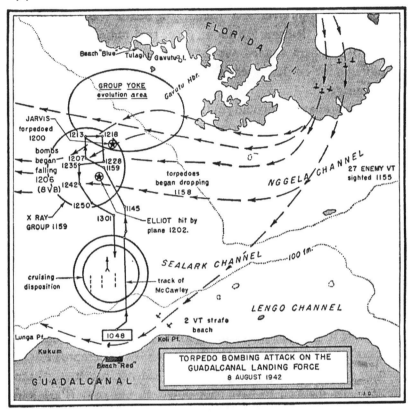

TORPEDO BOMBING ATTACK ON THE
GUADALCANAL LANDING FORCE
8 AUGUST 1942

18 "Zekes" in the two attacks. He was not at all pleased with the results of this attack, especially as his planes had been unable to find the carriers.[20]

When the enemy delivered a torpedo attack next day, the Task Force was better prepared to meet it. Admiral Turner, tipped off some 80 minutes in advance by the faithful coastwatcher on Bougainville, had both transport groups in cruising disposition, screened by cruisers and destroyers and maneuvering at 13.5 knots by simultaneous turns, in which he had vigorously drilled the transports en route to Guadalcanal.

[20] *War College Analysis* of Savo Is. Yamada mentions an attack by 9 large flying boats of which 2 were shot down and others made forced landings, but I can find no mention of these on the American side.

A few minutes before noon August 8, a large formation of enemy planes was sighted swinging over the eastern cape of Florida Island. The majority of them were low-flying "Bettys" armed with the deadly Japanese aërial torpedo. Three fighter planes from *Enterprise*, patrolling over Nggela Channel, took out four of them. One peeled off to strafe Beach "Red," but the rest had to pass the gantlet of the screen's anti-aircraft fire and then that of the transports. They came in very low, some only 20 feet above the water; and those that got as far as the transports were so groggy with machine-gun hits as to remind one officer of heifers loose in city streets. Only nine out of 26 torpedo-bombers were seen to pass through the transport formation; the Japanese admitted that 17 were shot down. The only hit they obtained was on destroyer *Jarvis*. A few minutes later, a small formation of the "Bettys" came in. They too took a bad beating, but two of them when lethally hit tried suicide tactics, one with success. The Japanese pilot just managed to steer his burning plane into transport *George F. Elliott*, with deadly effects.[21]

If the air battle of the 7th was won by the carrier planes, this defeat of a major threat by the torpedo-bombers was largely due to the ships' anti-aircraft gunners and to excellent ship handling. Admiral Turner always turned his transports to parallel the line of the planes' approach; and, as torpedo-bombers have to come in on a wide angle in order to drive their "fish" to a target, this quick maneuver baffled them and gave the anti-aircraft gunners a chance. Ship losses might have been nil had damage control been up to par. What happened on board *Elliott* is not entirely clear; but it seems that a fair part of the crew abandoned her prematurely, the one destroyer which helped the fire fighting was insufficient, an attempt to smother the fire below by the time-honored method of closing all hatches proved unsuccessful, and by the time darkness set in the transport was a mass of flames. A destroyer sent to sink her fired four torpedoes at close range

[21] Same. Admiral Yamada, however claimed that his planes had sunk 2 heavy cruisers, 2 destroyers and 10 transports. He lost 2 out of 17 escorting "Zekes."

without effect and *Elliott* became a burning derelict which made a handy mark for the enemy that night. She was a total loss.

Thus, during the first two days of Operation "Watchtower," the enemy had managed to inflict a few losses without accomplishing anything more than a slight delay in the American time-table. Before midnight August 8 the beachhead, airfield and enemy encampment on Guadalcanal, and the three islands wanted on Tulagi-side, were secured; everything looked rosy. But the critical period in an amphibious operation, under World War II conditions, was not the actual landing; the crisis came when the enemy counterattacked in strength. That moment had now arrived. A few minutes after midnight, the Battle of Savo Island opened.

Index

Index

Names of Combat Ships in SMALL CAPITALS, except
I-boats, S-boats, PTs and YPs
Names of Merchant Ships in *Italics*

The following Task Organizations containing lists of American and Japanese ships and commanding officers are not indexed: —

Battle of Coral Sea, pp. 17–20; Battle of Midway, pp. 87–93; Aleutians Operation of June 1942, pp. 172–74; Operation "Watchtower" (Guadalcanal–Tulagi), pp. 270–75.